JACK BENNY

JACK BENNY

*Mary Livingstone Benny
and Hilliard Marks
with Marcia Borie*

Doubleday & Company, Inc.
GARDEN CITY, NEW YORK
1978

Library of Congress Cataloging in Publication Data

Benny, Mary Livingstone.
Jack Benny.

Includes index.
1. Benny, Jack, 1894–1974. 2. Comedians—United
States—Biography. I. Marks, Hilliard, joint author.
II. Borie, Marcia, joint author.
PN2287.B4325B4   791.4′092′4 [B]
ISBN: 0-385-12497-x
Library of Congress Catalog Card Number 77–80902

In addition to the marvelous contributions of those people close to Jack who have shared their memories with us, the authors would like to acknowledge the generous assistance received from the Waukegan *News-Sun,* the Chicago *Tribune,* the reference library of the Academy of Motion Picture Arts and Sciences, and Mr. Brooke Whiting and the Department of Special Collections, Research Library, University of California, Los Angeles.

PREFACE

ON JANUARY 14, 1927, MY LIFE BEGAN. That was the day I became Mrs. Jack Benny. I never knew happiness until I married Jack. I adored my parents, my sister and brother, but my life was not really complete until I became Jack's bride.

I was a kid when I married him. It was an impulsive act that turned into one of the great love stories. Until the day Jack died, he was still holding my hand. Jack thought I was everything . . . I thought he was everything. We lived together for forty-eight years. We worked together. We shared a lifetime—together. I adored that man . . . I always will.

For the last thirty years of his life, Jack never really had a family, except for his sister, Florence, who lived in Chicago. We spent the majority of our time in Hollywood. Here, my mother and father became like parents to Jack. Until they passed away, he was constantly over there. Invariably, he would call me from their home, having stopped in to share breakfast or coffee with them.

Although many of you know me as Mary Livingstone, performer, I am basically a shy person, which is why I finally stopped working professionally with Jack. But even when I quit the show, my life was full from morning until night, because I shared every moment of my husband's world.

To me, Jack isn't gone . . . Often, I sit in his room, and he is there with me. We used to have so much fun just being together. We were inseparable.

The last few weeks of his life, I got up every ten minutes to check on him. Finally, he let me hire a nurse. He didn't want me to get sick, too. During the last day that he was able to sit up in bed, I walked into his room to bring him something. He was propped up against the pillows watching television. When I came in, he took hold of my hand. "You know, doll," he said, "I love you more now than I ever did in my whole life . . ."

I started to walk out of the room. When I reached the door, I turned back and said, "Doll, you're full of ——!"

He started to pound on the dressing table and screamed with laughter. He always did think I was funny.

Jack had a fabulous professional life. He stayed on top for so long . . . and he always shared his spotlight with others whom he had made famous.

Over the years, countless people tried to analyze him. Why, they asked, was Jack Benny so special? How come, they wondered, did his popularity last so long? Well, there are many theories. But personally, I believe one of the reasons Jack was such a special man is that he never looked back . . . He had a favorite saying: "Yesterday is your past. Today is your future. Tomorrow is a secret." Well, Jack believed wholeheartedly in the *first* part, but for him tomorrow was *never* a secret. He always *knew* what he was going to do.

Jack was continually busy moving forward. He was the only performer I know who hated nostalgia. Talking about the old days bored him. Whenever someone asked him about something he had done in the past, he really did not want to discuss it. The old days were fun to him—but they were over. Done with. All he wanted to do was talk about tomorrow. This attitude—this constantly enthusiastic optimism—is what kept him going, what kept him so perpetually young.

Up until the day Jack died, he never lost his timing, his instinctive knowledge of what his audiences wanted from him. He never lost his unique charisma—that way of walking out, taking command of a stage and making people love him—because he loved them back.

Offstage, however, Jack lived such a comparatively ordinary life. Away from the lights, he was a simple, modest man. In the world of show business, his very normalcy made him "abnormal." Over the years, this paradox intrigued people, and numerous publishers wanted Jack's autobiography. They were anxious to print a book which would zero in on the essence of Benny.

Finally, some years ago, Jack agreed. He hired a writer, accepted a publisher's advance, and set about to work on his life story. However, when the writer brought a draft of the book for his approval, Jack was disappointed. The manuscript did not please him. He felt it did not reflect his life as he knew it to be.

The publisher's advance was returned. The writer was paid for what he had written. What happened was that Jack purchased his own life story—and packed it away on a closet shelf!

Then, in 1974, when Jack decided to write his autobiography again, he selected as his collaborator someone who knew him intimately—someone he loved and trusted—my brother, Hilliard. We've called him Hickey ever since our daughter Joan, as a baby, couldn't pronounce his name and started calling him Uncle Hickey.

When they began to work, there was a spontaneous outpouring on Jack's part. Sometimes they would write. Other times, they would just sit and talk, dredging up anecdotes, reminiscences, memories which the two of them had shared over the years. Putting *everything* down, not knowing which line, which phrase, which "happening" would eventually wind up in print. It was in this manner that the over-all pattern for the book was conceived.

As Jack once wrote, "Hickey is a fine writer. One of the best in the business. He thinks like I do—which is invaluable. Together, we get results which are most important to me. He started writing my radio show in 1938, along with Bill Morrow and Ed Beloin. He was very young. Morrow and Beloin received credit for the shows, as well as for writing several films I did at Paramount. But Hickey worked on them, too. I'm sorry he never received credit. For a long while, he had to be content just *knowing* he was contributing.

"Eventually, Hickey graduated to producing both my radio and television programs. Over the years, he grew to know exactly what I wanted in written material, what fit me in delivery. What I would accept, what I wouldn't. By the time he became my head writer, he knew my every thought. He is the only one I keep continuously on salary for fifty-two weeks a year . . .

"Not a week goes by that we are not writing together. I'm pretty good, too—you know. We work on material for television, speeches, banquets, theaters and concerts, as well as on my appearances in Las Vegas and Lake Tahoe. Usually, I prepare speeches myself, including an occasional eulogy. Then I ask Hickey to look at what I've written and try to improve on the weak spots. He claims I'm rather good at speech writing.

" 'You don't have much to embellish,' he tells me. That's when I'm very proud of myself . . .

"No one can write about me and with me like Hickey can," Jack said. "No other potential biographer ever shared a dressing room with me while I changed . . . Or stood in the wings while I was performing . . . Or even walked on stage and did routines with me. Hickey knew me intimately for nearly fifty years. We spent decades just saying 'good morning' to each other. Not a day passed when Hickey and I and Mary were not either together, or on the telephone to each other. We shared breakfasts, lunches, dinners, business trips, vacations . . ."

They were working on the book when Jack passed away, and my brother felt obligated to continue working. A few months later, I decided to join in as the co-author. Both of us feel so strongly that we owe it to Jack's memory to set the record straight.

William Paley, the head of CBS, who isn't given to tossing profuse compliments around, went on television after Jack died to eulogize him. Among the things he said was that Jack Benny had more guts than any performer he ever knew. The courage to pause, to just keep quiet, and to evoke screams of laughter from an audience who *knew* why he paused, who *knew* exactly what Jack was thinking. And, in the knowing, laughed with him and loved him all the more.

The image Jack created and perpetuated for so many decades

lives on. People still think he was cheap. He was always so believable that he became synonymous with his "character." At the mention of his name people immediately thought of cheapskate Jack and his lousy violin playing . . . He was always the foil for those of his radio and television family who surrounded him.

Jack dared to be less than a hero, and wound up being Everyman. Every stingy thought each of us has ever had was manifested in the role Jack played—and made his own.

When you live with and love a legend like Jack Benny, what is written about him is terribly important. Jack and Hickey dearly loved each other. I am happy my brother and I have joined together to write this book.

Mary Livingstone Benny

JACK BENNY

CHAPTER ONE

THE PARADE ROUTE along Genessee Street was lined with a crowd estimated at over twenty-five thousand. Men, women, and children stood, all anxiously awaiting the start of Waukegan's Centennial-Armed Forces Day Parade. It was June 24, 1959, at nine-forty in the morning. Mayor Robert Sabonjian and hometown hero Jack Benny entered the lead convertible. Behind them, numerous military units, gaily decorated floats, dozens of marching bands, and drill teams from nearby naval and marine installations gathered in their proper order. Awaiting the ten o'clock signal to begin, the lead car was parked at the corner of Genessee and Belvedere streets.

As he sat there, Jack kept looking around. "I know this place," he said to the mayor. "It's so familiar to me . . ." Suddenly, as he looked up at one of the buildings, tears came to his eyes. "Upstairs, right there," he pointed, "that's the last place I lived when I was a boy. I can still see my mother, father, and sister sitting in that apartment by the window."

He turned in the other direction. "And down there, right across the street, that's where my dad had his haberdashery . . ." He lowered his head. The mayor turned away, respecting Jack's momentary reflection, focusing his own eyes on a small grocery store, the Little Food Market, which stood on the ground floor beneath the apartment which Jack had singled out.

"Do you think I could go up and just look around for a few minutes?" Jack asked. The mayor nodded and immediately called the chief of police over. Following instructions, the chief went up and asked the occupants if Jack Benny could come through their home.

Minutes later, he returned to the car. "They said they weren't expecting any company today, and that things are in a mess," he reported. "But if Mr. Benny wants to come up, it's okay with them."

Jack and the mayor got out of the car and disappeared on the stairwell leading up to the second floor. They walked all through the small apartment; then Jack paused a moment to look out the front window. Choked up, he left without even thanking the family for their courtesy. When they came down and re-entered the car, Jack sat in silence. But a few moments later, when the parade began, he raised his arms and waved, the familiar Benny smile on his face.

Along with Jack, the honored guest that day was Secretary of the Air Force James Douglas, Jr. On the reviewing stand at Genessee and Washington streets, Admiral E. P. Forrestel, Ninth Naval District Commandant, stood as the colors were trooped by him and the celebration got under way. When the morning's festivities were over, Jack and the mayor had lunch with the military dignitaries at the Swedish Glee Club.

At three-thirty that same afternoon, Mayor Sabonjian, members of the city council, and the local school board accompanied Jack and his sister Florence to a seventeen-acre site just north of Golf Road and west of the North Shore tracks, a plot of ground facing on to Montesano Avenue. There, in a brief ceremony, Jack picked up a gold-plated shovel and began breaking ground for the $1,250,000 Jack Benny Junior High School.

As he turned over the first small mound of earth, the crowd pressed in on him until he was surrounded by hundreds of people. Small children darted in and out trying to get closer to Jack.

School board president James Rust made a short speech. ". . . Jack, the people of Waukegan have always appreciated the fine way you have co-operated with the city. We trust that the children who go to this school will be as successful in their life's work as you . . ."

When the ceremony ended, Jack and his sister led the way across the grounds. From out of the crowd, a man named John Whyte emerged and handed them an old photograph. It was a picture of South School's kindergarten class of 1899. Jack and Florence studied the photo. After a few moments, Benny pointed to a tiny kid. "Look, I found me," he grinned.

That evening, Jack attended and spoke at several banquets, judged a fiddle contest, and wound up at the apartment of his cousins, Cliff and Sudie Gordon.

The following morning, before leaving Waukegan to catch a plane home from Chicago, he made an appearance aboard the U.S.S. *Worland,* a patrol craft escort ship, which had steamed into the Lake Michigan harbor and docked at the pier. Ex-sailor Benny was "piped" aboard and spent an hour with the officers and men, sharing coffee and memories of his own naval days.

A week after Jack returned from his visit, he dictated a letter addressed: TO EVERYONE IN WAUKEGAN which he sent to the Waukegan *News-Sun* so it could be printed for all to see . . .

Now that I am just about getting over the most exciting day that I can remember—I want to send these few words of sincere thanks and gratitude.

I can only repeat an honest statement that I made during several speeches in Waukegan and that is—my day there in conjunction with the Centennial-Armed Forces Parade was the most thrilling that I have ever experienced throughout my entire career in show business. I will never forget it. The warmth and hospitality displayed by everyone will remain with me always. I am very proud to be one of you.

Having a junior high school in my honor may seem a little incongruous—but it is the finest tribute that any entertainer in America has ever received. I deeply appreciate it. Again may I say —I will always be grateful.

Affectionately,
Jack

"I've been mayor of Waukegan for twenty years now . . ." Robert Sabonjian recalled recently. "And I knew Jack for a long

3

time before I took office. He was our Ambassador of Good Will, dropping the name of Waukegan into every home in America and all around the world. In my mind, he was always associated with laughter, but several times during that particular visit, I saw him in tears . . .

"You know," the mayor continued, "we all read Jack's letter in the paper, and were touched by the sincere affection he expressed. But it wasn't until three months later that I found out how the story of Jack's Centennial visit *really* ended. Quite by accident, I discovered that, as soon as Jack had returned to Hollywood, he arranged for the family living in his parents' old apartment to get all new furnishings. He sent them a living room set, appliances, lamps—everything. He did it without fanfare, without publicity. It was his way of thanking the people for allowing him to walk through their home . . ."

In June 1959, within the space of a few hours, Jack had bathed in the warmth of Waukegan's love for him. He had seen the apartment of his parents, Emma and Meyer Kubelsky, which he had left forty-seven years before . . . He had shoveled a small bit of earth which symbolized the beginning of a school that would become a living memorial to his fantastic success . . . He had participated fully in the activities of a town and a way of life he loved and cherished . . .

Those were extraordinary moments for Jack Benny, a simple, humble, almost childishly naïve man, whom peers considered a comic genius . . . A brilliant talent who, during the course of his years on earth, was one of that select handful of entertainers seen, heard, and loved by millions of people around the world.

CHAPTER TWO

MEYER KUBELSKY was born in Lithuania and came to America in 1889. Like those tens of thousands of immigrants who preceded and followed him, he was sent to the United States to escape the oppression of Jewish pogroms. It took nearly ten years for his father, a wine merchant and dispenser, to save the necessary money to send Meyer to America.

Finally, passport in hand, all the years of hard work about to be rewarded, the elder Kubelsky was informed by the government that, despite the issuance of the passport, his son would be forbidden to leave. In desperation, and with the help of a man who delivered empty bottles to Kubelsky's wine shop and tavern, a plan was hatched. The boy would be smuggled out of the country under a shipment of bottles.

The ruse was successful. Meyer Kubelsky made his way to Hamburg, Germany, where he boarded a ship for America, traveling steerage class. He arrived in New York Harbor several weeks later, seasick, homesick for his family, unsure of his future, but determined to make a new life for himself.

He stayed in New York only a few days, then headed for Chicago to look up some people from his East European village. His father had carefully printed their names over and over on many slips of paper—just to make sure his son would arrive in the blessed land of America with a written record of friends to seek out.

Chicago was *not* the Old Country . . . For poor people, it usually wasn't a paradise, either. But to Meyer, Chicago seemed like heaven, even though he spent his first year working twelve to fifteen hours a day in a variety of sweatshops. At least he was free —no longer did he have to live under the threat of tyranny! There was also opportunity just waiting to be accepted. Every night, after work, he attended school, learning to read and write English. Meanwhile, he saved every penny he could hang on to. His goal— God willing—was to go into business for himself.

Finally, the time came. He rented a horse and wagon, and invested in a supply of household goods—stocking up on everything from pots and pans, and needles and thread, to underwear and kitchen aprons. He became an "entrepreneur of commodities," traveling along the shores of Lake Michigan, stopping at all the little towns in between Chicago and Kenosha, Wisconsin. He stayed at cheap boardinghouses, budgeting himself at fifty cents a day—twenty cents for meals, thirty cents for his room.

He was an enterprising young man, and enjoyed the challenge of traveling and selling. But now, he constantly thought about earning enough money to be able to open a tavern like his father's.

One of the regular stops on Meyer's route was in Waukegan, a quiet little Illinois town, which held a particular attraction for him. Being Orthodox, he could always look forward to a kosher meal at the home of the Solomon Schwartzes, one of the five Jewish families who lived there.

Out of kindness, Schwartz extended his hospitality free of charge. Out of loneliness, he was hoping to convince Jewish travelers to settle in Waukegan. So, during Meyer's periodic stops at the Schwartz house, the older man filled the boy's head with wondrous stories about the attributes of his thriving community.

In fact, it wasn't too long before Mr. Schwartz had appointed himself the boy's "official mentor," listening to Meyer's dreams and encouraging him. When the boy confessed that his main goal was to own a tavern like his father's back home, Schwartz not only became enthusiastic, he actually found a saloon-billiard parlor which was for sale.

Meyer stayed in Waukegan for the next two weeks, watching the place every day and actually counting the steady flow of customers. Satisfied, he committed himself, signed a lease in the fall of 1892, bought fixtures, and became the operator of a saloon.

Now that Meyer had become a resident, Schwartz felt the young man needed one more thing in order for his life to be complete—a wife. He told Meyer about a person he knew in Chicago, a matchmaker (a male counterpart of the character Dolly Levi, whom Shirley Booth, Carol Channing, Pearl Bailey, and Barbra Streisand were to immortalize in story and song).

Three weeks after opening the saloon, Kubelsky traveled to Chicago, met the man, and filled out a questionnaire. Smiling to himself, he remembered Solomon's one admonition: "When you put down your occupation say you're in the refreshment business. After all, Jewish saloonkeepers *are* a rarity. Besides, it might scare off any prospective girls—or even worse—their parents."

When the application had been completed, the marital magician brought out a stack of dossiers on single girls. Carefully, he leafed through them, discarding this one and that one, until there remained only two applications on the desk before him.

"There are a couple of very good possibilities here. The first one—what a catch! She's a nice person, *only* five years older than you—and her family is comfortable. In fact, they're *very rich*. With her comes a dowry of several thousand dollars." He paused to let that fact sink in. "If the parents take a shine to you, I wouldn't be surprised if they buy all your household furnishings and pay at least your first year's rent. I ask you, isn't this truly a match in a million?"

Meyer nodded, then inquired about the girl whose name was on the second piece of paper.

The matchmaker started to speak, slowly. "Well, this one is *not* quite in the same circumstances . . . However, she *is* younger than you, quite beautiful, very religious, and her family is well thought of. The father is a hard-working man. They are immigrants from Lithuania, where you come from. But they've lived in Chicago for quite a few years.

"With this one comes beauty—but *no* dowry . . . *No* year's rent. *No* furniture—except for one item—a piano . . ."

Meyer agreed to mull over the situation. He returned the following week and asked to be introduced first to the beautiful girl —the one without the dowry. He was taken to an apartment in the Humboldt Park section of Chicago to meet the Sachs family.

Slightly ill at ease, Meyer attempted to exchange pleasant conversation with the parents, and then she appeared. Emma Sachs was as beautiful a young girl as he had ever seen.

His fate was sealed. Taking the matchmaker aside, he said simply: "If she'll have me, this one is my choice."

Emma's reaction was equally instantaneous, and the courtship began in earnest immediately. Every Sunday, for nearly three months, Meyer dutifully boarded the Chicago & Northwestern train, traveling thirty-six miles so he and Emma could be together until it was time to catch the last train home.

Finally, one day, Emma got up the nerve to ask Meyer exactly what this "refreshment business" of his was really like. She was horrified to discover her "intended" was, in actuality, a saloon-keeper. But he soft-pedaled the fact by describing his place as a "sort of restaurant" where working people could relax, have a drink, enjoy good food, and play a game or two of billiards . . .

Emma Sachs and Meyer Kubelsky were married early in 1893 and settled down in a two-room apartment on Sheridan Road. A couple of blocks away was Meyer's saloon, on the corner of Genessee and Washington streets.

Ten months later, on Tuesday, February 13, 1894, Emma, aged twenty-four, accompanied by her husband, traveled to Chicago, where she checked in to Mercy Hospital to await the birth of her first-born.

The following morning, a son arrived. They named him Benjamin—a St. Valentine's Day gift to the Kubelskys—one day, a gift to the whole world.

When Benny was born, Queen Victoria was still residing at Buckingham Palace, and Grover Cleveland was beginning his second term in the White House . . . Actress Sarah Bernhardt, the Divine, was the critics' anointed darling, and Scott Joplin, the King of Ragtime, was offering his unique keyboard compositions on river boats cruising up and down the Mississippi.

People were being stirred by John Philip Sousa's marches, dancing the cakewalk for pleasure, singing "East side, west side . . . all around the town . . ." and Isadora Duncan was on the brink of making her professional dancing debut.

Tom Edison's electric lights were slowly replacing the nation's incandescent glow, and in the Midwest, neighbors were taking bets as to whether or not Alexander Graham Bell's telephone would ever become a popular instrument.

Entertainment on a mass scale was unknown. Instead, it was a time of traveling circuses, and great troupes of repertory companies crisscrossed America, playing in big theaters as well as small towns, helping to transport the local populace into a fantasy world they would never have otherwise known.

It was close to the middle of the decade known as the Naughty Nineties, when "fast" women shed bustles and big puffed sleeves and donned ankle-length skirts and peekaboo blouses that most "decent" folks thought shocking . . . It was the era of courting by horse and buggy along pitted dirt country roads . . . or for taking trips from somewhere to anywhere, on trains that crept along at twenty-five miles an hour belching cinders and smoke.

It was the year in which the New York *Times* Publishing Company copyrighted their newspaper, whose daily edition, consisting of twelve pages, sold for a penny . . . and cigarette boxes were decorated with Lillian Russell's face and form.

This was the era when men religiously read the *Police Gazette* while discussing breathlessly the latest fisticuff exploits of John L. Sullivan and Gentleman Jim Corbett . . . and Enrico Caruso made his debut in Naples.

Today statistics tell us that in America in 1894 slightly over two million live births were reported. Of those near turn-of-the-century babies, perhaps a million and three quarters grew to maturity. Among the survivors, a relatively infinitesimal handful achieved national recognition, even fewer became internationally known.

Yet, one day, this *particular* child, Benjamin Kubelsky, would be known to the world as Jack Benny. He would become one of the "chosen few" . . . And, for the fifty years of his professional life, he would be analyzed, dissected, interviewed, talked about, written up, photographed, microscopically examined, all in an effort to come up with a definitive list of specific reasons for his fame.

If the magic Jack created could have been reduced to a tangible mathematical formula: three words, a pause, a hand applied to the cheek; two words, stare, a tug at the ear; eight words, raised eyebrow, a finger rubbed under the bridge of the nose; six more words, another pause, a wringing of hands, there might have been spawned a whole generation of imitation Bennys—all equally able to make millions laugh. But, to the contrary, Jack's uniqueness was illusive. He remained all of his life a one-of-a-kind comic actor—a seducer, if you will, of generations of people who grew up with him through vaudeville, radio, films, and television—recipients and participants in a mutual love affair.

CHAPTER THREE

ALTHOUGH HE WAS A BABY in diapers during his father's saloon-keeping days, in later years Jack Benny would relate stories of the period based on what his mother had told him concerning their family life in the late 1890s.

"My dad was possessed of the philosophy of the Tevye character from *Fiddler on the Roof*," Jack began. "He didn't mind poverty as long as *he* didn't quite reach that level. But the only time in his young life that he was really successful was as a bartender. Dad knew how to handle the saloon . . . how to cope with his type of clientele. Ironically, he very seldom touched a drop of liquor, and never smoked.

"My mother hated every minute of Dad's association with the customers who frequented his joint—and it really was a joint—with very cheap pool tables and free lunch every day. She kept begging Dad to give it up, pull out, rent the place, or just sell it at *any* price he could get. Dad, of course, was reluctant to toy with her suggestions as long as the dough was coming in through three different swinging doors.

"However, one day a situation arose which made him change his mind. A drunken bum came in the place, started shooting pool, and wanted a free drink. My father wouldn't give it to him. In about ten seconds flat, Dad was the recipient of a lump on the head from a pool cue, the donor, of course, being the bum who'd requested the drink gratis. The following day, there was a sign prominently displayed in the window:

SALOON FOR SALE

"However uncertain their future was, my mother felt much happier . . . Eventually, Dad opened a haberdashery and was fairly successful."

10

Jack's earliest memories of childhood began around his sixth birthday. He received two very special and meaningful presents— a baby sister, born on September 12, whom his parents named Florence—and a violin. The sister he was thrilled about. As for the other gift, the truth is he had hoped his father would buy him a tricycle.

Who knows what fates combine to bring born genius into contact with those tools, those elements, those environmental situations which allow innate instincts to emerge, to flourish, to grow? In Jack Benny's case it was that first violin—a far cry from the Stradivarius he would one day own—and his parents' determination that, if he studied hard, he could one day become a great artist, a symphony violinist. "In that way," Meyer Kubelsky would say over and over to his son, "your mother and I will be able to repay our debt to America . . ."

Benny began taking lessons from a local teacher. In a short while, he became so proficient it was recommended he be sent to the Chicago School of Music. The lessons, plus his son's transportation to and from Chicago, were expensive, but there was no sacrifice too great for Meyer and Emma.

Two years later, Benny was considered such an outstanding musician that the civic fathers of Waukegan held a meeting and came up with a plan. Surely, they agreed, Benny was a prodigy. He needed the finest opportunity to study and perfect his craft. The townspeople would get together and raise a fund large enough to send the boy to a fine European conservatory. The Kubelskys were overcome with joy and gratitude, but Benny refused to go.

It was a flaw within himself. As a boy, he was a dreamer. He would practice for hours—but only while standing by the open front window, so he could play and simultaneously look out at Lake Michigan. He loved watching the boats go back and forth across the lake. He could also see the railroad tracks. Trains coming and going. People getting on—traveling places. He wanted to go, too. But not to Europe—that only meant more lessons, more hours being cooped up, *studying*.

So he stayed at home, halfheartedly going through his daily routine. His father was a strict man. Authoritarian. Demanding.

Every morning, Benny began a full day at school, followed by long hours of violin practice.

He would have preferred time to play ball and just roam, but he kept to his rigorous schedule, using up his free time on weekends earning money playing violin at local weddings and anniversaries. When he was fourteen, Benny began playing the fiddle with local bands. The musicians he worked with were "older" guys, nineteen and twenty.

"Besides fiddling with dance bands, I played with orchestras at some of Waukegan's theaters. Once, I even worked at the Opera House . . . It was during a performance of *The Bells,* a melodrama about a rich man, the town's leading citizen, who, years previously, had murdered somebody and used the proceeds of his crime to finance his future success . . .

"In Act II," Jack recalled, "the character was supposed to fall asleep and have a nightmare in which the ghost of his victim returned to haunt him. I had a special solo during that scene. I was to play what they called 'trembling music' under the dialogue—but I missed my cue. You see, even when I was a kid, I could fall asleep, anytime, anyplace. So, seeing this actor pretend to sleep on stage, an eerie blue spotlight focused on him, I dozed off, too.

"The next thing I knew, the stage manager, not hearing my trembling tones, ran down to the basement, directly under the stage where I was positioned, and woke me up with a good clout to the head . . ."

The man who gave Benny the clout on the head was actually a clothing salesman by day. He loved show business, though, and doubled as a stage manager by night, and on Sundays. His name was Julius Sinykin. He was five years older than Jack and, despite their initial run-in, they soon became very close friends.

Jack had the ability to fall asleep anywhere. Years later, he once appeared in a television show called "The Burglars," and one of the scenes took place in Jack's bedroom. It was a typical Benny bit. Jack was supposedly having trouble falling asleep. His bed had been rigged up so that, with one tug, it would turn into a large cradle—rockers and all. Once all preparation had been made, the director, Don Weis, called for action. As the scene started, two burglars came through the window, flashlights in hand. There was supposed to be an exchange of dialogue between the actors, but it was interrupted when the sound engineer yelled "Cut." Over the dialogue, he kept hearing strange noises. He couldn't figure it out, since they were filming on a soundproof stage.

He called the producer, Hilliard Marks, over and said, "Listen . . . what the hell is that noise?" Hickey put on his earphones for a few seconds, then started to laugh . . . Jack had actually fallen asleep during the take. What the engineer heard was his snoring.

CHAPTER FOUR

As a TEEN-AGER, Benny was a bright boy, but a poor student. As much as he disliked the boring practice of scales—preferring to attack *real* violin pieces—he hated school and homework even more. This lack of scholarship was a disappointment to his parents, and they breathed sighs of relief when he graduated from the eighth grade and entered Central High.

Then began a period in his life when, unbeknownst to his mother and father, he began playing hooky, fleeing the classroom as often as he dared, preferring to wander the streets or sit down by the lake and just dream away the day. One time, he decided to run away from home and talked his cousin Cliff Gordon into going with him. They had no idea where they would wind up but, at least for Benny, this was a way out of his situation at school—which he felt was hopeless.

When they reached Kenosha, the boys found an empty barn to sleep in. At the next town, Racine, they stayed with family friends, after first swearing them to secrecy. Then they kept on walking, hitching rides when they could. After three days, it began to rain heavily. They were tired and hungry. Finally, they limped into Milwaukee. They had traveled a little over fifty miles before admitting defeat. Benny sent a collect telegram to Meyer asking for money to get home by train. It arrived in short order.

The boys traveled back to Waukegan somewhat afraid of exactly what fate might await them. Cliff's family greeted him with open arms, just as the Kubelskys welcomed Benny. Meyer didn't punish him—the boy had learned his lesson. He *had* made it all the way to Milwaukee with enough sense left over to call for help!

For the next couple of months, Benny settled down and made an effort to study. It was no use. He had to face facts—he did not care enough about school to give up daydreaming or playing truant.

At report card time, the number of missed days added up to quite at sum. Frequently, when he did manage to show up at school, he was a disruptive influence. Talking during English, cracking jokes through history, passing notes to his friends when he should have been studying math.

Years later, when he had become Jack Benny, star, the local Waukegan newspaper interviewed a high school classmate of his.

"Was Jack really as much of a cut-up as he says he was?" the reporter asked.

The woman laughed as she remembered back over the years.

"Well, yes," she replied. "It was obvious he didn't like to study . . . He thought of some pretty funny ways to avoid settling down. One day, he hid a piece of Limburger cheese behind the radiator. It was in November, I'll never forget . . . It was cold and raining. The classroom windows were shut and the heat was going full blast.

"Gradually, this awful smell filled the room. Our teacher told us to stand out in the hall, then she went to get the janitor. It only took a few minutes before the two of them discovered cheese melted all over the back of the heater. We were all instructed to come back after school and serve detention. But Jack 'confessed' he had been responsible . . . He was sent to the principal's office and the rest of us got off the hook.

"Once Jack walked into class carrying a stack of shoe boxes. He started down the aisle toward his seat and, when he was almost there, purposely tripped himself . . . Boxes went flying all over the room. Thank goodness, they were empty!"

However memorable Benny's high school hijinks were—even years later—to his school chums, for his parents it was a trying period. But there *was* one area of visible accomplishment. He was the outstanding member of the Waukegan Township High School Orchestra, playing first violin.

In 1909, the group gave a public concert. Benny arranged for his parents and sister to have seats right down in front. Proudly they beamed as they listened to the musicians—still children, really. There was Nathan Blumberg, Emma Baddaker, and Ben Swartz on the top row of the risers. In the middle were Cliff Forrester, Nellie Henderson, Harold Griffin, Hazel Cole, and Johnny Palmateer. And on the bottom row—right in front—were Phillip Kraft, Nathan Rosenblum, and Benny Kubelsky.

When her son stepped forward in mid-program and played his solo from *Il Trovatore,* Emma began to cry. Leaning over, she whispered to her husband, "All our sacrifices have been worthwhile. Maybe he isn't such a scholar . . . but he makes beautiful music!"

Benny spent the next year continuing to bluff his way through Central High. At the end of his second term, the principal informed Meyer that his son was flunking every course. There was no alternative. Benny was expelled.

Just how deeply affected Jack was by this turn of events would be manifested in everything he did later on in life. The look of hurt and shame on his father's face and the tears in his mother's eyes were pictures he carried around inside of him for years.

Although he didn't know it at the time, his lack of a formal education would actually work for him. He began to compensate in a variety of ways. He became an avid reader. He acquired a thirst for knowledge. On his own, he learned lessons about life that did not come from textbooks. All through this molding process, he retained a sense of humility, a simplicity that would eventually endear him to audiences all over the world.

After Benny was tossed out of school, his father was determined to keep his son "in harness." He was put to work in Meyer's haberdashery store. But after he botched up a few sales, and allowed customers who had no credit to charge merchandise, he was fired.

At his father's insistence, he then enrolled in the Waukegan

Business College, run by a Mr. B. A. Munson. This proved as unchallenging to Benny as Central High. After a few weeks, he failed. His father was beside himself. What future could a boy expect out of life when he refused or was unable to succeed at anything? It's possible he could wind up—God forbid—a bum!

Strange as it seems, throughout this period of trial and error, Benny remained in some ways a cocky kid. He was just sixteen, had been expelled from high school, fired by his father, a failure at business college, yet he still was successful at one thing—daydreaming. Who knew whether someday he might not be one of those passengers boarding the train, his arms full of luggage, headed for . . . somewhere. Maybe even the big time. At least he thought so, especially after he turned to his friend Julius Sinykin, who got him a job playing violin in the pit of the Barrison Theater —Waukegan's top vaudeville house.

The Barrison pit band consisted of drums, cornet, piano, and violin. The pianist was also the leader: Cora Salisbury. At one time, she had played in vaudeville, doing a talking and piano act. But after her husband died, she retired from show business and settled down in Waukegan to nurse her sick mother. Then came the chance to go to work at the Barrison.

She was a lively, intelligent woman, with an enormous bouffant hairdo and an even more enormous bust. At forty-five, she was a fine musician, and could improvise, sight-read, and also compose music.

Cora was the motherly sort and took a helpful interest in Benny's career. She encouraged him to think he had a promising musical future in vaudeville. She saw to it that Benny became a card-carrying member of the Waukegan local of the American Federation of Musicians.

Ironically, another woman came into Benny's life at this time— a woman who *indirectly* played one of the most important parts in Benny's life. Her name was Minnie Palmer. She was the mother of the Marx Brothers and traveled with the boys' vaudeville act. A brilliant woman, she had a keen instinct for show business talent, and during the period around 1911, she had devised an act for her sons that would soon make them the rage of vaudeville . . . top headliners.

But in 1911, with stardom still a few years away, the Marx Brothers and Minnie arrived in Waukegan to play the Barrison Theater. Jack remembered, "It was during a Monday rehearsal when the members of the pit band were given the music for those acts requiring it. Mrs. Palmer watched me pick up the notes fast . . . and she saw how well I played for her sons. Like every act which had music in it, the Marx Brothers carried their own orchestrations. I knocked her for a loop, and she asked me if I wanted to travel with the boys' act, play fiddle for them in the pit, and do a few comical musical cadenzas. She promised to double whatever salary the Barrison was paying me. That wouldn't have been difficult. I was only getting $7.50 a week. She also agreed to pay my transportation and room and board. The idea of leaving home, being on my own, touring with a gang of lively fellows of my age was very exciting.

"When I put the proposition to my parents, they turned me down flat. They wouldn't even listen to me." Jack sadly said good-bye to Minnie and her boys and remained behind. Exactly eleven years later, Zeppo Marx, one of Minnie's sons, and by then a close pal of Benny's, would be responsible for introducing him to the girl who eventually became his wife—Mary Livingstone!

CHAPTER FIVE

AT THE END of 1911, when the Barrison Theater closed, Cora Salisbury, the sole support of her mother, decided she would earn money by going back into vaudeville. She asked Benny to be her partner on the road. She proposed that they work up a piano-and-violin act, *strictly music*, no patter. So they designed what they thought was an act with real class: Salisbury and Kubelsky: "From Grand Opera to Ragtime."

When Benny spoke to his parents about going into vaudeville, they went into a state of shock. They knew that this time their son really meant business. He was eighteen. He wanted to make his own decisions. Still, they could not see it his way. They thought he would be ruining his life forever.

The discussion went back and forth for days. Finally Benny was granted one concession. His parents agreed to meet Cora face to face . . . to invite her to their apartment and at least discuss the situation. Jack's sister Florence, who passed away on August 9, 1977, was of enormous help to us in reconstructing Jack's early life. When we were in Chicago with her last year, she recalled vividly a scene which took place sixty-four years ago.

"Mrs. Salisbury arrived, dressed beautifully, so conservatively, so matronly. She immediately impressed our parents as a soft-spoken, respectable woman. I was sitting on the couch. My brother was pacing up and down, nervously. Mother was making a pot of tea in the kitchen, while Dad was seated in an overstuffed armchair, his hands folded, his eyes glistening, all prepared to stare Mrs. Salisbury down and be done with this vaudeville non-sense. But when he realized she was *older* than his own wife—really the motherly type—he relaxed a little bit.

"As Cora began enthusiastically talking about my brother's talent, Mother poured tea, plying Cora with home-baked cake, and seemed to be calmer and more collected. As they continued chat-ting, my brother stopped pacing and joined them at the dining room table. Cora was doing a whale of a selling job . . . Jack was beginning to see a glimmer of hope in the situation.

"Mother was afraid that Jack, an innocent young boy, would be tossed among the wolves—meaning those fast show-business girls she had heard all about. Cora put her mind at ease on that score, as well. She promised to be personally responsible for taking care of seeing to it my brother lived in respectable boarding-houses . . ."

After Cora left, Benny gave his mother an imploring look. Emma Kubelsky knew in her heart that her only son had to be al-lowed this opportunity. So she started to work on Meyer, slowly wearing down his resistance. Finally, Benny's father gave his con-sent—but only for a trial period: "Three months . . . no longer!"

Benjamin Kubelsky, suitcase and violin in hand, walked a few blocks to the Waukegan railroad station, accompanied by his mother, his father, and Florence. There were last-minute goodbyes, plus Meyer's repeated warning: "Remember, Benny, three months, I'm only giving you three months!"

* * *

Benny and Mrs. Salisbury boarded the Chicago & Northwestern. After finding seats, he pressed his face against the window and waved a last goodbye to his family.

As the train pulled out, Cora put her head back and closed her eyes. Benny, to the contrary, couldn't look hard enough at the landscape disappearing before him. In the days of his boyhood, the city of Waukegan, in Lake County, Illinois, was—and still is—a comparatively small Midwestern town. It is situated on a bluff which rises eighty feet above Lake Michigan, one of the most naturally beautiful communities in America.

The streets are quiet. Tree-lined. Neighbors are very close. The whole town indulges in a variety of group activities, from quilting bees to softball games. Everywhere, neat clapboard houses are fringed by multi-colored flowers and trim green lawns.

All over town, numerous New England-style church steeples rise high above the city's modest buildings. And, on one corner, the Kubelskys' Temple Am Echod stands. Down the street, the Elks Club Lodge Hall and restaurant overlook the lake. Nearby is the city hall and a courtroom. And today, on Madison Avenue, the Plaza Hotel still stands, a monument to old age, its three-story red brick construction intact, complete to the iron fire escapes on front of the building. Even Cora Salisbury's three-story wooden frame house, built in the early 1800s, is still standing.

From almost everywhere in town, there is a view of Lake Michigan stretching as far as the eye can see. It is rimmed by factories with white smoke pouring from their stacks. Today, the population is close to seventy-five thousand.

For comedian-to-be Jack Benny, it was the ideal backdrop, a perfect launching pad worthy of a young boy who would one day conquer Broadway, Hollywood, and the rest of the English-speaking world. A close-knit community worthy of a man who would travel hundreds of thousands of miles and yet never really leave behind that Waukegan home-town sweetness and shyness that was a basic part of his very being.

It was on a September day in 1912 that Benjamin Kubelsky, age eighteen, left Waukegan. He would never come back home again—except to visit.

CHAPTER SIX

SALISBURY AND BENNY debuted their act, being featured as the second spot on the bill, during a three-day engagement at the Majestic Theater in Gary, Indiana. They opened with a very snappy version of the *"Poet and Peasant* Overture." Cora, a consummate show woman, and an early-day exponent of the flashy Victor Borge-Liberace-style piano virtuoso, raised her hands high above the keyboard, then proceeded to race through a series of impossibly difficult musical runs. Simultaneously, Benny's fiddling fingers flew up and down the polished instrument, his bow fairly flying in mid-air as he executed a series of nimble notes that, strung together, sounded like a symphony.

To add to their startling renditions, they further took the audience by surprise by being—for those days—a very high-class-looking act. Cora's heaving bosom was skillfully draped in folds of soft velvet, which cascaded to the floor. Her pompadour and up-swept coiffure sparkled all the way to the very back row as spotlights hit the rhinestones in her tiara, forming patterns of diamond-like crisscrosses which were fairly dazzling.

As for Benny, the kid, he was as elegantly turned out as the classiest maître d' at the Plaza Hotel, wearing a tuxedo, formal shirt, and precisely the correct bow tie, an outfit Meyer carefully had tailored for his son once he'd given up trying to convince the boy that life on the road was pure folly.

The act went over so well, the management added a Benny

solo. He stood stage center, bathed in the warm glow of a maternal spotlight, and played "The Rosary." There wasn't a dry eye in the house!

Although it didn't seem possible to have their debut marred by any problems, barely three weeks after they had started out on the vaudeville circuit, Benny was in trouble. In those days, word of new acts flew faster than the supersonic Concorde. Somewhere in the Midwest, an already established violinist, Jan Kubelik, took note of an upstart kid violinist using the last name of Kubelsky.

He contacted his attorney and instructed him to inform the boy to cease and desist—immediately. The lawyer dutifully reported "the infraction" to the arbitration board of credits' authority located in the home office of the Western Vaudeville Circuit. Benny was then notified in writing of the complaint being lodged against him. He was told in no uncertain terms that he would face court action unless he stopped using the name.

Despite Benny's protests, aided by Mrs. Salisbury's confirmation that his name *really* was Kubelsky, he was informed that the fact ("if it *was* a fact") did *not* alter the situation. He was to change his name, or else!

So the act became known as Salisbury and Benny, the boy using the full name Ben K. Benny, thereby warding off his first possible conflict with the law. He was *officially* in show business now—and learning very fast!

Having weathered the "Kubelik storm," Salisbury and Benny found themselves working constantly, playing a chain of small-time theaters in the Illinois, Wisconsin, Indiana, Missouri, Ohio, Minnesota, and Michigan areas.

Years later, during numerous cross-country excursions by car—trips Jack absolutely adored—he would frequently detour, sometimes a hundred miles or more, to investigate the scene of some theater in which he had appeared twenty or thirty years before.

Jack, who had the world's worst sense of direction, constantly getting lost in a two-room hotel suite, nonetheless had an uncanny road-map-like mind when it came to making precisely the correct series of turns and maneuvers guaranteed to bring him right out in front of either the original theater, now in a dilapidated state, or, more nearly, to a completely new building. Still, he would always get out of the car and, sniffing the air like a bird dog, hunt around until he found even some small shred of evidence, some link with bygone days.

Invariably, he would remember the exact location of the local boardinghouse in which he had stayed . . . what kind of dressing room he had shared . . . how the audience had reacted . . . if he had dated any of the girls in town . . . He even remembered each theater manager's name. As he walked around town, when people came up and asked for his autograph, Jack would oblige and then, in turn, ask them: "What ever happened to the Majestic Theater that was here on the corner?"

The answer most often came back, "Why, *that* was torn down thirty-five years ago!"

During these vacations back in time, Benny, who usually hated *talking* nostalgia, but loved *driving* it, would occasionally recall his early vaudeville days.

"It wasn't easy. The whole thing was a grind. We usually played split weeks. We would hit a town, head for the cheapest boardinghouse, locate the theater, make sure we had enough glossy photos for the management to display outside, then go and unpack.

"We would do four, maybe five shows a day. Each time, I had a nervous feeling in the pit of my stomach until I got the sense of the audience . . . until I knew which numbers they really liked . . . and what they barely tolerated.

"Cora and I would run from town to town. At first, I was always tired, but at least I was young. I don't know how the hell *she* kept up the pace. Still, every other night, no matter where we were, like the dutiful lady she had promised to be, she made sure I sat down and dropped the folks a note.

"Eventually, two things saved me. First, I used my knack for falling asleep to good advantage. I snoozed on hard wooden train station benches . . . in hot ratty dressing rooms . . . on boardinghouse beds with springs so tough and mattresses so thin I'd wake up with scars on my back. Then, there was coffee. Boy, did I develop a craving for the stuff! Hot. Strong. Black. Constantly.

"Today, I look at some of these young entertainers. They're handed everything: plush studios, air-conditioned cars to trans-

22

port them from place to place, fancy dressing rooms, and accommodations at the finest hotels. I think to myself, kiddos, if you only knew how it *really* was. But hell, that was *then,* this is now. I'm all for an artist getting whatever he can. Succeeding is hard enough without all the other crap . . ."

Despite the hectic pace, Salisbury and Benny played an entire year's engagements without more than a few days off here and there. However, as they began their second year together, Cora received disturbing news from Waukegan. Her mother was seriously ill. Although reluctant to leave Benny, to give up the act, she had no choice. So Cora went home, and Benny headed for Chicago to look for someone else with whom he could form a team.

CHAPTER SEVEN

JACK ALWAYS considered his next move to be an act of providence.

"It was just such luck, running into this guy named Lyman Woods. He was so smooth, so very tall, slim, and handsome, with a pencil-thin moustache. A real Doug Fairbanks type. Lyman never had any formal musical education. He couldn't read a note of music, but he didn't have to. He was a natural. He could hear a tune once and then sit down and play it, note for note. It was positively uncanny . . .

"We got together, only this time, *I* took top billing. You see, I had decided to change the spelling of my name to *Bennie*. I thought it looked much classier! The act became Bennie and Woods: 'From Grand Opera to Ragtime.' I borrowed a page from Cora's book, and we opened with the *'Poet and Peasant* Overture.' Then Lyman would do a medley of a Brahms' 'Hungarian Dance' and a Chopin nocturne—he sounded like Van Cliburn.

"Next, I'd come on with 'The Rosary,' played straight, and immediately segue from that into a snappier version called 'When

Ragtime Rosy Ragged the Rosary.' The audience howled. Then we had a few more standards like 'Waitin' for the Robert E. Lee' and 'Twelfth Street Rag.' We would walk off to applause, pause, then return, stage center, to finish with a duet of 'Alexander's Ragtime Band,' a number we purposely joked up. It was always calculated to bring us—*mainly me*—lots of laughs. I really used to ham it up, gesturing broadly, wildly rolling my eyes. Still, as with Cora, during our entire act, neither of us said a word . . ."

It wasn't long before the boys were getting better-class bookings, pulling down $350 a week, a very big sum for those days. In addition to playing nicer theaters, they were also hitting bigger towns: Boston, Portland, San Francisco.

During those days, Benny was considered quite the Beau Brummell. He spent nearly every dime he earned on fancy clothes, jazzy ties, a diamond stickpin, and a flashy pinkie ring. He also wore shoes that did everything but glow in the dark. If it hadn't been for his old buddy, Julius Sinykin, Benny would have wound up completely broke for all his efforts. However, the pal who had gotten him his start at the Barrison Theater had also made a pact with Benny when the boy first went on the road.

"Send me a few dollars every week . . . a five spot when you can manage it," Julius had advised. "I'll open a bank account for you. Then, God forbid, if you have any layovers, or things don't go right, you'll have a little something to fall back on. After all, you don't want to have to depend on your father again for money, do you?"

The moment he heard the latter remark, Benny readily promised to send money to Julius every week. The last thing on earth he wanted was to come crawling home to his dad for dough. After all, he'd been given permission to go out on the road for only a three months' trial run . . . but it was now *three years* since he had been on his own. Even though he was determined to make good, if things ever went wrong, at least he could come back to Waukegan with a little bit saved. "Sinykin's nest egg" was Benny's salvation.

During the years from 1912 to 1917, usually in the summertime, when bookings were slim, Benny returned to Chicago. He and Julius would meet there, take a suite at the Edgewater Beach

Hotel, and Julius would dole out a generous portion of Jack's "mad money." Then the two of them would go out on the town for the weekend with the "fastest girls" Benny could dig up—a big factor in Sinykin's *willingness* to supply Benny so liberally with money!

Julius had remained behind in Waukegan when Benny went on the road. He was still a "small-town boy," while his crony seemed to become flashier with every rise in billing. To Sinykin, Benny was the conquering hero home for a frantic weekend "from the front," all geared for three days and nights of debauchery—which Julius loved to share. To Benny, Sinykin was the thrifty, prudent "savings and loan" tycoon who made all of their fun financially feasible.

"Bennie" and Woods worked together successfully as a team for close to five years. Then, in 1917, the big time was finally within their grasp. Arthur Klein, their booking agent, one of the best in the business, finally decided the duo had "apprenticed" long enough. The proper moment had arrived for the boys to be booked into the *ne plus ultra* of vaudeville—the Palace.

Bennie and Woods got their big chance—*and bombed*. It happened on a Monday evening, September 9, 1917. The first act on the bill was a clever animal group, Everest's Monkeys, who worked hilariously together on stage without the benefit of their trainer. He stood in the wings and cued them.

Bennie and Woods came next. They were followed by a series of enormously famous and talented people, including Walter Kelly (Princess Grace's uncle), doing his well-known Virginia judge routine, and Smith and Dale, performing their Dr. Kronkite sketch, which was then, and still is, considered a classic.

To say Bennie and Woods bombed is being kind. Actually, they were greeted with *indifference*. The day following their debut, they were briefly reviewed in the New Acts section of the show-business bible, *Variety*:

BENNIE & WOODS
11 Mins. One. Palace, New York

Two young men, pianist and violinist, open with a syncopated duet, piano solo medley with the player travestying the long haired musician type. "Poor Butterfly" duet exaggeratedly rhapsodized, etc. Both with violins for encore, laughs, and the pianist through holding the fiddle awkwardly. Pleasing turn for an early spot.

On the face of it, the reviewer had not gone out of his way to be brutal. It was what he *didn't* say, rather than his comparatively tepid words, which indicated to those "in the trade" that Bennie and Woods obviously didn't have what it took to become big-time vaudeville headliners.

A short time afterward, the guys from "Grand Opera to Ragtime" dissolved their partnership, playing their final engagement in Milwaukee. It was not only the Palace flop, but circumstances which precipitated the split. Jack had received tragic news from home. Years before, it had been Cora Salisbury who broke up the act to return home and attend to her ailing mother. This time, it was Jack's turn to go home in sadness. His mother was dying.

As Florence Fenchel recalled, "My mother's illness had begun two years before. Early in 1915, she had gone to Chicago to be with her father just prior to his death. Afterward, she stayed on to make the funeral arrangements. While she was there, she accidentally discovered a lump in her chest area. Fearful, she went to a doctor immediately. He advised surgery, and the lump was removed.

"Mother came home feeling weak, but nevertheless apparently recovered. Of course, Dad and I got in touch with Jack. He came home and stayed until Mother felt stronger before going back out on the road.

"Months passed. Mom began feeling very bad. This time, the doctor told her she needed a radical mastectomy—both breasts were removed. It was a terrible ordeal for her. The surgery had to be performed with only a local anesthetic. Mother was a diabetic and they were afraid to give her full anesthesia. There was no insulin then, and diabetic patients were pure surgical risks.

"After the operation, the doctor told Dad Mother had, at most, sixty days to live. But she was a big woman, with a great deal of will power, and kept fighting the disease. She lived on for more than a year, but the illness took its toll. She went down to eighty pounds . . .

"The last time Jack came home, near the end, it was heart-breaking. She was barely recognizable. Finally, mercifully, her suffering ended. She died in November of 1917, at the age of forty-seven. Jack was then twenty-three, I was seventeen . . .

"My brother took her death very hard. He was doubly saddened because it was she who convinced Dad to let him go on the road . . . who always interceded when she felt our father was being too strict . . . I guess it hurt Jack most of all because she passed away without ever having seen him live up to his potential as a classical violinist . . ."

CHAPTER EIGHT

THE POSTERS were in store windows all over town: bearded, paternal, inspiring Uncle Sam, wearing red, white, and blue . . . Kindly eyes looking directly into yours . . . Arm extended, index finger pointed, as the words I WANT YOU fairly leaped off the sign. Three weeks after his mother's death, Benny took the poster personally. He enlisted in the Navy.

For as far back as anyone can remember, everything Benny did was tinged with a special style. The day he left home was no exception. He packed his personal belongings and said goodbye to his father and Florence. Then he rushed down the stairs to an awaiting car.

There, sitting in front of the Kubelskys' Genessee Street apartment, was the shiniest, flashiest Stutz Bearcat in town. Behind the wheel sat Benny's former classmate and close friend, Stubb Wilbur, revving the motor and tooting the horn.

The two boys roared down the streets of Waukegan. When they had traveled a total distance of eleven and a half miles, Wilbur stopped. Benny got out, shook hands, and made a mock salute. He had arrived at his destination: the newly established Great Lakes Naval Training Station.

For the past few years, he had been Ben K. Bennie, vaudeville performer. Now, once again, he was Benjamin Kubelsky—just another body for boot camp.

Jack remembered his days as a sailor with mixed emotions—mostly affectionately. "The first three months at Great Lakes, I went through the usual training, learning all the nautical procedures, marching in every type of weather: actually there were two kinds on the Lake Michigan shores that year, sleet and snow. I was not wild about drilling, or taking orders from chief petty officers, but I obeyed. It almost cost my father heart failure.

"I was performing one of my 'nautical duties,' piling large pieces of lumber into neat stacks, when who should come visiting but Dad and Florence. He took one look at me, and all he could think to yell out was, 'Benny . . . Benny . . . your hands! Watch your hands!' Quite obviously, he felt my violin playing ranked above stacking wood for the Navy!"

Benny mostly hung around with a few sailors who had been in show business before the war. Among them was Edward Elzear Confrey, nicknamed Zez. Confrey was from the Chicago area, and the same age as Benny. Before enlisting, he had been playing various instruments in pit bands of vaudeville houses around the Midwest.

To pass the time, the twosome joined forces, playing ragtime duets, Benny on the fiddle, Zez on the piano. They made such syncopated harmony together, they decided to team up after the war and do a vaudeville act.

Meanwhile, every Saturday, a whole group of "show-business sailors" put on impromptu evenings of entertainment. Benny either played violin solos or did his duet with Zez. One night, he made the mistake of playing "The Rosary"—perfectly straight—and found himself the target of booing from his fellow bluejackets. Dave Wolff, a close pal who was standing in the wings, walked out on stage and whispered something in Benny's ear, just as though it were a planned part of Kubelsky's routine.

What Wolff actually said was, "For God's sake, Ben, you're dying. Put down the damn fiddle and start talking!" In desperation, Benny looked out at the sea of faces and ad-libbed, "I was having an argument with Dave Wolff this morning . . ."

Benny paused, not because he had already developed his great sense of timing, but rather because he couldn't think of what to say next. "Well . . . anyway . . . this morning, I was having this argument with Dave about . . . the Irish Navy . . ."

The sweet sound of laughter erupted, giving Benny confidence to go on. "You see, I claim the Swiss Navy is bigger than the Irish Navy . . . but that the *Jewish* Navy is bigger than both of them put together . . ."

He brought the house down.

Encouraged, Benny went on with several more one-liners—and the gobs laughed and applauded loudly. Technically, this was the *first time* he had ever spoken words on a stage. In his seven years in vaudeville, with both Cora Salisbury and Lyman Woods, he could have been a mute for all his audiences knew. He had never uttered one line on stage. But now, with the sound of laughter ringing in his ears, a seed was implanted that would grow and flourish. As a performer, he *could* get laughs—*without* rolling his eyes and cutting up on his violin!

Around this time, the commanding officer of Great Lakes, Captain William A. Moffett (later Rear Admiral Moffett, Chief of the Naval Bureau of Aeronautics, who died in the crash of the dirigible *Akron*), was approached by his wife, the head of the Navy Relief Fund. Mrs. Moffett suggested the boys put on a show to raise money for her cause.

The captain agreed, and a notice was posted in the rec hall:

WANTED
Talent with some previous professional experience for show to be produced called *The Great Lakes Revue*. All interviews will be held at Navy Relief Headquarters, Main Camp.

"When I saw the sign, I couldn't run fast enough. Zez and I were picked to do a fifteen-minute specialty of ragtime pieces. Both of us figured this would be ideal experience for breaking in our future vaudeville act. We billed ourselves as 'Kubelsky and Confrey: Fooling Around with Piano and Fiddle.' Fortunately for Mrs. Moffett, there was a lot of other talent floating around camp!

"Originally, all I was supposed to do was the act with Zez. Dave Wolff, the guy who had whispered in my ear during 'The Rosary,' wrote and directed all the sketches, as well as setting up the sequence in which his 'talent' would be presented.

"One morning, at rehearsal, they were putting in a new sketch in which a buddy of mine, Bob Carleton (the composer of 'Ja-Da'), was to play an admiral. They needed somebody to act as his orderly. It was a snazzy part consisting of *two lines*. Dave looked around at the group of guys waiting on stage to rehearse, then pointed to me. It was one of those fluke things. I guess he figured if I could work my way out of 'The Rosary,' I could certainly deliver a couple of lines of dialogue. I read for the part in my flat, Midwestern tone. Then Dave heard a few more guys. By contrast, all of them overplayed the bit, so he cast me in the role . . ."

As rehearsals continued, Wolff kept increasing the part. By the time the revue opened at the Great Northern Auditorium in Chicago, Benny had become the comedy hit of the show, playing Izzy There, the admiral's disorderly.

The boys toured for two weeks, traveling to Detroit, Battle Creek, St. Louis, Kansas City, Cleveland, Cincinnati, and Milwaukee. The run ended with two final performances at the New Majestic Theatre in Waukegan.

His hometown paper hailed Benny in glowing terms as, "Waukegan's own stage star and particular pride . . . Benny and Confrey have a neat little act in the vaudeville portion of *The Great Lakes Revue* . . . Along with considerable laughable nonsense, they dispense some teasing tunes of a decidedly 'raggy' nature. Benny uses his eyes to such effect in this act, that more than one critic has called him the sailor with the come hither eyes. Some orbs, they are . . ." The paper then went on to praise his performance as being the standout comedy hit of the show.

After the armistice, in November 1918, it wasn't long before Benny Kubelsky was once more a civilian. There was only one problem: the Navy would *not* release Confrey—he was the only ragtime piano player they had! After waiting a frustrating length of time, Benny decided he had to go back to work. Rather than going on a search for another partner, he decided to do a single. Later on, incidentally, Confrey would become famous as both a performer and a composer, writing, among other songs, "Kitten on the Keys."

There is one postscript to this period. Also stationed at Great

Lakes during this time were two other young Midwesterners, Pat O'Brien and Spencer Tracy. But they never met Benny until years later, when all of them wound up in Hollywood as top stars.

Pat O'Brien recalls, "There were sixty thousand men at Great Lakes. Spence and I were childhood friends and enlisted together, but we never bumped into Jack. By the time my career took me to Hollywood, he was already there, and I had read stories about him which mentioned his Great Lakes background. When we finally did meet we became fast friends.

"Jack was a prince of a man. He was always doing such thoughtful things for people. I'll never forget my thirty-fifth birthday. As a surprise, Jack hired a huge beer wagon. He and Mary, George and Gracie, the Jimmy Cagneys, and the Robert Youngs all climbed on board and came roaring up my driveway. When I heard the noise, I ran outside. What a sight! Jack was sitting right up front, getting such a kick out of my stunned delight.

"Over the years, whenever we met," O'Brien continued, "we never failed to try and pull some gag on each other. Once, I was going to New York on business, when I found out that Jack was back there, staying at a certain hotel. On the day I arrived, he was playing gin rummy at the Friars Club with George Burns and Jack Waldron.

"I was walking down the street, thinking of some joke I could pull on Jack, when suddenly I turned the corner and saw fire engines in front of his hotel. I walked over and discovered there was a small conflagration going on inside. Immediately, I ran to the nearest Western Union and sent Jack a wire at the Friars:

> DON'T GO BACK TO YOUR HOTEL . . .
> IT'S ON FIRE. LOVE. PAT O'BRIEN

"A couple of hours later, when I walked into my own lobby, there was a telegram waiting for me:

> BE A NICE GUY. STOP BY MY HOTEL,
> GO THROUGH THE FLAMES AND SEE IF
> MY ROOM IS BURNING. LOVE. JACK

"The son-of-a-gun had received my message, but never missed a hand in his gin game!"

CHAPTER NINE

IT WAS 1919. America was still reeling from the aftershocks of World War I. In Chicago, a young chap played his first single engagement in Springfield, Illinois. He was billed as Ben K. Benny: "Fiddle Funology," and his act consisted of a potpourri of things he had done before, including the *"Poet and Peasant* Overture," done now in syncopated ragtime.

It was a struggle trying to make it on his own. Lacking the money to buy a complete routine, Benny made up a few jokes, added several comic bits on the fiddle, and also started to sing, in a rough, untrained baritone voice.

Once he had the act refined to the best of his ability, he got himself booked on the Western Vaudeville Time, the Gus Sun Time, the Poli Time, the Loew Time—all circuits in and around the same towns he had played before the war. He was still holding down the number-two spot, and audiences were still shuffling in while he was trying to perform.

Sudie Gordon, a native of Texas, has lived in Waukegan for fifty-seven years. She is a "double relative" of Benny's. Her maiden name was Sachs—the same as Jack's mother, Emma. Her father and Emma were first cousins. She grew up to marry Cliff Gordon, whose mother and Meyer Kubelsky, Jack's father, were sister and brother.

Sudie recalls, "When I was a young girl, one of Jack's favorite stops on his vaudeville tour was my home town, Dallas. We were always such a close family, and Jack looked forward to playing our local theater, the Majestic, because that meant he could come and stay with us.

"I guess he had his fill of boardinghouses, because he sure went for my mother's cooking. Every night, my father would get out the family car and we would all drive to the theater together to see one of Jack's early evening performances. Then, afterward, Daddy would go back to see Jack's last show, and wait to drive him home.

"Those were wonderful days for all of us. Of course, Jack wasn't any big star then—not to the public. But to the Sachs family, he was always a 'top headliner!' "

For Jack, these years represented a period of trial and error. He was struggling hard to stay alive—buying a novelty routine here, a few jokes there, whatever he could afford. Despite his lack of headliner success, however, he *did* run into another snag. Vaudeville star Ben Bernie reported him for using a name "obviously geared toward cashing in on *my* name and fame." So, once again, Benny was jolted into coming up with a new identity.

At this time, there was a sharp comic making big inroads. His name was Jack Osterman—and Benny was in awe of him. Borrowing Osterman's first name, and using his *own* first name last, Ben K. Benny became Jack Benny. He did not like it very much —but he had little choice!

As Jack recalled, "In January of 1921, I decided to debut with my latest routine at Proctor's Fifth Avenue. It was the place where many other new acts tried out. None other than Sime Silverman, founder, editor, and publisher of the show business bible, *Variety,* reviewed me. He was one of the most powerful behind-the-scenes men on Broadway . . ."

Here's part of what Silverman wrote:

NEW ACTS
(January 21, 1921)

Jack Benny
Monologist
14 Mins.; One
5th Ave., N.Y.

"Jack Benny has a violin and talk. Mainly talk. He handles himself as though having played small time, though his talk material is new. When Benny said he had stopped smoking, as smoking is now too effeminate, he waited for the expected laugh which was not as hearty as he looked for, so he repeated the gag. Later when nearing the finish and the right exit, he pointed to his name on the

33

card, while playing the violin and saying, 'Jack Benny. That's me. They couldn't get my right name on it . . .'

"In outline of turn, Benny has been a student of Ben Bernie, it seems. He talks much like Bernie, but has none of Bernie's gags. His violin playing is negligible for results. He holds the instrument in the regular way under the neck, whereas Bernie holds it carelessly, often against his body . . .

". . . But Benny seems able to help himself. His only worry just now may be how he is going to follow Bernie if he can make the big time. The answer seems to be for Benny to throw away his violin while Bernie is using one, and try another method of working in his talk, if he doesn't care to become a monologist, outright . . ."

"Although Sime was wrong comparing me with Ben Bernie," Jack said, "I suppose it was only natural, since I had taken out an advertisement in *Variety* announcing my name change, and Sime knew that Bernie had lodged a complaint against me.

"But he was perfectly right suggesting I 'throw away' the violin and become strictly a talker . . . There was only one problem—I couldn't do it. I was so psychologically dependent on the fiddle that other acts on a bill, knowing this, sometimes tortured me. They would steal my violin and hide it backstage just a few minutes before the orchestra played my entrance cue . . . and I couldn't go on without it.

"Shortly after Sime's *Variety* review, I was booked to play a week at Keith's Syracuse, where I always had been a riot. I decided that was the place to experiment and go on without my fiddle.

"The first day, I walked on stage empty-handed. I literally forced myself to go on. I did fourteen minutes without the violin, and came off soaked with perspiration from head to toe. I was a nervous wreck. The next day, I did my routine *with* the fiddle again."

Years later, by the time Hickey Marks went to work for Jack as a writer, Benny was an enormous star. Hickey remembers, "One of Jack's idiosyncrasies was his desire for warmth. We would be in Las Vegas, where it was a hundred and ten in the shade, but Jack never turned on the air conditioner. Everyone around him would

Jack's maternal grandmother, Mrs. Sachs. (Benny Family Personal
Collection)

Jack at eight months. (Benny Family Personal Collection)

Hilliard Marks and his "big" sister, Mary. (Benny Family Personal Collection)

Jack Benny, boy violin virtuoso. (Benny Family Personal Collection)

Best Wishes from Salisbury and Benny

Jack and Cora Salisbury. (Benny Family Personal Collection)

Jack and Lyman Woods. (Benny Family Personal Collection)

Jack, Florence, and their father, Meyer Kubelsky. (Benny Family Personal Collection)

L. to R.: Al Jolson, Jack, Ted Husing, Rudy Vallee, Irene Bordoni, and Lou Holtz on the beach in Miami, Florida. (Benny Family Personal Collection)

Jack and Ann Sheridan in a still from Warner's *George Washington Slept Here*. (Benny Family Personal Collection)

be dripping with perspiration, while he remained cool, calm, and dry.

"He would put on a fresh blue shirt under his jacket, go on stage, perform under hot lights, return to the dressing room, remove his jacket, and there wouldn't be one drop of sweat! I always shook my head, went to change my own shirt—which was soaking wet just from *watching* him perform. Obviously as his confidence grew, when he became successfully established, Jack's nervousness disappeared—forever!"

At the end of 1921, Jack was doing yet another act, this time billing himself as Jack Benny: Aristocrat of Humor. The essence of the routine revolved around low-key topical jokes, plus long stories about his supposed girl friends—*dumb ones*—always good for a laugh.

It was at this time that Jack met some very special people who were to become associated with him in various ways throughout his lifetime. One was a beautiful, blue-eyed blonde named Mary Kelly, a partner in a dance act called Swift and Kelly. She was living at the Coolidge Hotel, rooming with two other aspiring vaudevillians, Gracie Allen and Renee Arnold. At the time, Gracie was rehearsing a new act with a comic named George Burns. Through Mary Kelly, Jack met Gracie and George.

Recently, as George reminisced about his best friend, the usual Burns funny façade was, for the most part, missing . . . replaced by words of deep love and respect.

"When I first met Jack, he was such a beautiful man . . . He was so handsome . . . so slim . . . so suave . . . He had those blue eyes and that velvet voice . . . Well, he was a knockout on stage.

"He was already making $400, maybe $450 a week. Very big money in those days. He was a great monologist, playing number four on the bill. It was a choice spot in a big-time show which had seven or eight acts. Then he was promoted to the next to closing spot. If Gracie and I were on the same bill with him, he would be fourth and we would be seventh. Jack was doing better in vaudeville than Gracie and I were.

"Even back then, he did stingy jokes . . . Like the one about taking his date to dinner—and she got so excited she dropped her *tray*. Or, his penny arcade routine. (If you blow up to one hundred, you get your penny back. His date couldn't find him; he'd collapsed under the machine trying to blow too hard!)

"The thing is, here was Jack Benny—all alone—about to wipe out a *whole* country. Previously, stingy jokes in vaudeville were always about Scotland and Scotchmen . . . Eventually, if another comic told a stingy joke, it was about Jack. Even in Scotland they told tight jokes about Jack—*they* were glad to get off the hook . . .

"Never forget, it is the audience that makes you a star. They help shape and create your act. Essentially, it's a marriage of a talent with an audience. If the performer is smart enough, he observes what his audience laughs at loudest . . . In this way his act was shaped, refined, honed to—in Jack's case—perfection.

"So, he did a few stingy jokes, and *that's* what they laughed at loudest. The stingy bit fit him perfectly because the whole thing was so incongruous. If there was ever anybody who *didn't* look stingy, it was Jack. He was so immaculate . . . so elegant on stage. When he told a stingy joke, the contrast was just ridiculous . . .

"Jack was still a bachelor then," George continued. "Although he and Mary Kelly were going together, he remained quite a Don Juan. Whenever he and Mary couldn't be together, when bookings separated them, while Jack was 'loyal,' he always had some cute number in every town . . .

"In truth, it was the girls who pursued him—he was that handsome. But he and Mary *did* 'go steady' for nearly four years. While Gracie and I were married during this period, things didn't work out for Kelly and Benny.

"It was just one of those religious things. Both Gracie and Mary were Catholic . . . Jack and I were Jewish. There was never any problem about the difference in religion between Gracie and me. All our married life, she remained a staunch Catholic, which was fine with me. But I think Jack and Mary Kelly had problems along that line . . . Problems they just couldn't work out . . ."

Jack's sister clarified that episode in her brother's life.

"Jack came home to Waukegan one weekday between bookings and confided in me that he wanted to marry Mary Kelly. I told him whatever he wanted to do was fine with me, but he'd better talk to our father first. Jack was nervous at the prospect of coming right out and telling Dad. But he agreed with me that it was the only thing to do.

"I'll never forget that night. Dad came home for dinner and Jack was nervously walking back and forth in the living room. It reminded me of the day, years before, when our father was about to confront Cora Salisbury about taking Jack on the road. This time, however, our mother was gone. Jack no longer had her to act as a buffer.

"I made a good dinner and, midway through the meal, Jack just blurted out, 'Dad, I want to marry Mary Kelly.' Our father just sat there for a minute, then said quietly, 'Well, don't you think you should at least bring her home first so I can meet her?' Jack was stunned. Step one had been accomplished. Dad wanted to see her —even knowing her last name was Kelly!

"Remember," Florence said, "my brother was no longer a teenage kid asking for permission. He was *thirty-two years old*. In the public's eyes, a successful man. Still, Jack had a great deal of respect for Dad . . . and always a bit of a fear of him.

"A few weeks later, Jack brought Mary Kelly to Waukegan. Despite himself and his Orthodox beliefs, Dad fell as much under Mary's spell as Jack. She was so lovely. Tall, slim, blue-eyed, with blond hair and the sweetest face. After they had sat and talked awhile, Mary came into the kitchen with me, while Jack and Dad went outside to take a walk.

"Later that same evening, Jack told me what Dad had said. 'Benny (he always called him that—name changes not withstanding), Benny, I would rather you had fallen in love with a Jewish girl . . . But if Mary Kelly makes you happy, go ahead and marry her. She seems like a lovely person . . .'

"After Jack and Mary left Waukegan, Dad and I figured it would only be a matter of time before the wedding took place. A few months later, when Jack was home again between bookings, telling me all the while about how he and Mary were going to be married very soon, a telegram arrived—from Mary. It simply said she was sorry but she had just married *someone else* . . .

"Jack was heartbroken. It wasn't until later that he learned

Mary's father, a Chicago policeman, and her brother, a priest, had threatened to disown her if she married him.

"I can still see Jack sitting on the couch, reading and rereading that telegram, and just shaking his head. They had gone together for nearly four years. Now, it was over . . .

"Jack stayed close to home all that week with Dad and me. Then he left for California to fill an engagement at the Orpheum Theater in Los Angeles. It was early 1926 and, while Jack was still not a top headliner, he was very close to it—more successful professionally than he had ever been before."

CHAPTER TEN

"I'M QUITE SURE I was not in love with Jack Benny when I married him. I'm convinced he was not really in love with me, either. At the beginning, we had nothing in common except our senses of humor, and the fact that, when I was little, I had studied the violin . . ."

Mary Livingstone Benny began to talk, softly, shyly at first, until memories came crowding back, and her words spilled out.

"On the night he proposed to me, Jack was a newly rejected suitor, just coming out from under a four-year love affair. When I accepted him, I was wearing another boy's engagement ring. What we had together—our great love for each other—came gradually over that first year.

"I was a teen-age bride. Jack was thirty-three. I didn't know what being in love was all about. Jack was very handsome, and I was in love with the *idea* of love . . . of getting married and traveling with a husband who had a profession that seemed glamorous and exciting to me. When I watched him perform from backstage, or from a seat in the second row, I'd listen to the laughs, the applause, the comments of admiration, and think how lucky I was.

But that certainly *wasn't* love—although at the time, I was too immature to recognize the difference.

"I do know that, on my wedding day, January 14, 1927, my life changed in ways I had never anticipated. Before Jack, I'd led a happy life. He opened up a whole new world to me. With him, I found complete and total fulfillment.

"We lived together for forty-eight years. We worked together in vaudeville, on radio, in motion pictures, and on television. We shared everything. We discussed everything. He adored me. I adored him . . . I always will.

"Contrary to all those publicized stories, my *first* meeting with Jack was *not* in Los Angeles at the hosiery counter of the May Company—*that* came later. I initially laid eyes on him in the dining room of my parents' home at 1649 Nelson Street, in Vancouver, British Columbia. I was going on thirteen—and I couldn't stand him!

"My mother and father, Esther and David Marks, were among Vancouver's most affluent, socially prominent citizens. Dad, an extremely successful businessman, was president of the temple and very active in civic affairs. He and my mother enjoyed entertaining. They derived a particular pleasure out of opening their home to show-business performers appearing in town at the Orpheum, our local vaudeville house. Friday night suppers were frequently gay and interesting affairs, as the country's top stars had an opportunity to relax in the warmth and comfort of a home away from home, so to speak . . .

"One Friday, during the Passover holiday of 1922, my father invited the Marx Brothers (no relation) to join the family for dinner. They were then heading the Orpheum bill. But only Zeppo arrived—bringing Jack Benny with him.

"Jack and Zeppo were close friends and frequently roomed together on the road. As I later found out, when Zeppo told Jack about the prospect of a good Passover meal, he also said that he had heard the Marks family had two daughters, 'very cute numbers'—so Jack had been more than anxious to go along!

"What greeted them when they entered our dining room was my older sister, Babe, my younger brother, Hilliard, and me. Incidentally, my name then was Sadie. After a brief time, I heard Jack whisper to Zeppo, 'What did you bring me to meet these kids for? Let's get out of here!' Shortly thereafter, both of them beat a hasty retreat!

"Needless to say, my first impression of Jack Benny was simply that he was a very rude man. Childishly, I wanted to get even. The next day I gathered a large group of my school chums . . . We went down to the Orpheum Theater and purchased front-row seats. When Jack made his entrance on stage, I noticed that some of the audience was still shuffling into their seats. That's when *I* added to the confusion. I signaled to my cronies—whom I'd coached in advance—and we all heckled Jack throughout his entire performance.

"It was not a very auspicious beginning to what became a great love affair . . .

"Four years passed. I'd grown up and graduated from King George High School in Vancouver. Then my family moved to San Francisco. Our stay there was brief—just long enough for Babe's lavish wedding to vaudeville performer Al Bernivici. He was a violinist, appearing in a musical act called the Bernivici Brothers.

"In actuality, Al's last name *wasn't* Bernivici . . . and the other fiddle player in the act was *not* his brother. They were typical vaudevillians, members of an honored profession in which almost everyone was not who they claimed to be. The only *authentic* part of their musical act was the violin each played.

"Shortly after Babe's wedding, the family moved for the last time, settling down in Los Angeles. By then I had decided not to go on to college, and had taken a job selling hosiery at the May Company.

"It was 1926—and Jack Benny came to town to play an engagement at the Orpheum Theater. At that point, he had been on tour with the Bernivicis, and had become acquainted with Babe, who simultaneously returned from her Chicago home to visit the family. When she discovered Jack was appearing locally, she went to see his show, and invited me to come along.

"I couldn't make it. I was steady-dating a young law student, Eddie Brand (now a retired Los Angeles Superior Court judge). For a whole week Babe kept going back to see Jack's show, and she repeatedly asked me to come along. My answer was always no

—until one night Eddie had to work, and I was free. But that evening, Babe already had invited a girl friend to go with her. At the last minute, she said I could come along, too.

"After the show, Jack, a fellow performer on the bill, Babe, and her girl friend went to a supper club. I tagged along. When the four of them got up to dance, leaving me alone at the table, I became bored. When they finally came back and sat down, they started a conversation which excluded me. So I got up and left. As for Jack Benny, four years' time *hadn't* changed him in my eyes. He still seemed to be a pretty rude man—he barely said a word to me all evening!

"The following day, I was behind my hosiery counter at the May Company, swamped with business, when I looked up and saw Jack coming toward me. He got within hearing distance of my customers, then said, 'Pardon me, miss, can you tell me where the men's room is?'

"I was so embarrassed, I snapped back, 'Ask the floorwalker!'

"Jack played in town for the next two weeks. One day, on impulse, I told Eddie Brand I'd heard about a great comedian appearing at the Orpheum—a guy Babe knew and raved about. I suggested we go to see the show, so Eddie got tickets in the second row. When Jack first came on stage, he looked out in the audience, saw me, and made a few remarks directly *to me*. Eddie heard all he had to hear. He got up and walked out, leaving me sitting there alone.

"When the show was over," Mary continued, "I didn't know what to do. I had no money with me . . . So I went backstage and asked for Jack. When he came out, I said, 'I've only come to borrow enough so I can take a cab home.' Without a word, he reached in his pocket and pulled out a few dollars. He gave the money to me and I just left.

"The following afternoon, I was busy behind my counter. When I looked up, I saw Jack just standing there, staring at me. The minute our eyes met, he smiled—and walked away. For several more days, he kept coming in, but never talked to me. Finally, one day, he came in and asked me to have dinner with him after that night's performance. Since it happened to be another evening when Eddie was working, I said okay.

"Jack took me to the Coconut Grove in the Ambassador Hotel, a plush, romantic room for dining and dancing. As we walked in, the orchestra was playing 'Who?' I could be corny and say that became 'our song,' but it's not true. Still, to this day, whenever I hear that melody, my first date with Jack becomes very vivid all over again.

"Over dinner, Jack told me this was his last night in town. He was leaving to go on the road with the Orpheum Circuit. 'Well,' I blurted out, 'if you were a gentleman, you'd ask me to go along with you!'

"Jack fell down laughing. At the time, I didn't know he *always* reacted to a line he thought especially funny by either pounding the table or literally falling to the floor. I therefore considered myself terribly sophisticated and witty. However, that was the *end* of the conversation—and the evening. Jack took me home and left town the following day . . .

"A week later, the phone rang at three in the morning. It was Jack calling me from Vancouver just to say hello. My parents were angry because he woke up the whole household . . . Then Jack sent me a lovely present, but my mother made me send it back.

"A month later, I took a trip to Vancouver to visit my grandmother While I was there, I met a boy I'd gone to school with. Before I knew what happened, we got engaged. The moment I arrived home wearing my ring, I excitedly called Babe, who was back in Chicago, to tell her the news. She was living at the Sherman House Hotel then, and was in the process of getting a divorce. When she heard about my romance, she was surprised. 'You're silly,' she said, 'and much too young to get married.' But *I* was happy. Her big-sisterly advice just washed right over me.

"Ten minutes after we hung up, the phone rang. It was Jack. 'I hear you're getting married.'

" 'Yes, I am,' I replied.

" 'Well . . . the last month or so, I've been thinking about you . . . And if ever I *wanted* to get married, I'd like to marry you . . . But I *don't* want to get married . . .'

" 'Well, that's fine *for you*,' I said, sarcastically. 'But *I'm* getting married!'

" 'Look,' Jack went on, 'why don't you come here and visit

Babe for a few weeks? My sister, Florence, is getting married, and there will be lots of parties going on . . .'

"It didn't sound like a bad idea, seeing Babe, going to parties. My fiancé was still in Vancouver, and I was lonely. Impulsively I told Jack I would come.

"I took the train to Chicago, and he met me at the station. He must have been up all night with some other girl—he looked awful!

"Jack took me to Babe's hotel and waited while I unpacked. Then the three of us headed for Waukegan to attend a party for Jack's sister. Florence had been Mrs. Leonard Fenchel for exactly one week. When the party was over, Babe, the Fenchels, Jack, his father, and I all drove the few miles back to his dad's six-room apartment in Lake Forest, where he then owned a haberdashery store.

"Everyone else went to bed, but Jack and I sat up in the living room talking until almost dawn. Finally, he said, 'I really do think you're much too young to get married . . . But if you *are* going to get married, why don't you marry me?'

"Without missing a beat, I said, 'Fine.'

" 'Well then,' Jack said, 'let's get married this Friday—*before I change my mind!*'

"We woke up the whole household and told them the news. Then I went to bed and fell sound asleep. I got up at noon, and thought to myself, what am I doing? This whole situation is ridiculous. I'm wearing another boy's engagement ring. I'll have to call and tell my parents . . . Suddenly, the whole thing just seemed crazy.

"I went into the living room and told Jack I couldn't marry him. He just stood there looking at me. I didn't know it at that time, of course, but I had just done to Jack what his former girl friend, Mary Kelly, had done to him shortly before I had turned him down. Rejected him. There was only one difference—she had done it by telegram, while I said no face to face.

"Without a word, Jack just turned and walked out of the room. A few minutes later, his father came in . . . 'You know,' he said, 'you would make a great wife for Jack. He's getting older and he should be married. I think the two of you would be good for each other . . .'

"The following Friday afternoon, January 14, 1927, I became Mrs. Jack Benny. Interestingly enough, several weeks before Jack and I were to be married, just before his sister became a bride, Mr. Kubelsky took his wife's wide gold wedding band to the local jeweler and had it split and made up into two separate rings. He gave one to Florence when she married Leonard . . . The other half was given to me when I married Jack. I've never taken it off . . . Even when I made a picture at Paramount called *This Way Please,* or did TV shows, I made them put a piece of tape over it so it wouldn't show.

"The only other piece of jewelry I never take off is a silver bracelet with a heart charm—it was the first gift Jack ever gave me . . .

"Our wedding took place in the afternoon, at the Clayton Hotel in Waukegan, in the small apartment of Jack's best friend, Julius Sinykin. It was not a large wedding. I only remember a few people being there: Babe, Florence and Leonard, Jack's father, and Assistant State's Attorney Sidney Bloch.

"*After* Rabbi Farber performed the ceremony, I called my parents in California and broke the news. They were shocked. I can still hear my mother saying, 'Your father and I wish you every happiness—but I don't think it will work out.' I hung up and promptly fainted!

"I could be dramatic and say my swoon was a reaction to the big event. In truth, I've been prone to fainting all my life. I have low blood sugar. A chronic condition. Fainting is about the easiest thing I do. But at that moment, my groom was pretty alarmed.

"Over the years of our marriage, Jack witnessed hundreds of such attacks. All brief. None painful. Once, when Jack was playing Las Vegas, he was in the coffee shop having something to eat between shows when someone rushed in shouting, 'A woman just fainted at the blackjack table. Is there a doctor in here?' At which point, my husband automatically stood up and said, 'Don't be alarmed, it's only Mary!' "

CHAPTER ELEVEN

AT THE TIME of their marriage, Jack was performing in a Shubert Brothers' show, *Great Temptations*. It was a big, bawdy (for the times) revue predominantly featuring scantily clad dancing and chorus girls, whose routines and numbers were interspersed with comedy sketches, songs, and blackouts. Featured along with Benny were Arthur Treacher, Jay C. Flippen, and another great comic by the name of Jack Waldron.

One of the other hit acts of the show was a nude European dance team. Even the critics were somewhat shocked by the *male* nudity. They were *used* to naked and semi-nude girls.

Jack had several spots, including one routine with a young girl who was to become famous in Hollywood later on as "Blondie," Penny Singleton. Although the audience enjoyed the risqué numbers, the biggest hit was made by a beautiful, fully gowned singing star, Hazel Dawn. Among her numbers was the dramatic "Valencia," which she trilled with great style, thrilling the audience.

In Act I, Jack did a funny monologue, and even played a violin solo, as well as introducing several of the other numbers. All of this preceded the spectacular first-curtain finale—dozens of nude girls parading up and down a huge staircase. As a whole, the production was one of the most opulent of that season—or any other.

Great Temptations had opened in May of 1926, and nine months later, Jack was still in it—but Mary had never seen the show.

"The first part of my wedding night was spent in the audience watching Jack," Mary remembers. "But I was so tired from all the hectic running around during the week between Jack's proposal and our wedding day, I fell asleep long before the first curtain.

"We spent the rest of our wedding night in Jack's room at the Blackstone Hotel, where we continued to live until the show moved on. Since I hadn't really seen the revue on the night of January 14, I went to the theater with Jack the following evening.

"I was a bit unnerved by all those naked chorus girls. After the first act, I went back to Jack's dressing room. It was then I discovered that my husband of less than twenty-four hours apparently *shared* a dressing room with some of those cuties.

"I don't know if it was 'official policy,' but while I sat in the corner waiting for Jack, half a dozen girls raced in and out, stripped, and put on their next bit of sequins and fluff for the second act.

"Finally, Jack came in and saw me sitting there. He started to get a little red in the face, especially when another girl suddenly pranced in and started casually to undress in front of us. 'I forgot to tell you,' he said to the chorine, 'I'm married now . . . Please, get out of here!' "

Jack Benny, in 1927, was, as George Burns has said, "a real Don Juan." Mary was to discover just how right Burns was during the early weeks of their marriage.

"Great Temptations played in several other cities during the first month or so we were married," Mary continued. "I knew about his love affair with Mary Kelly, but I was unprepared for all the other girls he'd obviously romanced in every city where the show played. We would arrive in a town, drive by the theater, and see Jack's name on the marquee, then head for wherever we were staying. Invariably, the phone would begin ringing. The calls were always for Jack. *Always from women.*

"Realistically, I knew my husband was a great performer—and God, what a handsome man—but the calls got to me! I was so jealous of Jack. On my wedding day, I was a pleasingly plump one hundred thirty pounds and stood five foot five and one-half inches tall. In the first six weeks of being Mrs. Jack Benny, I went down to one hundred fifteen pounds—subsequently, even less. I was young, but not so young I didn't notice the slim figures of all those naked chorus girls! The first time I answered the phone and heard a sexy female voice ask for Jack, I just handed him the receiver. I stood there while he politely hemmed and hawed and finally said, 'I'm sorry—I can't make it tonight,' and hung up.

" 'Why didn't you tell her you were married?' I asked. 'Gee, Mary,' he said, with those innocent blue eyes, 'I guess I forgot.'

"In the third town, I was in the other room taking off my makeup when the phone rang and Jack answered. As I listened, I heard the same routine. A polite apology following a long and somewhat tender conversation. When he came back into our bedroom, I threw a jar of cold cream at him—and *just* missed!

"By the fourth city, you would have thought I'd be used to the calls. After all, Jack *never* left my side except to go on stage. Still, I was very immature and unable to cope with the jealousy I felt . . . The phone rang. Once again, Jack picked it up, was very sweet, and ended the conversation by saying, 'Well, I'm awfully sorry, but I'm afraid I can't see you tonight . . .' *I'd had it.*

"When he hung up, I walked over and, with my fingernails, scratched the whole side of his cheek. I think it was then Jack finally got my message. This incident occurred just before he was to go on stage . . . He walked out in front of the curtain holding one hand up to his face. Years later, when I told Jack's close friend Freddie de Cordova (now producer of Johnny Carson's 'Tonight Show') this anecdote, he just looked at Jack and said, 'All these years I thought it was *you* who had invented that great touch of pausing and putting your hand to your cheek. Now I realize Mary was responsible for *that* bit!'

"Despite my impulsive behavior that first year, I have to say that ours was the happiest of marriages. Jack and I loved being together. We always had so much fun. He was the most generous man. He was constantly giving me sentimental gifts of the most romantic nature. All of my jewelry is engraved. All with beautiful, thoughtful words. He even gave me presents on *his* birthday. I have one circlet ring of heart-shaped rubies set in gold. Etched on top of the band are the words: '2/14/40 . . . 13 years of happiness and we haven't even started. Love, Doll.' He gave that to me on his forty-sixth birthday.

"Over the the years, I still have to admit that, once in a while, immature jealousy reared its impetuous head. I'll never forget 1942 . . . Jack was making a picture co-starring Ann Sheridan, the 'Oomph Girl.' It was a film called *George Washington Slept Here*. Ann was married to actor George Brent, but they had recently been divorced . . .

"I could tell from things Jack said that he liked Ann. It upset me. Then George Brent called to say that he knew Jack had sent Ann flowers. My husband was always sending people flowers, but this time I wasn't thinking of Jack's perpetual generosity. I got mad. I had made it a practice never to go on any of Jack's sets when he was doing movies. This time, I decided I'd better see what was happening.

"I went out to Warner Brothers, and the moment Jack saw me, he came over, kissed me, put his arm around me, and took me to meet Ann. 'This is my wife, Mary,' he said. She said, 'Hello,' and I replied, 'How do you do.' That was the extent of the conversation. That evening, over dinner, Jack suddenly asked me why I didn't like Ann Sheridan. 'Why don't I like her?' I repled indignantly, 'All I said was, "Hello."' To which Jack replied quietly, 'I *know*.'

"Several weeks later, I was giving a big dinner party. On impulse, I picked up the phone and made a call. 'Miss Sheridan,' I said, 'this is Mary Benny. Jack and I are having a party and we'd love you to come.' There was silence on the other end of the phone . . . a very long pause. Then she said, 'I'd love to come.' I asked if she wanted me to send a car for her, or if she wished to be escorted by one of the other guests. She said no, that she could make it on her own.

"I still can't believe my own audacity," Mary laughed. "It was such a lovely party. At one point in the evening, I looked over and saw Ann sitting by herself. Something propelled me to her side. I smiled. Then I said, 'Miss Sheridan, I don't know whether you like Jack, or he likes you . . . But you *are* making a picture together . . . and I wanted to remind you of something. Jack wouldn't give my little finger for your *whole body!* Now, have a good time . . .' Then I just walked away.

"The next day on the set Ann obviously told Jack of our conversation. He came home that evening and confronted me. 'Mary, that was an awful thing you said to Ann Sheridan.'

"I just looked at him. 'I know it was awful . . . but I meant it.'

"He stared at me for a few seconds, then broke into a smile. 'Well, you were right, doll, you never have to worry about me . . .'

"I kissed him and then made my final statement on the matter. 'Believe me, Jack, when you make pictures with Ann Sheridan, or other beautiful girls, I worry! Look, doll face, if you ever do like someone else, don't tell me Don't let me find out. I never want to be humiliated. If you're going to cheat—do it quietly!' He took me in his arms and looked at me with an expression of amazement. I guess, being so naturally shy about some things, Jack was astounded at the passion of my words. But I meant them. God, I loved that man!"

CHAPTER TWELVE

"ALTHOUGH I DID NOT REALIZE it at the time, when I became Mrs. Jack Benny, I not only got a husband, but a career," Mary said. "During our first year together, Jack had a girl working with him in his act. She played the part of a typical dumb bunny. But after *Great Temptations,* when Jack was booked to go back on the vaudeville circuit for an extensive engagement, he wanted to save money and asked me if I thought I could do the girl's part. Without so much as batting an eyelash, I said sure. I was at that brash stage in life. I thought I could do anything—and I did—going on stage without any previous experience Sadie Benny became Marie Marsh. Later I changed my name again—to Mary Livingstone.

"Wherever the act played, local managers would send in reports on how everyone was doing. I didn't know it at the time, but the reports sent in on Jack and me were very positive. We traveled across America and Canada playing various towns, including Vancouver, where the boy I had been engaged to came to see the show—and wished me luck.

"For me, it was a happy time. I was no longer sitting backstage waiting for Jack. I was actually on stage, participating. I wore a short black skirt, a white blouse, and a black beret—not bad for a kid from the May Company!

"After touring for nearly a year, we arrived in Los Angeles, where Jack was booked to play the Orpheum. This was the big time and, by prearrangement, Jack sent for his regular girl. I wasn't in the least offended. After all, I did not consider myself a pro and I was happy for Jack that the girl agreed to come from New York to fill the engagement.

"The first two days, Jack and the other girl did the act. The third day, while I was sitting with Jack in his dressing room, the manager came in. Without any preliminaries, he said, 'The reports I received from all over the country have been marvelous. What happened all of a sudden, Jack? The girl is lousy.'

"Jack replied, 'To be perfectly honest, the girl who worked with me on the road is sitting over there. She's my wife.'

" 'Well,' the manager said, 'put her back in the act, for God's sake,' and slammed the door. So Jack sent the other girl home. That's when I *officially* broke into 'professional' show business. In fact, during the engagement, they even added a couple of songs to my routine. In those days, I had a lot of nerve!"

Early in 1928, the Bennys were back in New York, where they did a one-reeler for Vitaphone Studios. *Variety* reviewed the seven-minute film as follows:

The inimitable Jack Benny offers *Bright Moments,* a nifty little skit in which he is assisted by Marie Marsh. Benny's subtle comedy is well known to vaudeville audiences and his appearance before the camera loses none of his personality . . .

He gives Miss Marsh a chance in his act and her zealous efforts to make good provide a wealth of comedy. This is one of the best entertainment numbers the Warners have concocted to date. . .

Also during 1928 and 1929, Jack, appearing most often without Mary, was acquiring a nationwide reputation as a master of ceremonies-monologist, playing in theaters from New York to Los Angeles, with numerous stops in between. Wherever he went, absolute raves greeted him.

In Chicago, a well-known reviewer wrote:

Jack Benny and Gus Edwards, although not teammates on the current bill, are its predominant personalities . . . Benny is master of ceremonies. With his well known suavity, he strides in between acts, making pertinent remarks about the interruptions by Ray Bolger and Virginia Martin of the Gus Edwards review . . .

When he played the Keith-Albee Palace Theatre in Akron, Ohio, an ecstatic newsman commented:

A young man named Jack Benny made his Akron debut at the Palace Thursday afternoon and when he left the stage he could have had the theater . . . Benny is without a doubt the smartest monologist seen in this city of smells in many a moon. His line is smooth—so smooth, in fact, the audience hardly knew how to take him . . .

During 1928, a year of personal triumph, Benny gave an interview summing up his act. As his words indicate, he had already refined his knowledge of audience tastes and had zeroed in on his own best assets.

". . . Panning, that's my business. I live on it . . . Look, I'll show you why people like to be panned. You can't praise anything and be funny. If you want the laughs, you have to put something, or somebody in a ridiculous light, even yourself . . . People wouldn't crack a smile if you said you loved your wife, or your mother-in-law, if they thought you meant it. But tell 'em you don't, and tell 'em why, and they'll roll in the aisles . . . Everybody wants to laugh and everybody has to laugh at somebody. They would rather laugh at themselves than not to laugh. That's my theory. Put anybody on the pan and the audience will think the act is as hot as a depot stove . . ."

The interviewer then went on to comment: "Thus, in his act, Mr. Benny follows his own advice. He ambles in and out of the wings cracking a whip of satire. His tongue is his lash, as he plays ringmaster in the Orpheum Circuit. Towns he defames mercilessly with his naive descriptions. Other acts on the bill suffer many a jibe. And national figures are also his meat . . ."

Following which, Jack made a closing comment exhibiting his innate good taste, along with his ability to define the limitations of audience receptibility to his style.

"But you can't put all national figures down," Benny explained. "I can put down Calvin Coolidge or Herbert Hoover, but not Lindbergh. The audience will throw things at any actor who takes a crack at Lindy . . ."

When Jack appeared at the Palace in New York in mid-1928, vaudeville critic Larry Lawrence wrote:

An actor who can carry the difficult role of being master of ceremonies at a vaudeville show and not turn into an utter ass and bore the audience has again been discovered. He is Jack Benny and you may listen to his drolleries any time this week . . .

When Jack again arrived in Los Angeles to play the Orpheum, the raves continued:

Jack Benny, the nonchalant comedian . . . returned to the Orpheum Circuit for a tour as a master of ceremonies, in addition to giving his own act.

As easy going and subtle as ever—and even funnier than in the past—Jack is bringing his limitless stock of "gags" and the violin he never plays seriously (although he can) to the Orpheum theater this week and is entertaining "the folks out front," as he puts it with a new menu of food for laughter every day. There are few "repeats" in Jack Benny's chatter, for he tires of a joke sooner than do theater goers . . .

Benny was held over for a number of weeks, an unprecedented move for the Orpheum Circuit.

During this time, someone told Louis B. Mayer Jack Benny was the country's best master of ceremonies. So Mr. Mayer, who always sought out the best, signed Jack to an M-G-M contract, making him "filmdom's first on-screen m.c."

Jack was excited about the prospect of moving to Hollywood and making pictures. Mary was equally pleased. Coming to Los Angeles meant living close to her family.

The Bennys rented a lovely place at the Chalfont Apartments, in back of the Ambassador Hotel on Wilshire Boulevard. For the first time in their married life, Mary set up housekeeping in earnest—and even began to cook.

Both L. B. Mayer and production head Irving Thalberg were pleased to have Benny tied to a six-month contract. First, Jack did *Chasing Rainbows* (also known as *Road Show*) with Marie Dressler and Bessie Love. He then went into *Hollywood Revue of 1929,* which starred Norma Shearer (Mrs. Thalberg), John Gilbert, Joan Crawford, Lionel Barrymore, Laurel and Hardy, and Bessie Love.

When *Hollywood Revue* played Waukegan, Illinois, the townsfolk turned out en masse, led by Meyer Kubelsky, and everyone stayed to cheer their hometown boy. But personally, Jack wasn't too thrilled with film work so far. It didn't present the kind of challenge he was hoping for. Still, he was now a "movie star," which could do nothing but enhance his reputation.

Next, Jack made a two-reeler for Metro Movietone called *The Songwriters Revue,* in which he acted strictly as m.c. By this time, his M-G-M pact had come to a close. He was signed by Columbia for *The Medicine Man,* with Betty Bronson and Eva Novak. In this film, Jack got to play a real role—that of a medicine show doctor. To put it kindly, the picture was a bomb. Jack's stay in Hollywood was about to end.

Mary loved living in California, but she could see Jack was getting more restless with each passing day. Then Benny received a call from his agent, Tom Fitzpatrick, advising him that Earl Carroll was casting a new show called *Vanities,* and wanted Benny as one of his stars. The offer was for $1,000 a week.

Jack discussed the situation with Mary. He was anxious to pick up, leave Hollywood behind him, and grab the offer.

"Jack," Mary advised, "ask for $1,500 . . . after all, you're a star of stage and *screen* now."

"Mary," Jack protested, "you've been in show business a fast ten minutes, and you're telling me what to ask. That's ridiculous . . ."

Mary insisted, so Jack called his agent back and said he would love to appear in *Vanities,* but his price was a firm $1,500. Then he hung up, looked at his wife, and said, "Well, I've lost *that* job . . ."

Half an hour later, the agent called. Earl Carroll had agreed!

Mary didn't say, "I told you so," but from that day on, Jack never signed a contract or made a deal without consulting her first.

CHAPTER THIRTEEN

ONCE AGAIN, the Bennys became residents of New York City, and Jack went into rehearsals for *Vanities*. For Mary, it was a time of settling down and seeing all of the friends she had become so close to after her marriage.

Socially speaking, the Bennys were riding high. They rented an apartment at 55 Central Park South. George and Gracie had the apartment right above them. A few blocks away, Eddie and Ida Cantor, Fred and Portland Allen, and Jack and Flo Haley all had apartments. It was like one huge sorority-fraternity row, made up of stars instead of students.

Mary and Gracie learned how to play backgammon, taught all their friends, and made the game the rage of Broadway. Also, during this period, Mary became a devoted listener to radio. Often, when Jack came home from the theater, she would talk to him about this new medium. Mary felt that Jack had a marvelous voice, and would be perfect for radio. She urged him to become involved.

Jack wasn't interested. He had a steady job and, although *Vanities* was a bawdy show, full of nudity and material some critics and vice officers considered "borderline," it was having a successful run. He wasn't about to dissipate his energies by trying to pursue a career in radio. Besides, personally, he considered it just a fad that would blow over.

Then, early in 1932, Ed Sullivan, a columnist for the New York

Daily News, invited Jack to appear as a guest on his radio interview show. Because Ed was a close friend, Jack agreed. It was on Sullivan's March 29 show that the audience first heard his mellow, velvety voice: "Ladies and gentlemen, this is Jack Benny talking. There will be a slight pause while you say, 'Who cares?' I am here tonight as a scenario writer. There is quite a lot of money in writing for the pictures. Well, there would be if I could sell one.

"I'm going back to pictures in about ten weeks. I'm going to be in a new film with Greta Garbo. They sent me the story last week. When the picture opens I'm found dead in the bathroom. It's a sort of a mystery show. I'm found in the bathtub on a *Wednesday* night.

"I should have been in Miss Garbo's last picture, but they gave the part to Robert Montgomery. You know—studio politics. The funny part of it is that I'm really younger than Montgomery. That is, I'm younger than Montgomery & Ward.

"You'd really like Garbo. She and I were great friends in Hollywood. She used to let me drive her car around town. Of course, she paid me for it . . ."

It may be difficult to imagine that anyone could make such corny lines sound funny—but Jack did. His Sullivan spot received such great audience reaction, numerous advertising agencies got the same idea simultaneously: why not put Jack Benny, the great m.c.-monologist, on his own show? It was Doug Coulter, an account executive with N. W. Ayer, who came up with the best deal.

Jack signed a contract, and his debut show aired on May 2, 1932. It was called the "Canada Dry Ginger Ale Program," and Jack was billed as the "Canada Dry Humorist." He acted as m.c. on the show, which also starred a popular orchestra leader of the day, George Olsen, and his band, as well as a top vocalist, Ethel Shutta, who was Mrs. Olsen.

Soon after the broadcasts started, Benny, with his innate sense of comedy, began kidding his sponsor—injecting humor into what otherwise would have been the normal straight commercial. On one show, he read a telegram supposedly received from a representative of the company who had come across eight tourists in the Sahara Desert. They had been lost and without water for thirty days. "I came to their rescue," the wire read, "giving each of them a glass of Canada Dry. Not one of them said he didn't like it."

"A couple of months after the show started," Mary remembers, "Jack came home and told me that, at rehearsal, the program had run a couple of minutes short. He asked if I would be afraid to go on and do two minutes with him. I said no. I made my radio debut on August 3, 1932.

"Jack and his writer, Harry Conn, had created a character for me—Mary Livingstone from Plainfield, New Jersey. But when it came time for me to deliver my dialogue, what I did mostly was to laugh—because, by then, I'd had enough sense to get nervous! I didn't go on a second time until three months later . . . Again, out of nervousness, I laughed. You can imagine my surprise when fan mail started pouring in addressed to 'The Girl Who Laughed, c/o Jack Benny's Canada Dry Show'!"

Jack did seventy-eight programs for Canada Dry, and then they failed to renew his contract. While audiences all across the country roared at Jack's comic antics and funny commercials, there were rumors, and even press comments, that the sponsors didn't particularly like Jack's poking fun at their beverage. Whatever the reason, Jack was fired—and replaced by a program of organ music!

By this time, however, Benny had a nationwide reputation. Sponsors were standing in line, and Jack decided to go with Chevrolet. There was only a four-and-a-half-week lapse between Jack's last Canada Dry show, January 26, 1933, and the beginning of his "Chevrolet Program," March 3, 1933.

Mary now became a regular. In fact, it had been a provision of the sponsor's deal that Jack hire "the girl who laughed from Plainfield, New Jersey" as a permanent cast member.

The Bennys fell into a set work-social routine that was to continue uninterrupted for the next couple of years. Three days a week, Jack worked with his writer, Harry Conn, usually from noon until two-thirty or three in the afternoon. Then he played golf, or went to the Friars Club and enjoyed a card game. Six nights a week, he, Mary, and "their gang" would have dinner and then go to the theater. Some nights, after seeing a play, the group would catch a midnight movie.

The Chevrolet show featured Frank Black and the NBC Orchestra, as well as Alois Havrilla as announcer. Once again, Benny began kidding his sponsor, and "someone" at Chevrolet didn't take the funny commercials too kindly.

But Benny's stock was soaring with radio audiences. He had inaugurated spoofs on current films back in his Canada Dry days, the first being a take-off on *Grand Hotel,* which Jack called "Grind Hotel." The movie spoofs continued, along with Mary's routines, and Benny was rapidly rising to the top of the popularity polls.

The show ran from March to June of 1933, then took a summer hiatus, returning in October of 1933, and it continued on until April 1, 1934. In between times, Jack made another movie, *Mr. Broadway,* in which he co-starred with prize fighter Jack Dempsey, Ruth Etting, Bert Lahr, Ed Sullivan—and Mary Livingstone.

In February 1934, the New York *World-Telegram* published the results of a nationwide poll it had conducted to name the most popular stars in various categories. The results were as follows:

RADIO FAVORITES

Comedian	Jack Benny
Dance Orchestra	Guy Lombardo
Popular Female Singer	Ruth Etting
Popular Male Singer	Bing Crosby
Harmony Team	Boswell Sisters
Musical Program	Fred Waring's Pennsylvanians
Dramatic Program	March of Time
Children's Program	Singing Lady
Symphonic Conductor	Leopold Stokowski
Classical Singer	Lawrence Tibbett
Sports Announcer	Ted Husing
Studio Announcer	David Ross
Commentator	Edwin C. Hill
Most Popular type of program	Variety
Outstanding Broadcast of '33	Roosevelt Inauguration
New Star	Joe Penner
Favorite Program	Rudy Vallee Variety Show

It was a fabulous vote of confidence for Jack, who won out over Eddie Cantor, Ed Wynn, and Fred Allen for the top spot. Two weeks after Jack's victory hit the papers, Chevrolet announced his contract would *not* be renewed. He was to be replaced by an all-musical program starring conductor-composer Victor Young!

Individual Chevy dealers all over America registered furious protest. When the word filtered down that Benny was being canceled because of *one* executive who felt cars could be sold better with music than comedy, the furor grew even louder. Then the top man at General Motors got into the fray. He made a decision rescinding the cancellation. "Get Benny back at any price," he said.

It was too late. General Tire had already made an offer Jack could not turn down. Four days after leaving the air for Chevrolet, on April 6, 1934, Benny's new program debuted. Call it pride, label it what you will, Jack insisted on taking the offer and going on immediately, because that meant he would then hold the radio record for one hundred consecutive broadcasts.

Alois Havrilla, Jack's announcer, was replaced by Don Wilson. He was a big man with a booming voice, who would soon become intimately identified with Jack's products—particularly Jell-O—his bulk quivering as he walked in what Jack called "Don's six delicious flavors sway."

Wilson's radio career had begun back in the days of the crystal sets, when he was first heard in 1923 over KFEL, Denver. Six years later, while head of the announcers department at a Los Angeles station, KFI, he decided to switch gears and specialize in becoming a sports announcer. From 1929 to 1933, Ted Husing and Don were considered the top two coast-to-coast sports broadcasters.

Early in 1934, Wilson had moved to the NBC staff in New York. It was during this period that Jack held open auditions for a replacement announcer. According to Don, "I guess I was just lucky—I laughed in the right places. Jack hired me as a straight commercial man, but after the fourth week, the guys started working me into the scripts . . ."

Meanwhile, with every program, Jack was building a new legion of devoted fans. The country was crazy about him, his cast, his unique ways of integrating funny commercials. More and more, the press began to extol his virtues. In an issue of *McCall's Magazine,* Heywood Broun wrote an article saying that radio audiences were becoming sullen about advertising interruptions to programs, and that the American sense of humor wouldn't stand for the awed reverence with which announcers spoke the names of the products they were advertising.

He closed by hoping that "in days to come a grateful people would erect a statue to Jack Benny, with the simple inscription: 'In memory of the first man to take the curse off radio commercials!'"

On April 10, 1934, *Variety* reviewed Jack's new show:

> It would seem from the unveiling performance that Jack Benny put on Friday night for General Tire that a switch in sponsors was a happy break for both the listeners and the comic himself. Relieved of having to give thought to what the fellow who signed the check personally liked, Benny delivered a series of laugh interludes that rate among the very best of his air career . . .
>
> For his new stand, Benny has moved over his style of comedy intact. Only changes in his support are the band and the stooge doubling announcer. With Don Bestor, one of the near topliner dance organizations in the business replacing the Frank Black's NBC studio unit, and Don Wilson, the Coast emigre who has been making good on the big time, holding down what had been Alois Havrilla's assignment on the Chevrolet session, the exchange stacks up as an even one . . .

CHAPTER FOURTEEN

ALTHOUGH he would soon establish thirty-nine as his age in perpetuity, in 1934, Jack Benny celebrated his fortieth birthday. Twenty-two years after he had first left Waukegan to go on the road, his success was firmly established. If there ever really comes one time in a person's life when he *knows* he has it made, Jack had reached that moment.

Professionally, his radio show—albeit for his *third* sponsor in less than two years—topped the popularity polls. He was the recipient of mass adoration. And, behind the scenes, he was openly recognized by his peers as the Cadillac of comedians.

Personally, his seven-year-old marriage was as solid as ever. Mary was not only his partner at home, but in front of the microphone and on stage, as well; having her nearby, night and day, gave Jack that extra jolt of joy.

The only thing missing in their lives was a child, but Mary had difficulty in becoming pregnant. In 1934, they adopted a blond, blue-eyed infant and named her Joan Naomi. The Benny apartment was redecorated to accommodate baby and nurse, and Joanie's presence made Jack and Mary truly a complete family unit.

In addition to the radio show, the Bennys were in constant demand for personal appearances. In May, Jack headlined the stage show at New York's Capitol Theatre, on Broadway and Fifty-first, presenting Mary and a whole Benny revue. On screen, Clark Gable, Myrna Loy, and William Powell starred in *Manhattan Melodrama*. The combination bill was so popular, crowds lined the streets waiting for hours to get in.

In June, the Benny radio show moved to Hollywood for eight weeks while Jack co-starred in a Reliance picture for United Artists, *Transatlantic Merry-Go-Round*. Others in the cast were Gene Raymond, Nancy Carroll, the Boswell Sisters, Patsy Kelly, and tenor Frank Parker. Parker had come west to be on Jack's radio show. His presence on the coast gave producer Edward Small the idea of casting him, so as to cash in further on Benny's nationwide popularity.

The movie was a formula 1930s musical—with something added—a plot. The whole thing took place on a luxury liner, with Benny playing the ship's entertainment director. Between musical numbers and comedy sketches, there was also a mysterious murder.

While Jack's part was not actually large, it was a flashy role. His outstanding performance convinced certain film moguls he might be a great prospect for additional movies, but the Bennys left

Hollywood at the end of August. Once back in New York, Jack prepared several more programs for General Tire.

In early fall, Jack took on still another new sponsor. He was signed by General Foods to star on "The Jell-O Program." The show debuted on October 14, 1934, and ran for eight seasons. It was heard over NBC on Sunday at 7 P.M.—a time slot which Jack would occupy for the next twenty-one years.

It is ironic that the skillful ability of Benny and his writers would cause Jack periodic trouble throughout the early years of his radio career. Whenever a new personality appeared on the show as a regular, he became an integral part of "Benny's family." Conversely, any hint of departure provoked nationwide audience response, and sent Benny, his writers, and his production staff into a cautious search for a suitable replacement. This was especially true when it came to Jack's regular singers.

In mid-1934, Frank Parker, the immensely popular tenor, left the show—of his own choice. However, there *were* rumors he had been fired. Those were quickly squelched, only to have radio editors wonder in print if Jack's program could ever again be as good. After all, Parker's lush voice, and his deft reading of lines, had endeared him to millions. Despite the public airing of the situation, Jack refused to be stampeded into hiring someone else immediately. He had to be sure—absolutely sure.

Finally, a young chap named Michael Bartlett was selected. He had a lovely tenor voice, yet, try as they might, Jack and the writers could not mold Bartlett's personality to the Benny concept. After a few weeks, he was let go. The search began again.

At this period, there happened to be auditions going on, sponsored by a commercial firm, with the announced purpose of selecting the best new young singer. Dozens tried, and Kenny Baker won. Baker, a young native of California, from the small suburban town of Monrovia, was six feet tall, handsome, and built like a college halfback. The combination of his clear tenor voice and his boyish charm immediately struck a responsive chord in Benny and his people. Kenny, at the time of the auditions, was supporting himself working in a Los Angeles furniture store.

Jack signed Baker to replace Parker, personally working with him, skillfully *creating* the "public Kenny Baker." This time,

Jack's efforts paid off. In a few months, the press and public were extolling Kenny's virtues. Parker, while not forgotten, had been satisfactorily replaced.

For the first six months Jack was on the air for Jell-O, then a fairly new product, there were merchandising problems beyond Benny's control. All across America, those six delicious flavors: strawberry, raspberry, cherry, orange, lemon, and lime, were just sitting on the shelves—a fact hardly calculated to make a sponsor happy.

One day, Jack and Mary's agent, Arthur Lyons, showed up at the Bennys' apartment along with the Jell-O executive responsible to General Foods for the program. After a lengthy discussion, the executive got down to the bottom line. In order to keep the show on the air, General Foods requested that Jack and his entire cast take a cut in salary. Jack said he would discuss the situation and give them an answer within the week.

As it turned out, everyone agreed to the cut *except Mary*. Jack was astounded, but Mary stood her ground. Firmly, she told him: "I won't allow it to get around town that you've taken a cut in salary. It would be bad for you. I can't let that happen, Jack. It would be so unfair to you . . ."

Touched by his wife's fervent loyalty, Jack asked Mary if she had any other solution to the problem.

Mary nodded. "Let's you and I work *without salary* until the situation improves," she suggested. "I'd rather we earned nothing than let you accept less than the money you've been getting."

It was a revolutionary suggestion—but Jack went along with it. The rest of the cast continued to get the same salary they had been making. Mary and Jack worked free out of a sense of pride.

Two months passed. By then, Benny's show had swept the country. Jell-O was selling so well, grocers couldn't keep the product on their shelves. The sponsors showed their delight by giving Mary and Jack a dinner party to celebrate the good news. But first, the guests gathered at the Bennys' for cocktails.

One of the General Foods executives toasted them and made a flowery speech about being grateful to Jack, Mary, and their whole radio family for doing such a great sales job. Jell-O was a huge hit, and all because of the Benny show. At the end of his speech, the gentleman reached into his pocket and took out a check, which he presented to Mary. It was made out for a very large sum—the combined regular salary which Jack and Mary had given up for a total of eight weeks.

Meanwhile, in the kitchen, the Benny's maid-cook, Henrietta, had been preparing to serve hors d'oeuvres when there was a knock on the back door. It was a uniformed messenger with a large, specially wrapped gift. Inside the box, she found a huge silver platter—well chilled. On the platter, decorated with fancy garnishes, sat a six-tier mold in the form of a cake—*made out of Jell-O*. It was so fancy, if she had stuck a tiny bride and groom on the top, it would have been very appropriate for a wedding.

Because it was not part of the planned menu, she carried the platter into the dining room and said unceremoniously, "Mrs. Benny, what do you want me to do with this crap?"

The people from General Foods gasped. Jack's face turned the shade of the first three layers—strawberry, raspberry, and cherry. It was left for Mary to smile and turn orange, lemon, and lime!

CHAPTER FIFTEEN

DURING THE LATTER half of 1934, while Jack continued to do his radio show, he simultaneously went into rehearsals for a play, *Bring On the Girls,* written by George S. Kaufman and Morrie Ryskind. It was a political satire, the successor to the writing team's previous hits, *Of Thee I Sing* (a Pulitzer Prize winner) and *Let 'Em Eat Cake.* It was produced by Sam H. Harris, who had previously been responsible for such Broadway successes as *Dinner at Eight, As Thousands Cheer,* and *Once in a Lifetime.*

At the same time Jack's newest film, *Transatlantic Merry-Go-Round,* opened on Broadway, his play had its premiere showing at the National Theatre in Washington, D.C., October 22, 1934.

On the face of it, the show had everything going for it—except the third act. Even the great talents of Kaufman, Ryskind, and Benny could not help it. After a short run, the play closed.

Meanwhile, Jack continued doing "The Jell-O Program." Tickets to attend the weekly broadcasts were at such a premium, people had to write months in advance. Jack was then one of the few radio comedians who insisted on performing before a studio audience. His desire to "perform live" was a carry-over from vaudeville days. The broadcast studio only held a few hundred people. His show was ostensibly aimed at unseen *millions* sitting in living rooms all over the country. But Jack wanted the give-and-take of an audience in order to make his unique comedy format as perfect as he could.

Strange as it seems now, Benny actually had to fight with his respective sponsors for permission to have a studio audience. There was a lot of negative comment on the sponsors' part about all the "extra trouble" presented by an in-studio audience. But Benny stuck to his guns.

His own personal favorite comedian in vaudeville had always been Ed Wynn, whom Jack considered the ultimate in good taste and talent. When Wynn preceded him on the airwaves, the "Perfect Fool" also had insisted on an audience. Jack used Wynn as his example, knowing that the timing of his own show would be extremely enhanced by live reaction to his weekly comedy.

Obviously, Jack proved to be correct. The best evidence of this was the continued popularity of "The Jell-O Program." In almost every home in America, Sunday at seven was held inviolate as "Benny time."

Early in the 1960s, when Jack went to Washington, D.C., to appear at the White House, President John F. Kennedy told him how his father had insisted that the entire family gather together in the study every Sunday to listen. "It was a mandatory event," Kennedy smiled. "In fact, Jack, you know we were a very *devout* Catholic family. I was thirteen before I found out you weren't Bishop Sheen!"

Week after week, Jack was revolutionizing radio comedy by the very nature of the character he portrayed: a highly faulty, very foolish, but still totally believable human being rather than a comic caricature. By exaggerating his own eccentricities, Jack had fashioned himself into the common man, a readily identifiable character, even though he was both funnier and larger than life.

If satire is a mirror in which a person sees everyone but himself, then Jack Benny was America's looking glass. Fred Allen summed it up best when he said: "Practically all comedy shows on radio owe their structure to Benny's conceptions. He was the first to realize that the listener is not in a theater with a thousand other people, but is in a small circle at home. The Benny show is like a 'One Man's Family' in slapstick. When they tune in to Benny, it's like tuning in to somebody else's house. Benny was also the first comedian to realize that you could get big laughs by ridiculing yourself instead of your stooges. Jack became the fall guy for everybody else on his show."

His format was so popular, Jack was constantly being sought out to analyze himself. The fact was, from the very beginning, he had certain beliefs which stood him in good stead. Professionally, he always maintained: "You never compete against others on the air. You compete against yourself. It makes no difference if you're better than somebody else. You've got to be as good as you are at your best. If you start off with a bang . . . you've got to keep it up or you flop. Listening to others on the air doesn't mean a thing. What they're doing doesn't affect me directly. It's what I'm doing that makes the difference."

Late in 1934, Jack also said: "Few may realize it but comedy is going through great changes. The radio and screen have been the primary cause. Years ago, when comedians confined their efforts to the stage, it was fairly simple for them to make a hit. They were able to use the same routines for years and still retain their popularity. Now, however, the comedian has to be on the alert for new material, and as a result, his position is very uncertain.

"Comedy itself is based upon very old principles of which I can readily name seven. They are, in short: the joke, exaggeration, ridicule, ignorance, surprise, the pun, and finally, the comic situation.

"The joke is the simplest method of drawing laughs and most comedians—in fact almost all—use it too often. Because of its simplicity and repetition, the joke or gag tends to dull the audience. The constant use of this method, in my opinion, is the cause of so many failures among comedians who start their careers with great promise and then suddenly flop.

"As for exaggeration, perhaps the most popular exponent of this principle is Jack Pearl, who masquerades himself in the character of Baron Munchausen, the notorious liar. Pearl tells grossly exaggerated falsehoods which, when added to dialect, produce a good response from the audience. Dialect, of course, is not a principle of comedy, but merely a means of preparing the listener for a laugh . . .

"Ridicule is always effective, provided the right person is made fun of. This principle is Eddie Cantor's favorite, as can readily be seen when he makes those cracks about Rubinoff. Ridicule is closely aligned with sarcasm, although sarcasm is a much more intelligent form of ridicule.

"The ignorance principle, so well known, is the one which Burns and Allen depend upon . . . I use the comic situation principle, which I consider the best method of getting favorable results. The use of situations involves comic characters which grow in value as they become more and more familiar to the audience. The method is very complex, but it is this complexity that avoids dullness and repetition. Also, the use of comic situations gives the comedian many opportunities to get new material which will always provide the dramatic interest necessary for good comedy . . ."

At the same time Benny was talking about comedy, his weekly shows personified it. Whenever shifts in characterizations were necessary, Jack saw them first. A good example is the way in which Mary's character was changed after Kenny Baker replaced Frank Parker.

"When I first went on radio," Mary recalls, "the character I portrayed was that of a dumb girl. But when Kenny came on, the writers made him dumb, too. It didn't take Jack long to discover that two dopes weren't as funny as one. That's when I became Jack's smart-aleck girl friend . . ."

Jack was also constantly on the lookout for talent which might enhance his radio family. One night, he went to a Friars Club Frolic and saw a character actor, Sam Hearn, do a routine using the name of Schlepperman. Jack was so taken with Hearn's ability, he invited Sam to come on one of his shows as a guest. Hearn's appearance provided Benny with yet another big laugh-getter. Eventually, he became a semi-regular.

During his years on Jack's show, Hearn endeared himself to millions, and provided Benny's audience with countless laughs. Among his most memorable performances was a program on which Jack and company did one of their famous satires on great motion picture classics . . . in this case, *Lost Horizon.* Jack played the Ronald Colman part and Schlepperman was the High Lama. Also featured was that brilliant radio actor, Elliott Lewis.

The scene went as follows:

(Music fades—finish with Chinese wind bells)

ELLIOTT: Come, my boy, it's growing late, and I've promised to present you to the High Lama. He is *nine hundred years* old.

JACK: Nine hundred years old! . . . Isn't he awful wrinkled?

ELLIOTT: No, we have him *pressed* once a week.

JACK: *Gadzooks.*

ELLIOTT: Quiet . . . the High Lama approaches to greet us . . . be *prepared!*

JACK: Nine hundred years old . . . Gee, he must be all dried up.

ELLIOTT: Yes, don't light any matches around him.

JACK: Oh boy, am I nervous.

ELLIOTT: He will not harm you, my son. Here he is . . . *Behold. The High Lama!*

(Sound: Two gongs)

(Short trumpet fanfare—hold last note)

ELLIOTT: Your Excellency, I beg to present Jack Benny.

JACK: Your Excellency!

HEARN: Hullo, *stranzer.*

(APPLAUSE)

JACK: *Schlepperman!*

HEARN: Quiet, I'm a lama now.

JACK: A lama?

HEARN: And I thought I was joining the Elks.

JACK:	Well, tell me, Schlep, how are you doing in Shangri-La?
HEARN:	Oy, Jackie-boy, am I making money . . . Everybody here lives to be three hundred years old, four hundred, five hundred, there's no limit . . . I tell you, Jeck, I'm cleaning up.
JACK:	What do you do?
HEARN:	I sell birthday candles.
JACK:	Birthday candles? . . . You must be making a fortune . . . Say, is your wife here with you?
HEARN:	How else could I get nine hundred years old so quick?
JACK:	Oh, that's right.
HEARN:	Well, kiddies, I got to toddle along now to the Shangri-La airport.
JACK:	Oh, do you have an airport here?
HEARN:	Yes, this is where the bombers leave for Tokyo.
JACK:	Oh yes, I heard about that.

(Music into "With a Song in My Heart"—and fades)

Incidentally, just as Jack "on" and Jack "off" were two different people, so, too, the public Mary Livingstone was a complete departure from the real-life lady.

She was never what you would call a self-confident person. Meeting strangers frightened her half to death. There is no question that she would never have become an entertainer had she not married Jack. He understood this, and encouraged and helped her all he could.

"It made Jack happy to have me work with him," Mary comments. "Which is why I lasted as long as I did before retiring. In truth, in my own mind there were *never* two careers in our family. Jack was always the one and only star.

"Whenever we made personal appearances, for instance, managers would want to bill us as Benny & Livingstone, like they billed George and Gracie as Burns & Allen. I would never allow that. Jack was the star. I was always a featured member of his company. I never wanted us to be team—like ham and eggs. Jack was too special, and I never cared how they billed me . . ."

If a psychologist had ever examined one of Mary's own radio

scripts, he would have come to the same conclusion as Mary has just stated. By looking at the marginal notations on her pages, he could have seen just how truly dependent she was—or thought she needed to be—on Jack for everything she did and said.

"A little louder on the last word," Jack would tell her during rehearsal. Or, "Slow down on that second sentence and wait until I look at you before you speak again, please," he'd say. Dutifully, Mary would write in the margin: "Louder, Mary," or, "Slow down. Wait for my look, please" alongside the specific sentences, just as if Jack were speaking to her when she read her lines on the air.

Jack and the rest of the gang got a kick out of Mary's little notes to herself. She couldn't have cared less. She took the kidding good-naturedly. She felt that if she hadn't written Jack's instructions in the margin, she would not have gotten any laughs from the audience. Her problem was that as soon as she realized she was actually being co-starred on a coast-to-coast radio show, Mary Livingstone developed *mike fright*. Going on week after week put her in an almost total panic, a condition she managed to overcome with her husband's help—for years.

It was during the 1934 radio season that Jack needed to hire three character actresses to do a spoof on a then well-known singing trio. As Jack visualized them, one would be short, one would be fairly nice-looking, the third had to be obviously obese. A heavy-set blue-eyed blonde showed up on the day scheduled for auditions. The producer took one look and knew she was perfect for the role. She had a very pretty face, with several extra chins. She was a tall, heavy-set remnant of what once must have been a beautiful woman.

When Jack came in for rehearsal and looked at the three actresses, he did a double-take. Excusing himself, he went over to the heavy blonde and called her aside. The production team figured there was something wrong with the woman, and that Jack was being his polite self, taking her off to one side to tell her they couldn't use her.

In fact, Jack had *recognized* the woman. It was Mary Kelly, the girl he had gone with and loved for nearly four years! The sight of her filled Jack with sadness, especially since her part was one geared to make the audience laugh at her unusual bulk.

"Mary, how are you?" Jack began, not knowing what to say.

"The truth is, Jack, I've had some rough times," she replied, but didn't go on. It was obvious that Mary had had troubles. Jack literally pleaded with her not to take the part. It hurt him for her that, even on radio, where the listening audience couldn't see her, she would be the object of ridicule. Benny changed his mind after Mary said one simple sentence.

"Jack, don't turn me down . . . I need the job . . . I have to work . . ." After that, Mary Kelly was used as often as Benny could find room for her. In later years, she was under contract to Burns and Allen—the close friend and former room-mate that Gracie could never forget.

CHAPTER SIXTEEN

AT THE BEGINNING of the 1935–36 radio season, Jack, Mary, and the rest of the gang, except for Don Bestor's orchestra, made a permanent move to the West Coast. Jack was getting numerous big offers to make films, and living in California was the only practical solution.

Prior to leaving for Hollywood, Jack and Mary fulfilled numerous stage commitments, including one at the Hippodrome Theater in Boston. It was February 1935, and the world's attention was focused on a courtroom in Flemington, New Jersey, where the "criminal trial of the century" was in progress. Bruno Richard Hauptmann was being prosecuted for the kidnapping of the Charles Lindbergh baby. The trial attracted famous celebrities by the carload—all eager to get a glimpse of the proceedings. Jack and Mary were curious, too, so they headed for Boston by going first in the *opposite* direction, to spend a day at the courthouse.

After listening to the testimony and observing the defendant, the Bennys rushed on to Boston. There, waiting for them, were reporters, all anxious to know Jack's firsthand opinion of Hauptmann. Delighted to be questioned about something outside of his own career, Jack made a perceptive observation which landed on the front pages of Boston's daily newspapers.

"Hauptmann was more of an enigma to me after I listened to him being cross-examined," Jack said. "He's the sort of man who appears guilty if you believe him so and innocent if you don't. Personally, I saw nothing in his manner or words to convince me either way. You know, if you see a man shackled to a policeman in uniform, automatically that man looks guilty. But if you saw the same man seated in a chair talking amiably to a Chamber of Commerce official, he'd look as law-abiding as anyone else. That's the way I felt about Hauptmann . . ."

The reporters then returned to the usual Benny topic—his career —and one inquired about the way in which "Love in Bloom" had been selected as his theme.

"Well," Jack laughed, "the song was written by Leo Robin and Ralph Rainger for Bing Crosby's film *She Loves Me Not*. One night Mary and I were in this supper club and the band asked me to join them for their next number. I borrowed a fiddle and, just following the sheet music, I played 'Love in Bloom.' I guess it sounded pretty funny, the violin playing, I mean, not the tune! My spontaneous performance turned up being written about in some column, with the writer wisecracking that 'Jack Benny playing "Love in Bloom" sounded like a breath of fresh air . . . if you *liked* fresh air . . .'

"The following week, Mary and I went to another club. As we entered, the orchestra leader started playing 'Love in Bloom.' Obviously, he had seen the item in the paper. The thing just caught on, so I decided to adapt it as my theme song. Let's face it, it's also a pretty easy tune to play on the fiddle. I love it from that aspect, but actually 'Love in Bloom' has nothing to do with a comedian. I mean, 'Can it be the breeze that fills the trees with rare and magic perfume . . .' sounds more like it should be the theme song of a dog—not a comic!"

Back in California, Jack and Mary rented the beautiful Lita Grey Chaplin home, and settled down in Beverly Hills. Once again, Jack went to work at M-G-M, starring in a film called *Broadway Melody of 1936,* directed by Roy Del Ruth and co-starring the latest tap-dancing sensation Eleanor Powell, the equally new and extraordinarily handsome leading man Robert Taylor, pert and perky comedienne Una Merkel, plus comic Sid Silvers, Vilma and Buddy Ebsen, and songbird Frances Langford.

The film was based on an original story by Moss Hart, with music and lyrics by Nacio Herb Brown and Arthur Freed. Among the song hits from the picture were "Broadway Rhythm" and "You Are My Lucky Star." The movie was given a big, innovative *afternoon* world premiere at Grauman's Chinese Theatre on Hollywood Boulevard, complete with red carpet, stars arriving in limousines, and reporters and cameramen immortalizing the opening, as thousands of fans lined the boulevard waiting to see the celebrities.

Microphones were set up outside the theater, and Jack played m.c., entertaining the fans. There was an official ceremony, opened by the simulated roar of Leo the Lion, followed by a musical medley from the film played by a sizable orchestra. Benny then came out and traded quips with Sid Silvers, turning the whole affair into a quasi "Jell-O Program." Frances Langford and others from the cast sang. Eleanor Powell did a tap dance. Robert Taylor smiled—and the fans swooned. And Mary Livingstone, there with Jack, read a funny poem like those she had become famous for on radio. Climaxing the festivities, Jack came back on mike personally to thank everyone and to announce Jell-O's six delicious flavors as: "Strawberry, raspberry, cherry, Metro, Goldwyn, and Mayer."

The film was a smash box-office-wise all across the country. Everyone adored it, except close Benny friend Louella Parsons. She took exception to Jack's role—not the way he played it—that of a "gossip columnist," à la Walter Winchell, which she felt to be too satirically close for comfort.

The month before the film's opening, Jack ended his season on radio with a program on which he presented Portland Hoffa and Fred Allen as guest stars. The combination of the Allens and Jack and Mary made their last show before summer vacation a truly memorable one. Almost immediately, Jack was scheduled to begin another film for Metro. *It's in the Air,* co-starring Ted Healy, Una Merkel, and Nat Pendleton, to be directed by Chuck

72

Reisner. Before checking into the studio, he decided to take a brief driving holiday, and invited his brother-in-law, Hickey, to come along for the ride. (Mary, who had no patience for long automobile trips, decided to stay home.)

The twosome headed for Seattle to visit some of Mary and Hickey's relatives. The trip was a typical Benny outing—which therefore meant stopping at dozens of small, family-style cafes along the highway, where Jack invariably discovered "the best roast beef sandwich and coffee I've ever tasted," much to the delight of his young brother-in-law. It was during this period, incidentally, that he and Jack became especially close, and cemented a bond of friendship that was to last for Benny's lifetime.

Although Hickey volunteered to do all the driving so Jack could relax, Benny insisted upon taking his turn at the wheel. This prolonged the trip by an extra two days . . . Jack was always finding "interesting detours" which he invariably decided to pursue.

Once in Seattle, Jack and Hickey were the house guests of Ruby and Louis Wagner, Mary and Hickey's aunt and uncle. They owned a fifty-one-foot yacht cabin cruiser, *Nokomis,* and suggested their guests might like to take a leisurely cruise.

It was the Labor Day weekend, and Jack wasn't too keen on going. It was cold and foggy, and he really had to be talked into getting on board.

About fifty-seven miles west of Seattle, fire broke out in the engine room. They were not too far from shore and, just before beaching the boat, Hickey ran up front, where Jack was fast asleep in a camp chair. He awakened him and said, "Jack jump into the water . . . the boat's on fire!"

Jack took one look at Hickey, saw he was wearing a serious expression, and proceeded to jump overboard in a camel's-hair coat and cap. Fortunately, everyone made it to shore safely. A few minutes later, the yacht blew up.

A Coast Guard cutter came to their rescue and took them back to Seattle. During the trip, the skipper had one of his men serve hot coffee, meat-loaf sandwiches, and potato salad. Hickey said, "I'll never forget Jack sitting there on deck, a blanket thrown over his shoulders, a sandwich in one hand, hot coffee in the other. His only comment in the midst of the ordeal—which he never mentioned—was 'Hickey, this is the greatest meat-loaf sandwich I ever tasted!' "

Meanwhile, several hours later, Mary, back in Beverly Hills, was suddenly inundated by a flock of reporters wanting comments on her feelings about the accident. She didn't know what they were talking about. When one reporter told her a boat with Jack on it had blown up, Mary promptly fainted on her front lawn *before* they could tell her that Jack, her brother, uncle, aunt, and other relatives were unharmed.

She came to moments later just as the phone inside the house was ringing. It was a call from a Seattle newspaper assuring her all was well. But it wasn't until nearly midnight, when Jack finally got back safely and was able to phone personally, that Mary finally relaxed—but not before fainting once more—this time at the joy of hearing Jack's voice.

"Home from the seas," Jack began filming *It's in the Air*. The plot revolved around two confidence men, Benny and Ted Healy, who managed to stay just one step ahead of federal authorities. They were being pursued because of their various scams. Finally, they stopped running long enough to promote yet another "get rich quick" scheme, a balloon expedition into the stratosphere. They had no intention of actually going up in the thing—until necessity and the feds called for their hasty exit, upward, into the sky. In addition to its comic overtones, the film had elements of suspense, and became a big hit at the box office. When the film opened, Jack received the best acting reviews of his career to date.

"The Jell-O Program" coming from Hollywood, was as much of a smash as it had been during the two previous seasons. Johnny Green and his orchestra had replaced Don Bestor, and the comic byplay between the very elegant and polished Green and Jack, at his foolish best, went over big with audiences.

During this period, Mary spent as much time at home as possible. She was all wrapped up in being a good mother, and enjoyed discovering new delights every day. Joanie was an enchanting, extremely bright and responsive baby, and Mary reveled in the depth of her own maternal instincts.

As for Jack, no matter how hectic his schedule, every day began and ended with a visit to the nursery. Early on, he had discovered his baby's attraction to neckties—particularly bright red ones. Even if he were going out in a sports outfit, he would put on a tie when he went in to see Joanie. It made him happy to find the baby so alert, even if she did grab ahold of his tie and pull—hard.

This became an especially happy period for the Bennys after Burns and Allen also moved to the West Coast. George and Gracie had adopted a baby girl, Sandra Jean, close to Joanie in age, as well as a son, Ronnie, two years younger.

Toy shops in Beverly Hills were ecstatic whenever they saw Mary and Gracie walk through their front doors. Both ladies were pushovers for the latest in stuffed animals, dolls, rocking horses, and assorted children's games. Talk of baby formulas and the latest activities of their respective kids temporarily replaced backgammon as their favorite indoor sport!

CHAPTER SEVENTEEN

THE YEARS 1936–37 were busy ones for both Jack and Mary in films. Jack signed a contract with Paramount and made two pictures in a row. First he did *The Big Broadcast of 1937,* another musical which purported to be "the dancing, singing story of a small-town girl who wins her way to fame, fortune, and love." Jack "presided" over the film, mainly serving as an on-camera m.c. for the goings-on, which were very lavish. The cast included Burns and Allen, Bob Burns, and Martha Raye, and "the romantic triangle group," as portrayed by Shirley Ross, Ray Milland, and Frank Forest. Adding to the musical part of the film, there was Larry Adler and his harmonica, Benny Goodman and his band, and, making his film debut, Leopold Stokowski and his symphony orchestra. Paramount billed it as "the most exciting musical ever made."

In an interview which Jack gave Sheilah Graham just after the film opened, he spoke frankly. "I'm dissatisfied with my movies to date. I want very much to be successful in pictures, but so far I've only appeared in musicals. That is the drawback. Stories for song-and-dance pictures are secondary. The plot is made to fit the musical numbers instead of the other way around . . ."

Having said that, Jack went into his next musical for Paramount, *College Holiday,* again co-starring with Burns and Allen, as well as Mary Boland. In this opus, Boland tried to help a crazy college professor conduct an experiment in eugenics—the science of heredity which attempts to prove that offspring of certain ethnic and national groups are smarter than their peers. She enlisted Benny's help and he gathered together a "group of mixed students" from various backgrounds and colleges to take part in the experiment.

The kids on campus wound up being the nucleus for the obligatory musical show, in which everyone dressed in Grecian togas—except for Gracie Allen, who came as a Vestal Virgin. The reviews, putting it kindly, said the film had a rather flimsy plot!

In between pictures, Jack's radio show traveled to New York on several occasions. On one such trip, the writers created a character named Rochester, and made him a train porter. Six black actors tested for the role, which was won by a performer named Eddie Anderson.

Anderson, born in Oakland, California, came by his talent naturally. His father was a minstrel performer, and his mother one of the few black tight-wire artists.

During World War I, when he was thirteen, Eddie and his brother, Lloyd, sang and danced in San Francisco's Presidio and in hotel lobbies wherever servicemen gathered. Discovered by a pair of Western entertainers, the boys joined their company, performing up and down the California coast. However, when their father objected, the two Anderson boys returned home to learn a trade.

The "lessons" didn't take. Eddie's heart was elsewhere. Once again, he went back to show business, this time adding another brother, Carny, and forming a singing, dancing act, which they named the "Three Black Aces." In 1924, Eddie got a one-line part in a comedy stage play and decided *this* was for him—much more suited to his talents than just singing and dancing. A new career was launched and he went on to crisscross America playing in carnivals, vaudeville houses, and nightclubs.

In 1935, he won the part of Noah in the Warner Brothers film *Green Pastures*—and made a big hit. A couple of years later, when Benny's company held auditions for the train porter role, he was among the group that showed up.

Anderson, the second actor to try out, was so perfect for the part, the producer never even bothered to listen to the last four men. Eddie was hired for only one performance, on a show which was broadcast on Easter Sunday, 1937. His impact was so sensational, Jack signed him for a permanent spot in the cast.

Below is the actual dialogue from the first show Anderson did as Rochester. Visualize his cherubic-mischievous face, that marvelous gravel-like voice—and you get the full picture!

(Sound: Train effect)
(music fades)

JACK:	Gee, what a long trip.
MARY:	Say Jack, look out the window . . . (giggles) . . . They sure dress funny here in Hollywood.
JACK:	Those are Indians . . . This is New Mexico.
MARY:	Oh.
JACK:	Hey, porter, porter!
ROCHESTER:	Yas-suh.
JACK:	What time do we get to Albuquerque?
ROCHESTER:	What?
JACK:	Albuquerque.
ROCHESTER:	I dunno, do we stop there?
JACK:	Certainly we stop there.
ROCHESTER:	*My my!*
JACK:	Hm.
ROCHESTER:	I better go up and tell the engineer about that.
JACK:	Yes, do.
ROCHESTER:	What's the name of that town again?
JACK:	Albuquerque.
ROCHESTER:	(laughs) Albuquerque. What they gonna think up next?
JACK:	*Albuquerque is a town.*

ROCHESTER: You better check on that.

JACK: I know what I'm talking about . . . Now how long do we stop there?

ROCHESTER: How long do we stop *where?*

JACK: In Albuquerque.

ROCHESTER: (laughs) There you go again.

(Sound: Train whistle twice)

During Eddie's early years with Jack, racial and ethnic prejudice was still very much an unspoken problem—particularly in places like New York City. Jack, being Jack, never even gave it a thought until the first time he took his show East after Rochester became a regular. Jack and Mary usually stayed at the Sherry-Netherland, while the cast, crew, musicians, and writers stayed together at an equally fine hotel a few blocks away.

"We checked in early in the afternoon," Hickey recalls. "A few hours later, I got a call from the manager's office. We were old friends, so he selected me to be the social arbiter for the whole group. 'Hickey,' he said, 'I think we have a problem. Can I see you right away?' I said, 'Sure,' and he said he would be right up. While I was waiting for him, I kept thinking to myself, 'We've always stayed at this hotel before . . . What could be wrong?' Then it hit me. I assumed one of the guys in the band had had a few drinks too many and probably tried to seduce one of the maids!

"He walked into my room with a very long face. As he spoke, he seemed embarrassed. 'Look, we have several guests here from the South. They object to Rochester staying here . . .'

"I looked him straight in the face and, without missing a beat, I smiled and said, 'That's no problem. Eddie will move out tomorrow . . .'

"He was very relieved and thanked me profusely. The next morning, Eddie moved—but there were forty-four *other* checkouts. We left the hotel en masse!"

Hickey remembers another trip East with Jack and the gang when an incident happened at a very popular restaurant Jack especially loved.

"About fifteen of us walked in and took a couple of tables. A waiter came over, took one look at Eddie, and refused to serve any of us . . . Then he looked over, saw Jack, and said, 'Oh, I'm sorry we kept *you* waiting, Mr. Benny. We'll serve you right away . . .'

"Jack just looked up at him in disgust and said quietly, 'You had your chance . . .' And we all got up and walked out. Jack couldn't stand such insensitivity. After a while, the word got out . . . and we had no more problems."

On March 23, 1937, Waukegan honored its hometown boy with a huge Jack Benny Day. There was a parade, then Jack appeared at the local high school, met with his former school chums, planted an elm tree in front of city hall, and was guest of honor at a banquet attended by close to one thousand of Waukegan's finest citizens. Honorary chairman was Jack's old buddy, Julius Sinykin, while another school chum, Mayor Mancel "Bidie" Talcott, gave the opening speech. It was an exhilarating day for Jack, who always reveled in such hometown gatherings.

During the evening, Local 284 of the Stagehands Union presented Jack with a lifetime gold membership card. Way back on May 29, 1910, when Benny Kubelsky had just gone to work at the Barrison Theater, he had spent a few months handling props, as well as playing in the pit. Consequently, he had had to join the union, and had kept up his dues until he went into vaudeville. Twenty-seven years later, the union made it official—Jack Benny could handle props should the occasion ever again present itself!

In the banquet audience was Jack's sister Florence and her husband Leonard, as well as one of his first violin teachers, Charles Lindsey. His dad, vacationing in Florida, sent a telegram, as did Fred Allen, who had been invited but could not attend. Perhaps it was just as well. That evening upon request, Jack played "The Bee."

Speaking of "The Bee," the great classic Benny-Allen feud began on Fred's very first radio show of the 1937 season. It ended when Fred appeared on Jack's show the night of March 14. In between, for a fantastic ten weeks, millions of Americans sat glued to their radio sets awaiting the next installment of the feud—the next batch of insults to fly over the airwaves.

It certainly was *not* a planned affair. It all started rather innocently when Fred Allen had a young violin virtuoso, Stewart

Canin, on his show. Preceding the boy's playing a brilliant rendition of "The Flight of the Bumblebee," the following dialogue ensued. It will give you a rough idea of how the feud got under way . . .

ALLEN: Tell me, Stewart, how old are you?

STEWART: Ten years old, Mr. Allen.

ALLEN: Do you know Jack Benny?

STEWART: No, sir.

ALLEN: Well, did you ever hear Mr. Benny play the violin?

STEWART: Yes, sir.

ALLEN: How did his playing sound to you?

STEWART: Not very good.

ALLEN: Well, from what I understand, Mr. Benny is allegedly going to play "The Bee" next Sunday on his show and I want to be fair about the whole thing. So, Stewart, why don't you explain to Mr. Benny how to manage it. You know, you could tell him how to hold the violin and everything.

(Stewart obliges)

ALLEN: Are you listening, Jack? The violin is held in the left hand, the little finger resting lightly on the first string. The round end of the violin sets back into the neck, a little over to your left, with just a dash of your Adam's apple peeking around the corner. The bow, or crop, as you call it, Mr. Buck Benny, is held in the right hand. Now, to play the violin, what do you do, Stewart?

(Stewart scrapes out a few notes)

ALLEN: I see, you scratch the bow across the strings. Fine. And now that Mr. Benny knows how to hold the violin, little ten-year-old Stewart Canin will show little thirty-five-year-old Mr. Benny how to play "The Bee." Go ahead, Stewart.

(Stewart plays beautifully)

Thank you, Stewart. This was "The Bee," Mr. Benny, played by a ten-year-old boy. Aren't you ashamed of yourself now to go through with your threat? Why,

Mr. Benny, at ten you couldn't even play on the linoleum. Next Sunday, ladies and gentlemen, the world will realize that Aesop spoke two thousand years too soon when he said, "Nero fiddled and Rome burned." For if Jack Benny insists on fiddling, America will burn. I rest my case.

Technically, the feud ended in March 1937, but it would be years before reporters stopped asking Benny and/or Allen about it. On Jack's part, time after time, whenever he was asked "to confess" that the whole thing had been planned, he would reply, "Believe me, it *wasn't* . . . if it had been, it would never have lasted the way it did."

In 1940, Paramount made a film called *Love Thy Neighbor,* in which Jack Benny and Fred Allen co-starred, along with Mary Martin and Eddie "Rochester" Anderson. The plot of the film revolved around a reconstruction of the Benny-Allen feud. The picture's release helped to perpetuate the verbal duel, to this day spoken of as a radio classic.

In real life, of course, Jack and Fred were close friends. Allen, real name John Florence Sullivan, had been born in Cambridge, Massachusetts, three months after Jack, on May 31, 1894. Their paths first crossed during vaudeville days, and they both started on radio in 1932.

In his book *Treadmill to Oblivion,* Allen, in discussing the unplanned origin of the feud, his show's "most popular running gag," admitted that after his initial provocation of Jack, he waited eagerly for the following week to see if Benny would pick up on it.

"The Jack Benny program was the highest-rated show on radio at that time," Allen wrote. "With our smaller audience, it would take an Academy Award display of intestinal fortitude to ask Jack to participate in a feud with me. I would be hitching my gaggin' to a star. All I could do was to hope Jack would have some fun with the idea and that it could be developed . . ."

Over the years, professionally and personally, there was a great deal of mutual fondness, respect, and admiration between Portland and Fred and Jack and Mary.

On the evening of March 17, 1956, as Fred was walking his

dog along the streets of New York City, he had a heart attack and died. Benny, in Hollywood, was stunned.

"This is the most shocking thing," Jack said to reporters soliciting his reaction to Allen's untimely passing at age sixty-one. "The American public has lost its greatest wit. Fred's humor and brilliance was comparable to that of Will Rogers. I know I have lost a very dear and treasured friend. I spoke to his wife, Portland, this morning and I was stunned to find out that Fred had been given a clean bill of health in a physical checkup just yesterday . . ."

In 1971, thirty-four years after the original feud started, Jack gave a concert at Dartmouth College, where little ten-year-old Stewart Canin, by then forty-four, was the concertmaster. The highlight of the evening was Jack's explanation to a standing-room-only audience that, because of Stewart's playing on the Allen show, he, Jack Benny, had taken up the study of the violin seriously again after so many years of using it merely as a prop.

The audience gave Jack a standing ovation—after which he played "The Bee." As Hickey recalls, "The auditorium was rocked with applause and bravos. It was a deeply touching moment for Jack—and one that will long be remembered by those who attended."

CHAPTER EIGHTEEN

IN 1937, the Bennys were involved in the biggest domestic project of their married lives when they hired architect and builder Carlton Burgess to oversee the construction of a home in Beverly Hills. While radio audiences conjured up an image of Jack Benny living in penurious squalor—befitting his public cheapness—the elegant mansion was under way.

At this time, Jack's radio show was featuring a weekly sketch called "Buck Benny Rides Again." To commemorate this happening, steel beams of the foundation were covered with the character names: the Sheriff, Daisy Mae, Buck Benny, along with the real names of Benny guest stars, such as Andy Devine.

The home, Benny's residence for twenty-five years, soon became a landmark on those movie star maps sold by canny old women who stood on selected street corners of Beverly Hills, Brentwood, and Bel Air. In fact, 1002 North Roxbury Drive was a twice-daily stop on regular sight-seers' bus tours. Occasionally tourists got a glimpse of Jack or Mary, but there was one special day, and one special group, which Jack would talk about and laugh over for years to come.

Unlike his radio scripts, in which Jack supposedly lived next door to the Ronald Colmans, in reality, the adjoining house belonged to Lucille Ball. Lucy and her family and the Bennys were extremely close friends. Over the years, Jack made numerous, usually vain attempts to create situations geared to make Lucy and Desi Arnaz, and later on, Lucy and her second husband, Gary Morton, laugh.

On this particular day, he had dressed up as a strolling gypsy, complete with bandana around his neck and funny hat on his head. Then, fiddle in hand, he went out the back door, slamming it shut, and began playing away as he crossed the lawn to Lucy's.

Serenading his neighbors, dressed in a funny costume, did *not* bring about the laughs Jack had anticipated. Feeling slightly foolish, as Lucy endearingly loved to make Jack feel, as all his friends did when he tried to be funny off camera, Jack walked back across the lawn in his weird getup. But when he got home, he found himself locked out—and, on a rare day, the house empty. Mary was in Palm Springs. The servants were off. Joanie was away at school. So there he stood, fiddle in one hand, trying desperately to get into his front door.

At that precise moment, the tour bus came down Roxbury Drive. Jack could hear the driver over the P.A. system announce: "And on your right, the home of . . ." Without even thinking, Jack turned toward the bus.

The driver sputtered for a moment, then continued, "The house of . . . why, there he is now, Jack Benny!" Within seconds, the bus had emptied, and several dozen tourists ran across the front lawn to get his autograph.

Jack started to explain his getup . . . his predicament . . . but felt so foolish, he just shut up and spent the next half hour signing autographs and shaking hands. The fans were so excited, no one even remarked on Jack's strange outfit. Benny was nonplused by the experience until he realized that for tourists to see him dressed as a gypsy, violin in hand, vainly attempting to get into his own house, was *nothing unusual*—his "image," rather than being diminished, had been confirmed!

Jack's house cost a quarter of a million dollars to construct, decorate, and furnish, during days when that sum was an enormous fortune. It was a two-story home of the Georgian period, with a red brick exterior and an expansive lawn out front. Inside, everything was designed to make the Benny family comfortable, although parts of the house were more formal—for entertaining purposes.

Since a great deal of work on Jack's show was done at home, with the writers and production staff frequently in attendance, there was a spacious, informal den where Jack and his team could relax—and create. It was also the place where the Benny cast could come, on occasion, to read through the week's script.

Also, since Jack never "turned off," never was completely detached from his work, he needed his own bedroom suite where he could be free to get out of bed and write, or make notes, whenever the spirit moved him—no matter the hour of day or night.

On the other hand, since Mary was a late-night person, who adored staying up until the wee hours reading, and then loved sleeping until noon, she too, required her own suite.

Then there was Joanie, a small child when the house was first constructed, who grew to her teens in that home. She, too, had a suite—for years shared by a nurse-governess, and eventually turned into a teen-ager's dream.

Jack's "province" was a large bedroom-sitting room with several windows—always kept closed. He was perpetually cold and, no matter what the temperature outdoors, he loved literally to nest away there surrounded by assorted clutter—so incongruous with the immaculate image he presented on stage or television. So different, too, from the rest of the spacious Benny mansion, which resembled the manicured perfection of a *House Beautiful* cover.

Next to his bed stood Jack's oversized nightstand crowded with dozens of bottles in assorted shapes and sizes containing every color and type of pill imaginable. There was also a loose-leaf book with hundreds of telephone numbers of family, friends, acquaintances, plus assorted entries Jack could never figure out—although he had written them himself. Wedged in between was a cup full of sharpened pencils, writing paper, and the latest book he was reading.

In one area of the room there was a king-sized desk, constantly crowded with a large daily appointment calendar, assorted newspapers and scripts, various small items of memorabilia collected from his trips, plus a collection of road maps which he enjoyed "reading" as though they were novels.

On the floor between the desk, the bed, and several overstuffed armchairs, magazines, more newspapers, and scripts lay scattered about.

Across the room, the clothes he had worn the night before were casually tossed over a straight-back chair. Just behind it, there were shelves full of reference books and framed photographs of Mary, Joan, his parents and sister, interspersed with autographed pictures of the world's famous, plus awards he had won.

A corner table was covered with pennies, nickels, dimes—assorted change gathered up as a result of his emptying his pockets. Next to the coins lay his gold money clip usually containing a hundred dollars or so in crumpled bills. Also on the table was a tee, a golf glove with a ball in it—and an ash tray with a half-smoked cigar balanced precariously on one edge. On the floor just beside the table was his open violin case, with always easy access to the instrument which he loved.

The suite, done in tones of brown and beige, included a dressing room, done in brown leather, a porch overlooking the back garden, and Jack's bathroom, where he was free to leave the cap off the toothpaste, as well as to set up his music stand and practice his violin.

Mary's suite, by contrast, could have come off the pages of *Glamour*. The main room was done in soft blue, rose, and white, and decorated in an exquisite Victorian style. There was a black marble fireplace, upholstered chairs, and lounges in a floral chintz, the pattern of which was repeated on the wallpaper at two ends of the room.

Her larger than queen-sized bed, with its blue-tufted headboard, always contained half a dozen king-sized pillows for propping up and leaning against whenever the mood struck her.

Adjoining the bedroom was Mary's mirrored dressing room, which featured wall-to-wall white-cedar-lined closets. There was also a large bathroom and a tub rimmed with her favorite perfumes and bath oils.

Joanie, the smallest member of the family, not only had a live-in governess, Julia Vallance, but the biggest suite of all, consisting of a series of rooms which changed in decor as they grew from nursery into a young girl's dream place. As a teen-ager, her bedroom featured two beds, one for frequent overnight school chums. She also had a separate dressing room, with one whole wall of colognes and perfume bottles, and a private bath. Adjoining this was a huge playroom which changed over the years from a place for playpen and dolls, to a recreation room with a phonograph, hundreds of records—pop and classical—and a spinet piano. Around the room, Joan still kept her cherished collection of dolls and toy horses, plus her books and framed photos of her friends. There were also autographed pictures of movie stars, including her favorite—a blow-up of Van Johnson—which hung over her bed, and which Van himself had given her at the height of his teen-age idol days at M-G-M.

Downstairs, the Bennys had a formal drawing room, but Mary insisted on the room not looking like "a museum," and added upholstered pieces in shades of pale green, rose, and ivory. A large fireplace was added so the room could be at one and the same time both formal and cozy. It was here that the Bennys did the bulk of their entertaining.

Jack and Mary had a large formal dining room done in gray and gold, with a long, highly polished table, in the middle of which stood a magnificent English silver bowl, and above which hung an elegant crystal chandelier.

There was a handsome wood-paneled library with dark blue

oriental rugs and a Dutch tile fireplace—an elegant setting in keeping with the beauty of the rest of the house.

The family room, a downstairs playroom-den, was comfortable and spacious, and faced the garden and pool. Next to it was a cozy breakfast room, which seemed more like an outdoor terrace because of large standing silver urns overflowing with green vines. The den had a huge brick fireplace which took up half of one wall. The rest of the walls were paneled in walnut, and the huge sofa and oversized chairs were upholstered in a gay red and white apple-patterned print.

In front of the fireplace, there was a spacious red ottoman on which three or four people could sit comfortably. On the floor, a big multi-colored, hand-braided rug was dominated by the identical red of the chairs and sofa. Also in the room were a large card table and chairs, as well as several Early American Windsor pieces.

The Bennys' back yard had a gently sloping lawn and a large pool, with a mosaic tile octopus at the bottom, sans eyes. When the pool was newly finished, and Jack, Mary, and Joanie moved in, the baby was not quite five. The first time she went into the water, in her Uncle Hickey's arms, she screamed out in terror and managed to communicate the fact that the eyes of the "fish" on the bottom of the pool were looking right at her! So the Bennys had the pool drained and the octopus' eyes removed. Overlooking the pool was a large cabana, a barbecue, plus a complete outdoor kitchen and bar.

Mary, who had a reputation for giving the most elegant and charming parties of any hostess in town, frequently utilized the back yard-pool area, in addition to the living room, dining room and drawing room, especially for her larger parties.

Years later, Joan can still vividly recall some of the "extravaganzas" that took place in the Benny household.

"My parents gave the most lavish parties," she began. "When we were kids, Sandy Burns, or my other best friend, a girl named DeeDee, used to spend the night at my house whenever we knew a Benny gala was in the works—especially Mother's New Year's Eve parties. We would get ready for bed, dressed in our robes, then we'd lie down on the top stair of the landing, look over the railing, and watch as each new guest arrived.

"The parties were always big and fancy in what was the 'golden era' of Hollywood. Usually, they would have a huge tent put up in the back yard and hire an orchestra. There were flowers everywhere. The men came in black tie and the women in gorgeous formals. It was such fun watching. Every big star in town came, and we were as impressed by them as any kids from Ohio might have been . . .

"We'd ooh and ahh at Clark Gable . . . Jimmy Stewart . . . Robert Taylor . . . The whole Hollywood's Best Ten Box Office names. We even collected autographs. I don't think Sandy or I thought of our parents as being celebrities—at least not in the *same* way. I knew Daddy was famous, but I took that for granted. After all, he *was* my father. I mean, living as Jack Benny's daughter couldn't be compared to *seeing* Clark Gable and Carole Lombard in our hallway, or watching Van Johnson's freckles move when he smiled!

"Invariably, Mother would ask us which few celebrities we especially wanted to meet and talk to," she continued. "Always we would name two or three, and Mother would bring them upstairs. I'll never forget the first time she brought up Frank Sinatra. He was the bobby-soxers' delight then and we practically died! Van Johnson was one of my special favorites. He even painted a picture for me that hung over my bed next to his photograph. My personal female favorite was not a star herself. Her name was Mal Milland, and she was married to Ray. Mal was very young during those days, but she had prematurely gray hair. She almost always wore shocking pink and looked so gorgeous. We would invariably ask Mother to bring Mal up to see us. She was, in my eyes, the height of glamour . . ."

For close to three decades, 1002 North Roxbury Drive was a showplace the Bennys loved and shared with their family and closest friends. In the late sixties, they sold the home and moved, at first into a penthouse apartment, which they hated, and finally to another mansion, this time in Bel Air, where Jack and Mary were living when he passed away.

All his life, Jack was such a very simple man. The home on

Roxbury Drive was the place he loved the best. In fact, every once in a while, even after he had lived there for twenty years, he would look around and shake his head. Then he'd say, with wonder and pride, "Gee, it sure is a long way from Waukegan!"

CHAPTER NINETEEN

AT THE START of the 1937–38 radio season, General Foods was paying Jack $390,000 a year, $10,000 per week, based on a thirty-nine-week season. This was his personal salary. In addition, he received $15,000 a week for any other talent he cared to provide.

Fellow comedians who earned far less, or who had radio shows canceled after one or two seasons without new sponsor pickups, tried to figure out "scientifically" how Benny managed so consistently to make "his magic" work.

In truth, there was nothing magical at all which accounted for Jack's success—unless you consider his own genius to be "magical." Previous to going on radio, Jack had spent eighteen years in vaudeville and on the legitimate stage honing, refining, and shaping himself into a unique talent.

By the time he had played the Palace Theater the second time around, Jack had mastered himself and his material. Unlike 90 per cent of his fellow comics, Benny had ceased to depend on physical "shtik" or props for his success. Instead, it was his own personality which he used to wow audiences. In the language employed by the critics, Jack was a "smooth" comedian—his humor could be projected across the footlights by his voice alone.

During his first two years on radio, Jack had not yet hit his full potential as an artist on a mass medium. But by the time he went on for Jell-O, he had created a character for himself which when transferred to the airwaves had a unique universality to it.

Audiences howled at Jack, the self-confident man who made a

fool of himself. They loved him because he wasn't the wise guy who told all the jokes, who had all the funny lines. To the contrary, he was the target of the jokes and humorous situations. Audiences laughed *at* him, but also *sympathized* with him because, invariably, his best-laid plans blew up in his face. Jack was Everyman: the pleasant guy striding down the sidewalk supremely confident he was making a tremendous impression until he stepped into that rain-slick puddle and fell on his ass. He was someone everyone could and did identify with.

Hand in hand with Jack's radio persona went his uncanny ability to set up a situation so listeners could rapidly grasp the basic idea. Swiftly, he would lay out a crystal-clear picture of himself in a given situation and, because it was so plain, audiences followed him happily, zooming in on the funny complications which ensued from the specific situation. Week after week, they understood the basic humor of the plot and Jack's relationship to it.

In other words, Jack Benny had a special knack of making everything believable. For instance, when Jack got into his fleabitten Maxwell, the situation was so cleverly established that, instead of his being a comic standing in front of a microphone, making a joke of a prop jalopy, people thought of him as a real man, engaged in a real struggle with a real vintage 1920s automobile.

Jack's shows were never built around one-line gags or fast quips. Each program began with a funny premise and the dialogue was written to fit it, instead of being contrived in order to arrive at a preordained joke. On Benny's shows, the jokes were never an end in themselves—they just naturally evolved from basic situations.

Why did this formula work so well for so long? Because it was meticulously planned and executed. Every laugh was carefully constructed, built up gradually, so when it finally came, the audience was ready to respond. Jack also had the marvelous facility of creating certain basic situations which achieved amazing longevity, which he was able to use and reuse because they had been so carefully established and nurtured.

All of this was done in the most painstaking way. Unlike Fred Allen, a brilliant man who worked on inspiration alone, Jack struggled and labored over every line, every situation. Of course,

90

he had his writers, but in Jack's case, he was always the guiding genius, the mastermind, the final editor.

After Harry Conn stopped writing for Benny, Jack hired Bill Morrow and Ed Beloin. They worked in conjunction with Al Poasberg, a writer whom Jack had cultivated during his vaudeville days. But after Boasberg died, in 1937, the quality of Jack's shows still remained top-notch.

Recently, George Burns said, "I've been asked if I thought Jack was terribly ambitious. I don't think I'd use *that* word exactly. All I know is, he loved show business. The thing is, Jack fooled everybody . . . On stage, on radio, in films, and on television, he seemed to be a weakling. He *looked* fragile with those little thin wrists . . . the way he touched his face . . . his baby-smooth skin. He seemed so vulnerable, you wanted to take him home and adopt him. But you *couldn't,* because, in truth, he was very strong when he was performing. He was a giant, but he appeared, instead, like a little boy . . . And he always looked so amazed when an audience laughed at him. His expression would indicate a perpetual question: 'Why are you laughing at me?'

"Well, Jack Benny *knew* goddamn well why they were laughing. Believe me, he knew! That's why he was being paid all that money . . . Come to think of it, I guess Jack *was* ambitious. But, as I said, he fooled everybody because he *looked* like he wasn't. The plain truth is Jack always wanted to do very well. He was a perfectionist. He used to go over and over his lines, his script, until he felt every element was exactly in place . . .

"Basically," George continued, "there was a very strong side to Jack which people couldn't see. To be honest, I couldn't see it, either. But it was there—I'm positive of that. It had to be . . . And, if Jack wanted to get tough, he could—but in his *own* way. For the most part, his credo was, 'No means the same thing whether you say it low, or shout . . .'

"The small things in life were so damn important to him. A good cup of coffee, a cold glass of water. Whenever I say these things, they sound made up. But they're true—every word! Whenever Jack said something was the greatest, like the 'greatest apple,' it would knock me out. Once, he even came to me and said,

'George, let the guy downstairs shine your shoes. He's marvelous!' I just looked at him. Who the hell cared—except Jack!

"You wouldn't think that a guy making all those millions of dollars, staying in the finest hotels, eating the best food, living in an elegant house, would ooh and aah over a fresh glass of water. But *that* was Jack . . .

"I hate to shatter his public image, but Jack never really cared about money. What he cared about was *cash,* and not about thousands of dollars. If he had a hundred and fifty dollars in his money clip, it was always rolled up and crumpled. If he had that amount in his pocket, he thought it was a *lot* of money. On the other hand, he would think nothing of writing a check for twenty-five thousand dollars for charity. To him, when you wrote a check, it wasn't like money. I don't think he ever really knew how much he did have. He never worried about it—it was something that was there . . . I've always thought Mary was one of the luckiest women in the world because she married a fine, darling man. I would have said that even if Jack never earned more than fifty dollars a week. But to live all those years with a man who was so nice—and so successful—that's indeed being truly fortunate . . .

"Professionally, I would have to say that Jack was somewhat self-centered . . . constantly focused inward . . . Maybe you could call it guts . . . or courage . . . or chutzpah . . . All I know is, when he told a joke—even a lousy joke—he would stand there . . . then he'd pull his ear . . . rub his nose . . . fold his arms . . . All the while, he would just stare at the audience. Then, after he got to them, he would say softly, 'What the hell are you laughing about?'

"As a performer, Jack just can't be compared with anyone else. He could talk about the weather and get laughs. He got to be such an institution that it didn't even matter if he was funny. Any time Jack paused, people laughed. They were afraid *not* to react for fear of being accused of lacking a sense of humor.

"Jack was unique because he *wasn't trying* to be unique. He was such a nice person . . . They are really rare in this world. He was a very normal human being who liked a cold glass of water. Very few people take the time to appreciate things like that . . .

"No matter how successful Jack became, you couldn't be jealous of him. I can think of only one performer, back in vaudeville days, who was jealous of Jack—Phil Baker, also a big star. He just didn't think Jack had any talent. He could never imagine how Jack made it in vaudeville. He would say, 'Jack never does anything but stand there, touch his face, stare, and then say, "Well . . ."' He couldn't see what the hell was so funny about 'Well' . . . Phil thought *anyone* could say 'Well.' The sad truth is *no one* could, except Jack, not and get a laugh.

"The audience pushed Jack. The audience made 'Well' a hit . . . What was our life then except just going out and doing our fifteen minutes, and if we were good, we got to do seventeen minutes? Those minutes were a comic's life savings. His success. Believe me, you learned to do it successfully, or got out of the business . . .

"Jack fooled the whole world. He had this tremendous talent, but he looked like he didn't. He even read the telephone book on a show once because Louella Parsons said Jack would be funny reading anything—even the phone book. So he came on, told the audience what Louella said, then proceeded to read some names and numbers. The people screamed. 'After all,' he told them, 'you're not going to let Louella Parsons down, are you?'"

During the 1936 season, flashy Phil Harris joined Jack's show. Phil, a native of Linton, Indiana, was raised in Nashville, Tennessee. Although his main interest as a boy was sports, his musician father simultaneously instructed him in the fundamentals of music. Possessing a terrific sense of rhythm, Harris gravitated toward drums, and appeared with his father at carnivals and in vaudeville during school vacations.

Phil also gathered together a group of his peers, and they formed their own orchestra, which Harris called the Dixie Syncopators. The group was quite successful—with Phil doubling as vocalist—barnstorming around the southern states. Subsequently, they were booked for a full year's engagement at the Princess Hotel in Honolulu, Hawaii.

When the year was up, the group disbanded, and Harris, on his own, was signed to a contract by the Palais de Dance in Melbourne, Australia.

Returning to America, Harris worked at two popular spots in

Hollywood, the Coconut Grove at the Ambassador Hotel, and the Wilshire Bowl. He became so popular, RKO signed him to a contract. The first film he made was a short, *So This Is Harris*. Jack, on an out-of-town engagement, happened to drop into a movie house where the Harris short was on the bill. He had gone to see the feature film and had come out enchanted by the Harris charm. Phil was contacted, signed, and became a Benny regular. His hip, snappy patter and happy-go-lucky manner provided another perfectly balanced comedy character with whom Jack could get laughs at his own expense . . .

Early in 1937, Jack starred in another Paramount film, *Artists and Models,* with Ida Lupino, Richard Arlen, Gail Patrick, Martha Raye, and Ben Blue. He played a down-on-his-luck advertising man with multiple problems—paying his bills while simultaneously trying to impress a client by finding the right girl to reign as Queen of the Artists and Models Ball. The plot was further complicated when Jack became involved romantically with *both* Ida Lupino and Gail Patrick. It was a gals, gags, and music film, with the attendant number of leggy chorines starring in several elaborate song and dance numbers.

The picture turned out to be a huge box-office success, and Walter Winchell wrote: ". . . Jack Benny finally gets his best break in Paramount's 'Artists and Models.' The Benny magic, we mean, finally reaches out from the screen into the auditor's heart . . ."

A few months after *Artists and Models* was completed, Paramount came up with another musical which they hoped would star Jack Benny. This time, he balked. The name of the film was *The Big Broadcast of 1938,* which was to feature W. C. Fields, Dorothy Lamour, Ben Blue, and Shirley Ross. Part of the action took place on an ocean liner. Benny argued that he had already played a similar role in *Transatlantic Merry-Go-Round*. Besides, the role called for him to sing a romantic ballad near the end of the film—a little ditty called "Thanks for the Memory." Jack didn't think he could handle it.

For weeks, the studio applied pressure—but Benny stood firm. At the last minute, director Mitch Leisen was talked into hiring a vaudeville performer who had also appeared on Broadway, a young man who had had a couple of opportunities for stardom before, but who just seemed to miss—Bob Hope. The rest is history.

Over the years, Hope and Benny became close friends. Hope always said that if Benny hadn't turned down the part, his career might have floundered for several more years before he got his big break. Benny, modestly, never took any credit for "paving Hope's way." To Jack, it was just one of those lucky coincidences of fate, nothing more. To Bob, it was the beginning of everything!

During this period, Mary, also under contract to Paramount, co-starred on her own in a picture called *This Way Please,* with Charles "Buddy" Rogers and Betty Grable. The combined Benny income was astronomical. The radio show was the number-one program in the country. Socially, the Bennys were one of the town's most prominent couples—and Jack became the owner of a race horse.

It started as a publicity gag. Jack and his old friend Ed Sullivan were discussing horses, when Jack suddenly decided he would like one. Sullivan put Benny in touch with Jerry Brady, an experienced horseman, who worked for the Alfred Gwynne Vanderbilt stables. Through him, Jack found out there was a horse auction coming up in Saratoga, and Brady said he would be happy to select one for Jack. Benny was delighted. He and Mary were on their way to New York to board the luxury liner *Normandie* bound for England. First, they made a side trip to visit Brady and inspect their purchase.

The horse Brady had chosen was a beautiful colt, sired by Upset, the only one to beat Man o' War in the Kentucky Derby, out of Helen T. The blood lines were good, and the horse was beautiful. Jack and Mary named him Buck Benny. He was turned over to trainer Freddie Hopkins and after a suitable period was entered in several races—but always ran out of the money.

The horse was never brought to California, and Jack's enthusiasm for "the creature" took a back seat to his busy schedule. Benny just paid the bills and left the racing details to his trainer.

Some months passed. One morning, Jack and Hickey were at Paramount together when they bumped into Raoul Walsh, not only a top director, but a racing enthusiast as well. Through him, they learned Buck Benny was scheduled to run that very day. Jack turned to Hickey and said, "Shall we bet on it?" Hickey shook his head. "I'm not going to put a dime on that nag. If you want to bet, it's up to you." Jack decided to pass.

A few hours later, as they were leaving the studio, Walsh came running over to congratulate Jack. Buck Benny, a tremendous long shot, had come in first, paying $48 to win. Jack was so mad, he chased Hickey all the way across the Paramount lot.

Although Jack sold the horse at a claiming race a few months later, and recouped his investment, he never forgot about the day Buck Benny won—and he never let Hickey forget it, either!

CHAPTER TWENTY

BEGINNING IN THE EARLY days of commercial radio, a system of "packaging shows" for specific clients had come into being. There were a dozen or so top advertising agencies, each handling certain very large accounts such as General Foods, General Motors, and American Tobacco. From among the shows and talent available, a sponsor would decide on the type of program or specific talent he wanted. After they were signed, the agency would appoint one of its own staff to function as producer. This was in contrast to today's setup, in which the networks or independent companies assign their own producer and the ad agency representatives work in a liaison capacity, mainly handling the commercials which go on each program.

Up until the end of the 1938 season, Tom Harrington was the Young and Rubicam Advertising Agency producer assigned to Jack's show for Jell-O. When he was made vice-president of his agency, and left to go back to the New York office, Murray Bolen, his assistant, replaced him. Bolen stayed on as Jack's producer until 1942.

"Those were fantastic years," Bolen remembers. "I really had my hands full acting as both producer and liaison between our agency client, General Foods, Jack's company and NBC . . . I had to get clearance on every commercial from Charlie Mortimer, vice-president of General Foods. Most of the time, the sponsors loved the way Jack kidded the product. A few times, though, they didn't . . .

"Still, Jack had reached such a top position in the industry, he was rarely interfered with—and for good reason. Every agency made frequent checks to determine how effective their shows were. Young and Rubicam was no exception. By random selection, hundreds of people across the country were called and asked two questions: 'Have you listened to the Jack Benny show during the past few weeks?' And, equally as vital: 'Do you know who sponsors the show?'

"Jack had the only program on the air with a *91 per cent* immediate sponsor identification. No one ever topped Benny's record!

"It was a stimulating, creative atmosphere being around Jack and his people. I sat in on all the rewrite sessions and rehearsals. Jack was always so professional. Whether we worked in his home, or at our office in the Taft Building, on the corner of Sunset and Vine, Jack alway maintained a very businesslike attitude. He knew exactly what he wanted—and worked until he got it.

"He was a marvelous man, very unstarlike, but he demanded as much perfection as possible. Everyone who worked for him loved him. We all knocked ourselves out to please him.

"When I first took over the program," Bolen continued, "we were broadcasting from a studio on Melrose [now KHJ], doing two shows every Sunday. The network wouldn't allow Jack, or any other artist, for that matter, to record the first show for a later playback in order to accommodate the western states.

"Then, too, we ran into frequent technical problems transmitting shows across country over the telephone wires which we utilized. In those days, every station had to employ a stand-by musician, usually a pianist or an organist. Whenever trouble occurred, an announcer would come on and say, 'Ladies and gentlemen, please excuse this temporary break in transmission . . . There will be a brief musical interlude . . . We will rejoin the program in progress momentarily . . .'

"Our stand-by, a guy who literally had to hang around the studio all the time, was a fine pianist named Ben Gage. He eventually gave up standing by—and married Esther Williams."

In between the Bennys' first and second shows each week, Jack, Mary, and various members of the cast and production staff left the studio and headed for Mary's parents' home. Mr. and Mrs. Marks always had an elaborate buffet set up. Quite often, friends, such as the Jack Haley, Sr.'s, would join the Benny group for the buffet, then remain behind to listen to Jack's second show with Mary's family.

Flo and Jack Haley remember those days with great clarity.

"It was amazing how relaxed and casual Mary and Jack and the others were—even knowing that a second show faced them," Haley recalls.

"Not only that," Flo added, "but don't forget, Jack would often do different bits of business for the second show—just to keep his orchestra and cast laughing *spontaneously* and on their toes . . ."

"Jack had a very special quality to him," Haley continued. "Flo and I were friends of Jack's from our vaudeville days . . . you could watch an awful lot of performers, but only a few of them were blessed with genius. It's something you can't really define. My daughter-in-law, Liza Minnelli, has it; Jack Benny had it too . . ."

"Mary and Jack were such a perfectly matched couple," Flo commented. "Away from public view, Mary was as funny as Jack in front of a microphone. I can't remember an appropriate time when Mary didn't have a wise and witty comeback. She really was a great character!

"Once, she had an appendicitis attack, and Jack sent for the ambulance to take her to the hospital. As she was being put on the stretcher, Mary said, with a perfectly straight face, 'Would you mind going down Wilshire Boulevard? Magnin's has some new dresses in the window and I'd like to see them . . .' The attendants looked at her, saw she was completely serious, and followed her instructions. When they got to Magnin's, the ambulance slowed down. Mary sat up, saw two outfits she liked, and ordered them as soon as she reached the hospital!"

By this time, Jack had a firmly established work routine. After each Sunday's second broadcast, he and Mary chatted with members of the audience, gave out autographs, then Jack got together with his writers, Morrow and Beloin, and briefly discussed ideas for the following week's show.

On Monday, the writers met alone. They came up with a rough outline for the program and presented it to Jack on Tuesday morning. Then, together with Jack, they spent three or four hours on Tuesday, Wednesday, and Thursday polishing, rewriting, and shaping a rehearsal script. Friday was their day of rest.

Saturdays, the cast gathered, and Jack would read the entire script through, then solicit comments. Inevitably, little changes and deletions were made. Then everyone read his or her own part as they went through the script from the top. Following the run-through, the cast left. Jack, the writers, and certain members of the production staff would stay behind and discuss the program, often doing more rewrites, sometimes for hours on end.

At ten o'clock Sunday morning, the cast reassembled and rehearsed the revised script. At 4 P.M., they went on the air. Even as late as the *final* rehearsal, Jack would still go over each phrase, until he *knew* it sounded right.

It was this supreme effort, carried on week after week, thirty-nine weeks in a row, which set Benny apart from most of the other comics. Early on in his life, he had known what it was to fail. Once he became a star, Jack Benny refused to coast on his laurels, to take success for granted.

"During this period," Murray Bolen remembers, "NBC finally completed building new studios at the corner of Sunset and Vine, and Jack's show made the move. Shortly thereafter, a new system was inaugurated. Jack was permitted to do one live show for the East Coast, which was simultaneously transcribed for rebroadcast later that evening . . .

"The new system made things easier for all of us . . . Only one big problem remained. As producer, I carefully clocked each week's script with a stopwatch, so I could figure out how much time to allow for laughter. But Jack's audience was unpredictable. It was almost impossible to second-guess their enthusiasm . . .

"Week after week, we'd go on the air and, midway through the show, we'd be maybe thirty to forty-five seconds overtime. If I couldn't find a way to pick up the time, I'd call the producer of the show following Jack's, and ask to *borrow* the extra seconds. They always gave it to us, knowing they could make it up.

"This worked fine for a while. Then the network found a way to keep us 'honest.' Do you remember those three chimes which NBC began to ring at the end of each half hour—Bing . . . Bong . . . Bong? Although Jack never took 'credit' for it, NBC brought in those chimes so we would *have* to be off the air when our half hour was over. All the artists bitched about it, but no one realized that it was inaugurated to *prevent* Benny's laughter from spilling over. Nowadays, station breaks are computerized—but back then, we sure played havoc with the schedules!"

CHAPTER TWENTY-ONE

IN 1938, Hickey Marks was employed as a third assistant director at M-G-M. In between assignments, he spent a lot of time sitting in on Jack's writing sessions, watching and listening as Jack and Morrow and Beloin put the shows together. From time to time, he came up with ideas that everyone liked. Then, one day, Jack said, "Hickey, why don't you leave Metro and come to work with us on a steady basis? I'd like you to be one of my writers . . ."

For the next few years, Marks worked in that capacity on Jack's radio shows, as well as over at Paramount writing extra dialogue for Jack's films . . .

"It was a marvelous, productive period," Hickey remembers, "but also a hectic one, since Jack was making so many movies. Whenever he was shooting at Paramount, Bill Morrow and Ed Beloin and Jack and I would get to the studio at five-thirty in the morning and work on the radio show until at least eight. Then the makeup man would come in to prepare Jack for the day's shooting, which began at nine.

"Our office became Jack's dressing room. While Jack was on the set, the boys and I would go in for some occasional horseplay in between writing sessions. Bing Crosby had the next dressing room. At the time, his big hit record was a single called 'Please.' Ed and Bill and I bought a copy, and very carefully cut a groove in the disc. Whenever we heard Crosby come in, we'd put on the record. It would revolve on the turntable perfectly until it reached our artificial groove. Then it would repeat over and over: 'Please, lend a little ear to my pleas . . .' It drove Bing nuts. He'd pound on the wall, but we'd let the record go on and on. Finally, one day, in desperation, he walked to the open door of Jack's dressing room and tossed a wastebasket full of debris at us. Morrow, Beloin, and I collapsed with laughter—but we figured Bing had had enough. We broke the record in half and left it on his dressing table!

"It really was a fantastic time to be at Paramount," Hickey said. "Claudette Colbert was on the lot, along with other stars such as Gary Cooper, Ray Milland, and Paulette Goddard . . . Cecil B. DeMille always had lunch at his special table in the commissary . . . And, two dressing rooms away from Jack, there was a young actor making his first film at Paramount, *I Wanted Wings,* William Holden.

"In the picture, Bill played a character named Ludlow. He and I became good friends. A few years later, we both wound up in Santa Ana, California, at the same Army Air Force base, where I was producing, directing, and writing shows. None of the other guys could figure out why they called Holden lieutenant, and I always referred to him as Ludlow. Later on, when Bill appeared on Jack's show, it used to drive Jack nuts. I'd always call Holden Ludlow, and Jack just couldn't understand it.

"I must confess," Hickey continued, "it was also during this period that I began doing terrible things to Jack—just for fun, of course. He was so trusting, so vulnerable. It was very easy. I used to send made-up telegrams that drove him crazy. My invented wires would not have been so maddening to anyone else I know.

It's just that Jack was always so considerate of others, so anxious to acknowledge any act of kindness.

"For instance, I once sent a wire which read:

> HEARD YOUR SHOW. THOUGHT IT WAS
> GREAT. ALL OUR LOVE TO YOU AND
> MARY.
>
> DAVE AND SYLVIA

"I was with Jack when the telegram arrived. He read it, then showed it to me.

"'Hickey,' he said, looking very perplexed, 'who are Dave and Sylvia? Maybe it's a misprint. It could be from *Danny* and Sylvia (Danny Kaye and his wife, Sylvia Fine). Gee, I'd better call Danny and thank him—just in case.'

"Naturally, I would agree, and Jack would call dear friends, like the Kayes, and thank them. They never knew what in the hell he was talking about! This resulted in some pretty funny telephone exchanges, with the recipients always confused, but gracious, indulging Jack, but *not* knowing why. No matter how many times I sent phony wires, he never caught on . . .

"One Friday morning, when Morrow, Beloin, and I were working with Jack at his home, the butler came in and handed Jack a telegram. He opened it, read it, then turned to us and said, 'Well, this is the goddamnest thing I ever heard in my entire life.'

"It was either Ed or Bill who asked, 'What is it, Jack?' I already knew!

"'Listen to this,' Jack said, his voice rising:

> HEARD YOUR SHOW AND THOUGHT IT WAS
> ONE OF THE GREATEST. ALL OUR LOVE
> TO YOU AND MARY. HOPE TO SEE YOU
> SOON.
>
> CAROLE AND CLARK

"Jack's brow was a study in wrinkled confusion. 'Well, I just don't understand this at all. If the Gables heard the show *last Sunday,* why would they wait until *this Friday* to send me a wire?'

"He turned and looked at me. 'Jeez, Hickey, why?'

"Very seriously, I tried to explain the situation logically. 'There must have been some delay in getting the wire delivered, Jack

. . . Maybe Western Union made an error . . . Perhaps it was one of their operators who mislaid the message . . . Of course, they could have just forgotten to deliver it last weekend . . .'

"Jack shrugged, but completely accepted my half-assed, convoluted explanation. Fortunately, when he called Carole and Clark to say thank you, they were out of town on a hunting trip. That was one confused conversation I didn't have to listen to . . ."

The Hickey Marks phony telegram bit went on for many months—with Jack none the wiser. Then Marks decided to lay off for a while. Several years passed, then a perfect opportunity presented itself when Jack was making an appearance in Warwick, Rhode Island, and Hickey, as usual, was with him . . .

"First of all, you have to understand that, wherever I go, I'm a terrific tourist," Hickey explained. "I take every spare moment to go sight-seeing. This one morning, I left Warwick very early and made the grand tour, going as far as Hyannis Port, Massachusetts. I was about to head back when I spotted a Western Union office across from where I was parked. It had been a long time between telegrams—I decided to remedy that situation.

"Hours later, I arrived back at our hotel and entered my room to the ringing of a phone. It was Jack. He sounded a little frantic and asked if I would please come over to his room right away. I said okay, and walked across the hall. Jack inquired how my sight-seeing venture had gone, but I knew that was not the *real* reason he had called me. In his hands, he held a telegram.

" 'Jeez, Hickey, I've been trying to reach my sister . . . I've been calling Chicago for hours, but Florence isn't home.'

" 'What's wrong, Jack?'

" 'Well, there's *nothing* wrong . . . but look at this telegram I got:

> TALKED TO FLORENCE THIS MORNING.
> UNDERSTAND YOU'RE PLAYING WARWICK.
> ARRIVING IN PROVIDENCE THIS WEEKEND.
> WOULD LOVE TO SEE YOUR SHOW. ARE
> TWO TICKETS AVAILABLE? REGARDS.
> RUTH AND HARVEY

" 'I don't even know who in the hell Ruth and Harvey are! Now they want to see my show. This is ridiculous. Why in the hell don't people ever sign their full names, or at least let me know where I can reach them?'

"Soberly, I said, 'Jack, don't get so steamed. They'll probably get in touch with us when they arrive. If they are friends of Florence, either they'll call you or me . . .'

" 'No, I can't wait for that,' Jack said. At such times, he could become very adamant. 'I've got to keep trying to reach my sister . . .'

"Once again, he picked up the phone to place a call to Chicago. This time, I had gone too far. Jack was really very upset about possibly offending Florence's friends. He was so damn considerate about such things, I just didn't have the heart to string him along any more.

" 'Jack,' I started, then paused, trying to think of something to say. 'Jack . . . *put down the phone . . .*'

"He looked at me—hard. After years of receiving phony wires, suddenly he read an expression of guilt on my face.

" 'Hickey, you son-of-a-bitch,' he began, then proceeded to call me every dirty name he could think of. 'You've been doing this to me for years, haven't you?'

"I didn't know whether to laugh or cry. Instead, I just nodded. I could see Jack wasn't too sure himself whether he should get hysterical with laughter or punch me in the nose.

"For years after that day in Rhode Island, whenever Jack received a wire, he was never quite sure if it was for real or not. Invariably, he would find me and confront me, telegram in hand. He'd shake it at me and make me read it while he kept staring in my eyes—as only Jack could. Not a word would pass between us. Slowly, I would raise my right hand . . . 'Honest to God, Jack . . .'

"Whenever I said those words, Jack breathed a sigh of relief and took the wire seriously. He knew when I said, 'Honest to God,' I couldn't be lying . . . Jack was such a decent guy . . . so vulnerable. I've often wondered how I had the nerve to carry on my 'personalized' Western Union campaign for so long!"

CHAPTER TWENTY-TWO

KENNY BAKER STAYED with Jack four seasons. The combination of his singing voice and the boyish charm of his created character, as pitted against Jack's brashness, turned him into one of the country's most popular performers. But in June of 1939, Baker left Benny for what was announced as a better financial offer.

In a collective fit of naïveté, many members of the nation's entertainment press again wondered—in print—if the Benny show could survive such an important defection. It was an odd conjecture, given Benny's track record—and some other stars might have felt it necessary to respond with "fighting words." But Jack, true to form, refused to rise to the bait. Instead, he quietly decided that he and Mary would conduct a personal talent search during their summer vacation.

After a brief holiday together, Jack flew to Chicago to interview prospective tenors. Mary, on her own, went into New York for the same purpose. As soon as the announcement of Baker's leaving hit the papers, literally hundreds of singers began vying for the spot.

Dennis Day, real name Owen P. "Eugene" McNulty, vividly recalls the whole episode. Born in the Bronx, New York, Day was a young kid, just out of Manhattan College, where he had been president of the Glee Club.

"In the summer of 1939," Dennis recalls, "I had done a few local CBS radio shows, singing with conductor Raymond Paige, who had a replacement show for André Kostelanetz. Occasionally, they would take transcriptions of songs I sang right off the air. I was still pretty much an amateur, working under the auspices of what they called Columbia Artists Management . . ."

Across town, in the old Paramount Building, Mary sat in the

office of the Bennys' agents, Arthur and Sam Lyons. In front of her was a stack of several hundred photos which she leafed through as she listened to audition recordings . . . One face very much appealed to her. As she turned over the eight-by-ten glossy, she saw the name Dennis Day on the back. The young man had a handsome Irish kisser, and Mary asked if she could listen to his voice. Lyons made a telephone call, and CBS responded by sending over one of Day's on-the-air transcriptions.

"I even remember the songs Mary heard," Dennis recently recalled. " 'Don't Worry About Me,' and 'I Never Knew Heaven Could Speak.' Then the Lyons office asked CBS to send me over. Someone from the station phoned and told me the time and place I was to appear. They said I would be meeting some very important people. They wouldn't say who . . ."

Meanwhile, Jack had flown in from Chicago, and Mary had shown him Day's picture.

"I was very apprehensive that morning," Dennis continued. "When I walked in and saw Jack sitting at a desk, I nearly went right through the floor. Benny's show was the number-one program in the country. Jack just looked at me and asked if I would like to sing for him. I said I would be happy to. A date was set up for the next day. I rushed home and called my accompanist, Billy Bruce. The rest of that afternoon and evening we rehearsed about fifteen songs . . ."

The following morning, Day dutifully appeared at the RCA Building and took the elevator to the eighth floor. Jack and Mary were waiting. For about twenty minutes, Dennis sang. He was then told to take a break, and was standing in a corner of the studio, talking to his piano player, when Jack's voice came over the intercom: "Dennis . . ." To which Day answered, "Yes, please . . ."

"Jack later told me my reply was one of the decisive factors in my being hired. He liked the fact that I sounded both naïve and polite! But at that point, my 'ordeal' was just beginning . . ."

The audition over, Jack and Mary thanked Dennis, and he left. Three weeks passed. Once again Day was called to the studio, given a script, and asked to read. A transcription was made of his

Carole Lombard and Jack in *To Be or Not to Be*. ("To Be or Not to Be" Copyright © 1942, Twentieth Century-Fox Corporation. All Rights Reserved)

Jack in *Buck Benny Rides Again*, 1940. (© Universal Pictures)

Jack and Laird Cregar in *Charley's Aunt*. ("Charley's Aunt" Copyright © 1941, Twentieth Century-Fox Film Corporation. All Rights Reserved)

Jack and Mary in the doorway of their home. (Courtesy John Engstead)

The Bennys' Roxbury Drive residence for more than twenty-five years. (Benny Family Personal Collection)

L. to R.: Hickey Marks, Jack Benny, Ralph Levy (the director), and Barbara Stanwyck rehearsing for a television show, January 1952. (Photo by Gabi Rona, courtesy CBS)

Jack in an early version of "Singin' in the Rain." He was the m.c. in the film. (From the M-G-M release *Broadway Melody* © 1929 MGM Distributing Corporation. Copyright renewed 1956 by Loew's Incorporated.)

Jack and Noël Coward. (Benny Family Personal Collection)

Jack with Ernst Lubitsch, his *To Be or Not to Be* director. ("To Be or Not to Be" Copyright © 1942, Twentieth Century-Fox Film Corporation. All Rights Reserved)

Jack with Laurel and Hardy. (Benny Family Personal Collection)

speaking voice and air-mailed to the writers in California. Jack had wanted their opinion of how Dennis sounded.

"Three weeks passed," Day remembers. "I read in the paper where Jack and Mary had gone back to Hollywood . . . I thought any chance I had was gone. Then the Lyons office got in touch with me again. Jack wanted me to take another audition, so they sent me a round-trip ticket on the Golden State Limited . . . I was headed for Hollywood!

"I'll never forget going to the station with my mother and father. As we were saying goodbye, the famous vaudeville team of Tim and Irene walked down the platform. Mother immediately recognized them and went over to ask if they would please look after me! Irene's last name was Ryan. You may recall, she subsequently became Granny on 'The Beverly Hillbillies.'

"I felt foolish being 'looked after,' but it *was* my first trip west of the Mississippi. While we were on the train, Germany invaded Poland. I remember thinking to myself, 'Well, even if I get the job, it will be pretty short-lived.' The war was really heating up . . ."

In California, Dennis sang for some NBC executives and Jack's writers. He was then instructed to sit tight, stay under wraps, and not talk to anybody. He was told that no decision had been made . . . Jack had gone to San Francisco to play the World's Fair, and would be back in a couple of weeks. By then, something more definite would be known.

"I had to send home for money," Dennis laughed. "Jack's agents had given me a train ticket—but no cash. I rented a cheap room at the Hollywood Athletic Club and walked around town sight-seeing for two weeks, not daring to talk to anybody, or even to go anywhere near the network."

When Jack returned, Dennis was notified that he was being signed to a contract—*a two-week contract*. If he didn't make good, they could and would drop him. Fourteen days later, Dennis Day was given a contract for eleven more weeks. In fact, Benny and company were so unsure of Dennis' ability to fit into their format that for the whole first year, he had a series of thirteen-week contracts.

Just prior to the start of the 1939 season, Jack and his writers wrestled with ways to integrate Dennis on the show. While in New York, Jack had met Day's parents, Mr. and Mrs. McNulty, dear people with thick Irish brogues and very sweet old-fashioned ways. That meeting gave Jack an idea. Since they wanted to keep Dennis the naïve, boyish type previously identified with Baker, why not introduce the character of Dennis' mother? But instead of being like the real Mrs. McNulty, a sweet lady, the mother of six, who spoke with an Irish accent and played the concertina, she would be a heavyweight—very domineering—or, as Dennis subsequently nicknamed her, "my mother, the bricklayer." Brilliant character actress Verna Felton was signed for the part.

On October 8, 1939, Dennis Day made his debut. For the first sixteen weeks, Dennis' mother had the dominant role, while Day rarely said more than "Yes, please." Cleverly, "Mama Day" had been constructed as a woman who hated Jack, who thought Benny was taking advantage of her boy, and was determined to stick close by and act as a buffer between Benny and her son. The two new characters eventually became comedy classics—and Dennis had all of his options lifted that initial season.

On Day's first show, Jack and Mary set him up by discussing the impending arrival of a new vocalist . . . As you will note, it was "Mother Day" who dominated the scene . . .

(Sound: Door opens)

JACK: Well, how do you do, Mrs. Day . . . Come right in.

VERNA: Thank you. Come along, Dennis.

JACK: Well, I'm glad you found the studio all right . . . Did you take a cab like I told you to?

VERNA: Yes, it was a dollar sixty-five; here's the slip.

JACK: Oh . . . oh well, I don't mind.

VERNA: Then *smile!*

JACK: Hm . . . Oh, Mrs. Day, I want you to meet the members of my cast.

VERNA: How do you do.

GANG: (Ad-lib greetings to Mrs. Day)

JACK: And this is her little boy, Dennis.

VERNA: Say hello to the people, Dennis.

DENNIS: Hello to the people.

JACK: Oh fine . . . Now, Dennis—

DENNIS: Yes, please?

JACK: What song have you selected for your debut on "The
          Jell-O Program"?

DENNIS: I'm going to sing a—

VERNA: He's going to sing a delightful new number entitled
          "When You Wish upon a Star."

JACK: Hm . . . Now before you sing, Dennis, I thought our
          audience would like to know your age . . . How old
          are you?

DENNIS: Fifty-nine including Mother.

JACK: Well, that's not what I meant, but let it go . . . Now,
          go ahead, Dennis, we're all anxious to hear you . . .
          This is the microphone.

DENNIS: How do you do.

JACK: My, you *are* nervous . . . Go ahead, kid.

VERNA: Now remember, Dennis, breathe deeply.

DENNIS: Yes, Mother.

VERNA: Don't forget the words.

DENNIS: No, Mother.

VERNA: And come here, let me fix your tie.

JACK: Don't bother, Mrs. Day, you know this isn't *television*.

VERNA: You're quite fortunate, Mr. Benny.

JACK: Ha ha ha . . . Very good, Mrs. Day . . . Sing, Den-
          nis. (Oh boy, I'd like to give her a hotfoot.)
                  (Segue into Dennis's number)
          ("When You Wish upon a Star" by Dennis Day)

"Thank God for Mary Livingstone and Jack Benny. They
changed my life . . ." Dennis added. "I wound up being associated with Jack for thirty-five years. I often think back to
those first days, and I realize how much courage Jack had, giving
me a break. I was an inexperienced non-professional, blessed with
a natural voice. But I had only taken a few singing lessons in my
life. I certainly had never played any comedy parts before. Suddenly, to be catapulted to fame on the country's top show was an
unbelievable blessing."

109

Benny fans all over the country laughed week after week as Jack said: "Sing, Dennis . . ." and Verna Felton bellowed: "Not *now*, Dennis. *I'll* tell you when to sing." Jack's perpetual battle with Day's mother became a running gag which lasted on and off for several seasons.

"During my second year on the show, when Verna Felton only came on once or twice," Dennis continued, "her presence was so strongly established, the audience *thought* she was there. I'd say things like: 'Mr. Benny, my mother says it's time you gave me a raise . . . She thinks that for singing and mowing your lawn, I should be earning more than thirty-five dollars a week . . .' At which point, Jack would say with a disgusted tone: '*Your* mother . . . *your* mother, what does *she* know?' And, all across the country, people laughed as they visualized the dressing down my mother was going to give Jack . . ."

The Monday following Dennis' debut with Verna, the papers were full of good reviews, including this mention from *Radio Daily*:

> Dennis Day replaces Kenny Baker . . . Day is accompanied by a "stage mother" who is a natural for laughs. He displayed good range, a somewhat different and sentimental style, and his "Good Night, My Beautiful," was smoothly done . . .
>
> As "Mrs. Day," Verna Felton was the perfect choice. In previous seasons, she had played the mother of Don Wilson, Phil Harris and nearly every other member of the cast—each time with a new dimension of versatility . . .

At the end of the first season, Dennis was voted one of the top five most popular vocalists on the air . . . and the nation's radio writers joined in heaping praise on him. Not one of them wondered—in print—if the Benny show could survive Kenny Baker's loss. The answer was obvious!

CHAPTER TWENTY-THREE

CONTRARY TO THE TITLE of the Thomas Wolfe novel, Jack Benny believed you could go home again. Over the long years of his career, his association with Waukegan, Illinois, was a close and continuous one. Whenever they called on him for his time or his money, it was given freely, generously. Simultaneously, whenever the city could honor him, they did so, eagerly. It was a two-way romance—a love affair between a man and a town—with equal ardor on both sides.

In 1939, Jack made *Man About Town* with a stellar cast: Dorothy Lamour, Edward Arnold, Binnie Barnes, Monty Woolley, Betty Grable, Phil Harris, and Eddie "Rochester" Anderson. Directed by Mark Sandrich, with a screenplay by Morrie Ryskind, *Variety* said it was a "sparkling and cleverly contrived picture, precisely tailored for Benny's radio and screen personality and ample enough to enlist the best talent of every principal . . ."

Once again, Benny was surrounded by opulent musical production numbers, this time staged by LeRoy Prinz, and featuring, in addition to the main cast, a troupe of dancers, a group of acrobats, and Matty Malneck's orchestra.

With such good advance notices, Paramount decided to give the film an extra kicker by holding the world premiere in Waukegan. The city fathers were thrilled, and immediately began making massive preparations for the event.

Although the Genessee Theater was originally selected as the premiere site, there was such a demand for tickets, the film simultaneously opened in Waukegan's two other large movie houses, the Academy and the Rialto. The opening was scheduled for a Sunday evening, June 25, so Jack could broadcast his radio show from the theater stage.

For a full week preceding the premiere, the town celebrated, playing host to Jack's regulars: Mary, Don, Phil, Rochester, plus Andy Devine and Dorothy Lamour. The big event leading up to the actual showing of the film was a huge parade. For Jack, as always, it was a great treat "going home." But this trip had an extra touch which added to Jack's personal pleasure.

"When I was a boy," Jack once said, "I hated practicing the violin. Every once in a while, my dad would come home and hear me playing a piece I had learned the previous week. He would get angry and tell me to progress . . . to get on with my studies . . . to stop repeating what I already knew. 'Benny,' he would say, 'remember, if you ever want to get anywhere, *you have to keep practicing the hard parts . . .*'

"Over the years, as I grew more successful, one of the fringe benefits was the kick my dad got out of everything that happened to me. Although I heard via the grapevine that Dad always talked about me with a great deal of pride, he never had come right out and told me face to face exactly how he felt about what I had done with my life . . .

"When I knew Paramount's plans for the film, and heard there would be a big parade before the picture, and a big banquet afterward, I requested that my dad ride in the lead car, between Dorothy Lamour and myself, and that he have a front table at the dinner. It gave me a kick to think about how all this might affect him.

"Dad had just turned seventy. He was an old man. His frame had become lean and shrunken, but his eyes were still bird-quick, and his mind just as sharp as ever.

"All during the parade, as old friends and neighbors lined the streets and waved and cheered, my father said nothing. At the banquet, when I got up to make my 'impromptu' speech, and received some very big laughs, Dad remained silent. Every once in a while, I'd sneak a look at him, but his eyes were never on me. He was attentively watching the audience.

"Later, when I took him home, all during our drive, he didn't say a word. I walked him to his door and was about to leave, when he took my arm. Remember, it was 1939, when 'things' were beginning to boil over in Europe.

"'There's going to be another war,' he said. 'But we will win

. . .' He paused, and his eyes got that faraway look. 'There have always been pogroms in Europe. That's why your mother's family came . . . That's why I came to the United States, so when we married and had children our kids would never know the experiences we had been through. It always seemed to me we owed a debt to America . . . I wanted so much to pay it back. But I was only a small man—a *nothing*. When I gave you a violin, I thought if you could become a great musician, if you could make beautiful music, what a blessing that would be . . .'

"He sighed. 'That is why your mother and I were so sad when you stopped playing, Benny. That's why we hated to come and see you make a joke of the violin when you first went into vaudeville. But over the years, I've come to understand . . . You found you were better at making people laugh . . . and in times like we've had. it's very good, very important for people to laugh. How I wish your mother could have been with us tonight so she could have seen, as I did, that it was our Benny Kubelsky who made that laughter possible . . .'

"When Dad went inside, I just drove around town for a while. I kept hearing my father's words over and over again . . . and I remembered back to all those previous hours I'd wasted as a kid, when he had tried so damn hard to push me to apply myself. It was then I realized for the first time that all my professional life— in whatever I had done—one of the main things that had spurred me on, that made me such a perfectionist, was the subconscious voice of my father saying, 'Benny, remember, keep practicing the hard parts' . . . that, and the sad face of my mother just before she died . . . before I had begun to live up to my potentials . . ."

CHAPTER TWENTY-FOUR

EARLY IN 1940, Mary and Jack seriously discussed the idea of adopting another child. Joanie had brought so much love and pleasure into their lives, given them so much joy, that the Bennys made almost a firm decision to add a baby son to their household.

In mid-June, when the radio show was off for the summer, Mary and Jack, Joan, and her nurse sailed to Hawaii for a vacation. Hickey joined them later, coming over on a different ship. It was the only brief rest Jack would have that year. He had already done pre-production work on his next film, *Buck Benny Rides Again,* and was due at Paramount as soon as they returned from Honolulu.

Mary remembers that summer very well. "A few weeks after we returned, Jack was at the studio doing the film, and I was resting at home, feeling a little queasy. Jack was the hypochondriac in our family. I usually stayed clear of doctors unless it was absolutely necessary. That summer, *it was.* I saw my physician, he took all sorts of tests, then called me to announce happily, 'Mary, you're pregnant.'

"Jack and I were both thrilled at the news. Although it was very early in my pregnancy, Jack told *everyone.*

"He even went to some stag event, during this period, as a guest and after-dinner speaker. Although no one expected me, Jack proudly announced that I wasn't there because 'we were pregnant,' and one of us had to stay home and have the baby!

"We were especially happy because I had been unable to become pregnant earlier on in our marriage. But a few weeks after the doctor first told me the good news, I suffered a miscarriage. Jack was at the studio when it happened. He immediately rushed away from the set to be at my side. He was so concerned for my well-being. Naturally, I was quite upset. It seems my lifelong low

114

blood sugar condition—that which caused my periodic fainting spells—also prevented me from carrying a child full term.

"After this happened, Jack and I had another serious talk. Maybe having a second child, either naturally or by adoption, just wasn't in the cards. Professionally, we were both very busy. Free time was at a premium. Perhaps, we decided, it would be better to devote all of our love and effort to the baby we already had, who became, if that's possible, even more precious to us. We dropped our plans to adopt a baby son, and never regretted our decision . . ."

Joan Benny Blumofe, beautifully grown to adulthood, and herself the mother of four children, recalls her early life as the daughter of Mary and Jack Benny.

"I had a very happy childhood. People have asked, 'Was it awful being an only child?' 'What's it like to be adopted?' 'How does it feel to have famous parents?' My answer was always, 'I don't know. I've never had it any other way . . . There's nothing to compare it with.'

"When Daddy died I was, quite frankly, hurt by the obituaries. If I was mentioned at all, I was referred to as an adopted daughter —nothing else. It was like he and Mommy had me hidden in a closet somewhere. You see—my father and I were so close all through life. We were never really apart . . .

"I was terribly hurt by the obituaries because I sounded like an afterthought. I know they weren't *intentional* slights, but I still didn't think it was fair. After the funeral, they had all these TV panel shows where people got together and talked about Daddy. I would have at least liked to be asked. I guess in grief people tend to leave you alone. But at that time, I would have loved to talk about him. To tell everyone what he was really like . . .

"My mother and father were models for people who adopt children. I always knew I was adopted. How? Don't ask me. I can't tell you. Obviously, they started telling me I was adopted before I was really old enough to understand the word. But I know that I *always knew*. It must be terribly traumatic for a child if its parents wait until it's at the actual age of understanding to tell them. Then too, as a kid, my closest friends were Sandra and Ronnie Burns, George and Gracie's kids. They were adopted, too. A lot of my friends were. In fact, many of my parents' friends had adopted children. When I was little, I thought everybody was adopted. It seemed perfectly normal to me . . .

"We moved to the Roxbury Drive house right after my fourth birthday. Daddy and I really loved that place. One of his favorite pastimes, in fact I think it was his favorite, was walking. He loved to walk to his office from our home, or, most particularly, to visit our next-door neighbor, Lucille Ball, or walk down four houses to see the Jimmy Stewarts, or take an eight-block stroll and pop in on George and Gracie. Daddy would walk anyplace to see a friend. He really missed that after they moved from Roxbury . . .

"When I was growing up, I came to understand my father's priorities. His show came first. He came second. His illnesses came third. Then came the family. Daddy was not a curious man about things he did not want to be concerned with. He had a marvelous facility for blocking out everything irrelevant. He lived most of his life surrounded by a brick wall that shut everything else out and left him inside with his career. Which, in terms of our personal relationship, was a paradox—because we were very close —as long as it wasn't anything personal. He shied away from such situations . . .

"It's very hard to equate what I'm going to say with Daddy's image. On one hand, he was tremendously self-centered. A total egoist. But he *wasn't* egotistical. To the contrary, he was so kind, so wonderful. I mean, he wasn't one of those selfish s.o.b.'s always looking in the mirror. He wasn't conceited like that at all. He was an absolutely marvelous person, but you always realized his *total self-involvement*. It had a lot to do with his success . . .

"All my life, I learned to deal with Daddy on his terms—not mine. Somehow, I understood that his ability to be so focused in enabled him to sustain what he was in front of the public. It was an innate part of what made him so talented.

"Daddy had an enormous God-given talent. He worked on it, sure. But he always had a sixth sense about what was right for him—and he played it to the hilt all his life. Yet, the paradox is, Daddy was so *different* from other stars you might make the same comments about. They are the egotists. He wasn't, not in the same sense.

"For instance, when I was little, I'd go to the movies with him often. He loved films. Many times, we'd wind up standing in line for tickets at the box office. He never thought of just walking in. He was never bothered by having to wait. At some point, though, usually the theater manager would be told Daddy was standing outside and he'd come out and usher us in. Then, we'd get the star treatment. Daddy didn't mind that at all. He loved it! But he didn't automatically expect it, or demand it.

"There's that strange contradiction again. Humility along with egoism. It's hard to put together. How could one person be both things? Because he did have true humility. He never expected special treatment. Oh, there were certain things he took for granted. He loved being a celebrity . . . enjoyed people asking for his autograph. But he wasn't always Mr. Nice Guy. There were times when he was tired and didn't want to be bothered. They were *rare* times—only no one mentions them because that would shatter his perfect image. Well, Daddy wasn't perfect—but he was as close to it as they come! What he was was a very human being . . . sans halo . . .

"Whenever I had a problem, Daddy was *not* the one to discuss it with. It isn't that he wasn't interested, he was just sort of discombobulated. He didn't want to get involved. He would say, 'Do what you think best . . .' Children learn to deal with parents. In this area, I just knew Daddy wasn't the one to take my troubles to. Mother was the family disciplinarian. I learned not to run to Daddy if I wanted to do something and my mother had already said no. If I ever did go to him, invariably he'd just look at me and say, 'Ask your mother . . .'

"From the time I was very little, I instinctively understood Daddy's personality. He was just too soft-hearted when it came to dealing with people. He loved me so much, he just couldn't bring himself to disappoint me. Temperamentally, it was easier for him to have my mother say no to me. She loved me just as much, but she had a better facility for being the strict one. Even if Daddy was upset with someone, say a business associate, he rarely could articulate it. Most times he would write letters setting down the causes for his displeasure. Face to face, he was too sweet, too chicken to do it . . ."

CHAPTER TWENTY-FIVE

IN HIS SYNDICATED COLUMN of January 18, 1940, Ed Sullivan wrote:

> I see by the papers, as Will Rogers was fond of saying, that for the seventh successive year Jack Benny has been rated as No. 1 radio comedian of the national airlanes . . . That truly is an amazing record of consistency in a world that is anything but consistent . . . Styles and fashions change in everything; residential sections that are popular one year are unfashionable the next, magazines fold up and die from lack of circulation, political parties win one year and are tossed into the discard the next, movie stars and movie directors flourish and disappear from the popular orbit—it is an astounding thing that in a world of flex, Jack Benny has held his position for seven years, particularly when those years were as unpredictable as 1933, 1934, 1935, 1936, 1937, 1938 and 1939 . . . His startling hold on the good-will of the country, which is another expression of public opinion, is that in addition to his talent, the public recognizes the fact that here is a normal, decent sort of person.

* * *

> It is a heartening fact that a performer's true character must come through in his work . . . whether it is on the stage, in the movies, or on the radio, a player cannot conceal his innate characteristics . . . So when a performer lasts for any length of time, it is because the public has spotted certain qualities in him, above and beyond his professional skill, that ring true . . . The public analysis of Jack Benny is completely true . . . He is exactly as he appears to be, good-humored, loyal, appreciative, generous and simple in his tastes . . .

This word portrait, written by one of Jack's close personal friends, was 100 per cent accurate. Jack was indeed possessed with all the wonderful qualities Ed Sullivan wrote about. But, in addition, there was a certain duality to his nature, far too paradoxical to be summed up in one newspaper column.

On radio, the suave, vain, know-it-all braggart seemed so cool, so on top of things—even if his cast did make a fool of him every week. Behind the scenes, Jack was almost the complete opposite. At the end of every show, anxiety set in. What would they do next week? Benny, the consummate perfectionist, spent anxious days as the upcoming program was conceived, written, rewritten, rehearsed, edited, and finally put on the air. And on the air he always seemed so self-assured—and he was—but this came only *after* his meticulous preparation.

As Mary puts it, "Jack had an inner confidence. It radiated from him. But sometimes, even if he was the guest at a local dinner, before he left the house, he would be anxious. He'd jot down notes on index cards and go over and over them. But the minute we arrived at the dinner, and he was called on to say a few words, he would be perfectly calm and collected. It was always that way with him . . ."

As a "salesman," Jack Benny rated tops. Every product he sold on the air picked up in sales—even Canada Dry ginger ale and Chevrolet, albeit both sponsors fired him. Yet, always, Jack remained true to his own tastes. Unlike those radio and later television stars who literally drape themselves in the sponsor's product day and night, Jack "did his own thing." The product with which he was most closely identified for eight years—Jell-O—Jack never ate. Later, although he was on for Grape Nuts, he preferred a "sister product," Grape Nuts Flakes . . .

When he went on for American Tobacco, Jack did not take so much as one puff of a Lucky Strike cigarette. Dating back to his Earl Carroll *Vanities* days, when he had been forced to smoke a cigar in the show, he had cultivated a taste for them. He even appeared before live studio audiences during his Lucky Strike days smoking a cigar. He did make *one* concession, though—he smoked cigars made by American Tobacco—supplied to him by the boxful, first on the orders of the firm's president, George Washington Hill, and later by Hill's successor, Vincent Riggio.

Despite his cheapskate reputation, one that he always made so believable, Jack, in real life, was just the opposite. On the air, Mary used to tease Jack about being so poorly dressed. In truth, he had one of the most extensive and expensive wardrobes in Hollywood. When he relaxed, he liked to wear sports clothes, but always put on a neat business suit whenever he was going to appear before an audience. The others on his show followed his example.

Jack spent more than half his life trying, in vain, to live down his public reputation. In truth, he was a lavish, free spender, who took a personal delight in both spending and giving away large sums of money. In Hollywood, Jack was known as "an easy touch."

Whenever he traveled, Jack could *never* throw anything away. He was so associated with being stingy that if he stayed at a hotel and left behind a used pair of shoes, or an old bathrobe, invariably they were returned. Meticulously, the housekeeper would have the shoes resoled, or the robe laundered, and send them to his home in Beverly Hills.

It got to be such a "thing" with Jack, until Hickey came up with a solution. Whenever they traveled together, Hickey would carry a large pair of scissors. If Jack wanted to toss anything away, Hickey would first cut the item to shreds, and *then* Jack would throw it into the wastebasket. Eventually, *that* problem was solved.

If Jack took a taxi and gave the driver his usual ample tip, nine times out of ten the cabbie would smile, return the money, and say, "Please, Mr. Benny, don't disillusion me!"

Although more jokes were made over the years about Jack's toupee than any other Hollywood hairpiece, in reality, he never wore one. However, at an early age, he *did* begin to go prematurely gray. He was in his late twenties when his dark brown hair began to turn to silver—an inherited family characteristic. Because of his film and television work, he had his hair darkened.

Jack was a nail biter. Also, whenever he got nervous, he would rub his thumbnail back and forth across his second finger, until the thumb was worn to a frazzle. And, from the time he began playing the violin again, whether for fun or when he made concert tours, his nails were constantly full of rosin which he could never seem to remove.

He was a diabetic—albeit he had a modest case which did not require insulin. Jack himself diagnosed his condition. It happened while he was on his way East to do one of his broadcasts. Jack was sitting next to Hickey on the plane when the stewardess brought around some reading material. Jack selected a *Reader's Digest,* and immediately turned to the medical article. He loved the way the magazine presented diseases—in layman's terms.

The specific ailment Jack read about was diabetes. Since his mother had been a diabetic, Jack concentrated on the article with keen interest. The more he read, the more upset he became. When he had finished the final paragraph, he shook his head and said, "Hickey, something awful happened . . . *I just found out I'm a diabetic!"*

Because Jack was a notorious hypochondriac, his brother-in-law just laughed and changed the subject. However, as soon as Jack returned to Hollywood, he went to see his doctor immediately. After a series of tests was taken, it was determined that Benny had indeed been perceptive. He had a serious enough case to be put on oral medication, which he took several times a day, but not serious enough to require insulin injections.

From that day forward—with minor slips along the way—Jack maintained a diabetic's diet. The cook made special desserts for Jack without sugar. A supply of ersatz syrup was bought for the Benny kitchen, so he could still enjoy his pancakes. Whenever he traveled, he always took along a batch of dietetic cookies—a small quantity of which he kept in his coat pocket. Whenever someone would brush up close to him, instinctively his hand would go up to protect his "stash." Often he would say to someone approaching him: "Watch out for my cookies," to which the uninitiated Bennyphile would react with a raised eyebrow . . . And he rarely touched anything but dietetic ice cream. Happily, Mary even found a place where they made chocolate candy with a saccharin base.

Often, when people talked to him, Jack looked straight at them. He appeared to be listening, while actually allowing his mind to wander away to a subject of more importance: his next show, or personal appearance, or concert. It is *not* that he was intentionally rude—only that he was a genius with a one-track mind, always *focused in* on how to sustain the laughter he had received the previous week.

For the most part, Jack was very even-tempered. But he had a low boiling point. When he did get angry, he erupted like a volcano. Two minutes later, the anger was gone, forgotten. His mind was already elsewhere. He never carried a grudge, and always took the initiative of apologizing if he felt he had hurt someone's feelings.

The thing which seemed to bother him most was punctuality—a holdover from his vaudeville days, when meeting schedules and appointments was essential. If a rehearsal was called for noon, Jack would arrive no later than eleven-thirty, then pace up and down waiting for the others to arrive. He hated rudeness and considered being late the height of bad manners.

When he had a plane or train to catch, he fussed and stewed hours beforehand, and wound up arriving at the terminal or the station long before boarding time. In which case, he would wander around, often getting lost and having to be led back to the proper gate.

Mechanically, Jack was a washout. If anything more complex than changing a light bulb was required, he was completely helpless. Fortunately, he usually had people to do things for him—even open doors. Jack had weak wrists, and getting in and out of places could be a struggle.

At home, Mary took care of everything either personally or with the Benny staff. She was totally dedicated to Jack's well-being, and she saw to it that he was completely free just to be Jack Benny—star.

"It really wasn't that Jack *couldn't* do anything for himself," Mary commented. "It's just that Jack *didn't have to*—so he never paid attention to little details. His place was on the stage—only there could he be perfectly at ease. Many times, he would say to me, 'My only job is to walk out and be funny . . .' Consequently, wherever we lived, Jack didn't know much about the house . . .

even where the light switches or the heat thermostat was. I took care of everything for him . . .

"Yet, every so often, Jack *would* make an attempt to do things for himself. Like the night we came home from the theater, and Jack said he would like a glass of milk. 'I'll get it for you, doll,' I said. Suddenly, Jack turned to me as if I were balmy.

"'No, that's all right, doll, I can get it . . .'

"I followed Jack into the kitchen. He was all dressed in a tuxedo. Casually, he reached into the icebox, lifted the bottle of milk by its thin silver paper cap, and proceeded to spill the whole thing on himself. I just stood there and laughed. At first Jack kept a perfectly straight face. Then he doubled up with laughter too.

"'You see, doll,' I said, 'where would you be without me!' After that, Jack never attempted to get himself anything from the refrigerator . . .'"

The Benny home on Roxbury Drive had a unique security system. Throughout the house, there were special buttons which, when pushed, activated an alarm leading directly to the Beverly Hills Police Station. Time after time, if Jack wanted to call his butler, or a maid, he would forgetfully push one of the alarm buttons. Then he'd wait, unable to understand where they were—until an armed Beverly Hills policeman came walking through the front door!

But at the same time as people were waiting on him, Jack himself had a boundless supply of energy. As Mary recalls, "Jack hated going on vacations if he didn't simultaneously have something to do. He would usually plan his trips around an engagement. I wanted to just relax—not Jack. Yet after every working holiday, he'd turn to me and say, 'Okay, doll, now where do *you* want to go?' He'd take me anyplace I asked. And, when we were traveling, Jack *was* a perfect angel. He loved going shopping with me. He'd spend the whole day schlepping from store to store. He would sit patiently while I had my fittings for clothes, loving every minute of it.

"During all the years of our travels, he never bought anything for himself, only for me and Joanie, and the family and friends. Oh yes, once in London, he bought himself a pair of gloves—

that's all I can ever remember Jack getting for himself. I bought most everything for him. Still, when we were at home, he'd never spend a minute going with me for fittings. But in New York, London, or Paris, he'd sit for hours and enjoy himself. You figure it out!

"Jack's courtesy to and relations with people were extraordinary," Mary continued. "Whenever he went to a party, if someone rubbed me the wrong way, I'd comment to Jack on the way home that I didn't like so-and-so very much. Jack would always say, 'Well, doll, maybe they didn't like you, either. Why don't you give them a chance?'

"And, wherever he traveled to perform in theaters or nightclubs, Jack was the most undemanding star in the business. He never made a fuss if they gave him a small dressing room. In fact, he liked it. It reminded him of his vaudeville days. Whenever he was given the nicest dressing room, if he was appearing with a woman, he'd insist she take it—even if she wasn't a star. People around him made demands on Jack's behalf. He never opened his mouth. It wasn't in him. They always said Jack caused less trouble than any top star in the business . . .

"I don't think Jack ever had a true inner sense of his own worth. He knew people liked him, but I don't think he ever realized just how much people adored him . . . loved him. And he was the most patient, gracious man I ever met. Whenever he went, if a fan stopped him, he'd always stand and chat as long as they wanted to talk. Me, I'd die, but Jack would just stand there.

"He told me about a funny incident that happened to him one day after a theater rehearsal, when he came out of the stage door and a woman came up to him.

"'Are you Jack Benny?' she asked.

"'Yes, ma'am,' Jack replied. He always said 'yes, ma'am' or 'yes, sir,' when he talked to people. Even little kids!

"Anyway, when he said he was Jack, she looked him straight in the eye and said, 'No you're not!'

"'Yes, ma'am, I am,' Jack said for the second time, still patiently standing there. Four times she asked the same question and received the same answer. Finally, Jack said to the lady, 'What's *your* name?'

124

" 'Mrs. Goldberg,' she replied.

" 'No it isn't,' Jack smiled . . . and she walked away.

"What I've said is not meant to imply that Jack didn't have faults. He did. We all do. But with my husband, the good qualities he had so far outweighed the bad . . ."

CHAPTER TWENTY-SIX

ALTHOUGH IT'S HARD to imagine now, in the late 1930s and early 40s, movie studios were feeling the heat of competition from radio. Theater owners were complaining about former picture-goers staying home in droves listening to stars on radio. Why, they asked, did people need to pay money at a box office when they could stay home and be entertained for free?

The situation divided Hollywood for a time. It came to a climax when Darryl F. Zanuck, head of production at Twentieth Century-Fox, forbade his top male star, Tyrone Power, to appear on radio. The fight was on. Stars from every studio threatened to strike. Jack Benny was one of those who helped lead the way. After all, many of the most important film people were appearing as guests on his shows.

In light of the angry climate, the opening paragraphs of Hedda Hopper's column of April 15, 1940, had much significance . . .

Well, Jack Benny, our number one comedian, achieved the impossible. In "Buck Benny Rides Again," the lion and the lamb cavorted together, meaning radio and pictures. As you may have heard, they hadn't been too friendly, but Jack gives you the best elements of both. And if this picture doesn't lift the mortgage on your theater, then you might just as well give it over to war refugees.

I've known a lot of comedians, but Jack's the first one I've ever known personally who gave another comedian, Rochester, more funny lines than he kept himself. And Rochester didn't waste any time putting them over. Co-stars Ellen Drew, Andy Devine and Phil Harris are tops.

Benny's burlesque of a western chase and of all the cowboys who sing so much about "the deer and the antelope" laid the preview audience in the aisles . . .

Hedda's review was typical of dozens that flooded the country in advance of the film's national opening. Jack, in addition to tossing many of the greatest lines Rochester's way, also had insisted his sidekick have the spotlight during the New York opening. As a tribute to Rochester's outstanding performance, the world premiere of *Buck Benny Rides Again* was held in Harlem, at Loew's Victoria Theater on East 125th Street, the first premiere ever presented in the area.

It was the biggest thing to hit that section of New York since Joe Louis became champion of the world. There was a gala stage show preceding the film. Benny Carter's orchestra played. Ella Fitzgerald sang. Then the "Mayor of Harlem," Bill "Bojangles" Robinson, came on stage to introduce Rochester. Robinson said he knew of only three people to whom color meant nothing: Irving Berlin, who gave Ethel Waters her first big break in a musical show; Shirley Temple's mother, who gave him a chance in movies, insisting he appear on screen with Shirley, and Jack Benny, who gave Rochester the radio lines which had made him so famous . . .

Rochester came out on stage in a tuxedo, puffing "one of Mr. Benny's cigars!" He tried playing it for laughs, but was emotionally overcome by his reception. When he regained his composure, Rochester introduced Jack, who came on stage and traded a few quips. Then Benny said seriously, "As for giving me credit for tossing so many lines Rochester's way, if Eddie Anderson hadn't been a fine comedian, there's nothing I could have done for him . . ." The audience roared its approval. The lights dimmed and *Buck Benny Rides Again* began.

Meanwhile, back at home, Hollywood picture-makers had simmered down. After a short time, the movies studios versus the radio broadcasters feud was over.

But feuds were still a good subject matter for movie comedies. As soon as Jack finished filming *Buck Benny,* he had gone right into another picture, *Love Thy Neighbor,* a celluloid version of the Benny-Allen radio feud. The picture turned out to be so funny, Paramount rushed to make it their Christmas release.

"Ring this one up as one of the surest, biggest box-office hits that Paramount has made . . ." began *The Hollywood Reporter's* review.

"It was smart showmanship which led to the teaming of Jack Benny and Fred Allen and, particularly, to capitalizing to the full on their airwaves feud . . . Both Benny and Allen are at their insulting, irrepressible best . . ."

On December 18, 1940, at the New York Paramount, they held what was billed as "the biggest world premiere in Broadway history." Indeed, there was an all-out effort made to cash in on "a situation" Americans had laughed at and read about for years.

Love Thy Neighbor was produced and directed by Mark Sandrich, the brilliant young man responsible for some of Fred Astaire's and Ginger Rogers' earliest hit films. In this picture, Sandrich went all-out to utilize the Benny-Allen talents. In addition, the cast included Rochester, and brought Mary Martin to the screen singing her biggest hit number, "My Heart Belongs to Daddy."

On the day of the premiere, in addition to the film, moviegoers were treated to a fantastic stage show headed by Tommy Dorsey and his orchestra, featuring vocalists Frank Sinatra and Connie Haines, drummer Buddy Rich, trumpeter Ziggy Elman, and, to round out the group, the Pied Pipers.

The extra added bonus was the in-person appearance of both Jack Benny and Fred Allen—which accounted for continuous lines around the block, even though the theater seated four thousand people!

In between film making and personal appearances, Jack was hard at work on his weekly radio show. Several months into the 1941 season, an event occurred which was to become the biggest tribute to a radio star ever staged in Hollywood. NBC decided to give a dinner in honor of Jack's entering his tenth season on radio.

The closer the big evening came, the higher the bets were that the network wouldn't be able to pull it off—their plans were that spectacular. First of all, show-business greats from both movies and radio had been invited, along with dozens of top entertainment executives and political figures. Second of all, the invitations said white tie . . . and Hollywood insiders just knew that many glamour stars, who loved dressing casually, would *not* put on a white tie for anyone!

But when the night of May 9 came around, *Variety* called the event "a miracle." Twelve hundred people filled the Biltmore Bowl in Jack's honor. From the head table to the last seat in the rear, everyone was dressed elegantly—white ties, tuxedos, and sparkling formal gowns were everywhere the eye could see.

Among the guest speakers were Rudy Vallee, Burns and Allen, Bob Hope, Edgar Bergen, Fibber McGee and Molly (Jim and Marian Jordan), George Jessel, Fletcher Bowron, the mayor of Los Angeles, NBC president Niles Trammell, Colby Chester, chairman of the board of General Foods (Jack's sponsor), Y. Frank Freeman, Paramount's top executive and Jimmy Walker, the former mayor of New York City.

The whole setting seemed touched by a special magic . . . Floral tributes to Jack were in bowls and baskets all over the room, so many, they spilled over into the foyer of the Bowl in gay and fragrant profusion. And Gordon Jenkins and his orchestra provided mood music, while Martha Tilton sang.

As usual, speaker after speaker kidded the guest of honor. Throughout the hours of fun and tribute, Jack and Mary sat beaming, along with the rest of the Benny gang and close family members.

"It was one of the most memorable nights in Hollywood history," Jack's producer, Murray Bolen, remembers. "There were some pretty fantastic things going on behind the scenes, too. There was a woman named Bertha Brainard, who was the manager of NBC's program and talent sales. Along with the other top network executives, she had come in from New York for the occasion.

"Bertha was nuts about Jack . . . She was also a very powerful woman at NBC. As a surprise, she had talked the head of NBC into giving Jack a *special gift* . . . After all of the comics had done their turn, and the politicians and industry giants had taken a bow, Niles Trammell, head of NBC, called Jack up to the microphone. Following a standing ovation, Benny listened intently as Trammell presented him with a magnificent silver service, plus the master keys to all the NBC studios in both New York and Hollywood. Then Jack was handed a scroll, which entitled 'the bearer *to own the 7–7:30* P.M. *spot on NBC—forever.*' That had been Bertha's surprise—and Jack was deeply touched.

"The head of Paramount, acting on behalf of the Producers' Association, gave Jack a watch which was engraved, 'To Jack Benny—in appreciation of his services to humanity.' Then Jack made a sweet and funny speech, and introduced Mary and the rest of the gang. It was an unbelievable outpouring of love and respect for an entertainer . . . and no one deserved it more than Jack."

The dinner had been held on a Friday night, and running true to form, the following Monday, Jack checked onto the Twentieth Century-Fox lot to begin another film.

Charley's Aunt, directed by Archie Mayo, co-starred Kay Francis, Anne Baxter, Arlene Whelan, and James Ellison. The story, based on the classic Brandon Thomas comedy, as written in 1892 and performed over the years on stages around the world, gave Jack the opportunity to allow his comedic talents to flow to their ultimate degree. Dressed in long blond curls, lace bonnet atop his head, full-length black dress topped with a demure lace shawl, Jack, as Charley's Aunt, laid them in the aisles.

Billed cross-country as "the greatest comedian of our time," Benny's portrayal catapulted the film into one of 1941's ten top box-office attractions. He himself wound up on the top ten money-making star list, along with people like Gary Cooper, Clark Gable, Dorothy Lamour, Spencer Tracy, and Charlie Chaplin.

In midsummer of that year, Jack and Mary were in New York, having dinner with Sir Alexander Korda and his wife, actress Merle Oberon. Korda was set to produce an Ernst Lubitsch film, *To Be or Not to Be,* and Jack already had been signed for the male lead. Lubitsch, one of the industry's top writer-director-producer-creative geniuses, admitted to Jack that, while writing the screenplay, he had had Benny in mind all the time.

Jack was naturally thrilled to have been singled out for such a part. Korda, at that same time, was dickering with a well-known actress to play opposite him. Frankly, Benny was not too thrilled at the prospect. His own personal choice was Carole Lombard. Mary and Mrs. Korda concurred.

Over dinner, the Bennys managed to get Sir Alex slightly tipsy —drunk would perhaps be a more accurate word. Seeing Korda in this condition, Jack, Mary, and Merle all ganged up on the producer and insisted he cast Carole Lombard in the role. Being three sheets to the wind, Korda happily agreed. Whereupon Jack whispered to Mary, "Quick, get the agent on the phone and set the deal before Korda sobers up . . ."

So it was that Jack Benny, comedian par excellence, and Carole Lombard, Hollywood's highest-paid zany star and madcap leading lady, were assigned *To Be or Not to Be*.

Benny had known Carole's husband, Clark Gable, ever since his days at M-G-M. Personally, Clark and Carole were dear and close friends of the Bennys. Professionally, the combination of playing opposite Lombard and being directed by the master, Lubitsch, was the highlight of Jack's film career.

There had been a whole series of pictures stamped with "the Lubitsch touch." A native of Germany, a former actor himself, Lubitsch had gained a reputation for creating films of a sexual comedy nature, full of visual innuendo and subtle magic. He had done *Ninotchka* with Garbo, and films like *The Merry Widow* and *The Shop Around the Corner*. The fact that he personally wanted Benny, had even written the screenplay with him in mind, spurred Jack into the greatest performance of his career.

Beginning with the first Sunday in December, 1941 was to wind up a nightmare of a year—for everybody. And within a few weeks, Jack was to sustain a double loss which hurt him terribly.

Murray Bolen recalls vividly Sunday morning, December 7, when both Jack and Hickey arrived at the broadcast studio, in separate cars, around eleven-thirty.

"Jack walked in slowly, his eyes reddened, his head shaking sadly from side to side. In a few minutes, Hickey arrived . . . and I heard the following dialogue:

" 'Isn't it awful, Jack?' Hickey said.

" 'You mean you heard about it too?' Jack inquired.

" 'Well, of course I've heard, Jack,' Hickey retorted. 'The whole world's heard!'

" 'Wait a minute,' Jack said. 'What are you talking about?'

" 'Well, Jack, what are *you* talking about?'

" 'It's Sam . . . Sam Lyons [one of his agents]. He died at two-thirty this morning.'

" 'Jack, I'm so sorry,' Hickey replied. 'But a little later, the Japanese attacked Pearl Harbor. Jack, *we're at war!*' "

Benny, in grief over his long-time agent friend, had not turned on the radio and did not know the news.

The following day, everyone in Hollywood worked, war or no war. *To Be or Not to Be* was completed on schedule, just before the holidays. Jack was among the celebrants at the end of the film cast party on Christmas Eve. Carole was her usual self: gorgeous, witty, the standout in a group of famous people. The picture had been demanding, but fun, and everyone left wishing everyone else a happy holiday. Jack was especially pleased because Carole had promised that, as soon as she came back from her war-bond-selling trip, she would appear on his radio show.

The Bennys celebrated the entrance of 1942 as everyone else did in Hollywood—concerned about the war and anxious to give of their own personal efforts to make the situation easier on all concerned. Jack, his writers and production team began lining up a series of military installations to which to take the radio show; and Jack, along with a dozen other top stars, including Lombard, organized a Victory Committee to co-ordinate celebrity appearances.

On January 12, Carole, her mother, and her press agent, Otto Winkler, left Hollywood, scheduled to visit in various towns where Carole would make a personal appeal on behalf of war-bond sales.

"We had been out late on Friday night, January 16," Mary Benny recalls. "Jack and I had had dinner with some friends at Chasen's, and had sat talking until the wee hours of the morning. When we got outside to wait for our car, the man who put the papers in the small newsrack in front of Chasen's was just delivering the early Saturday edition. The headlines said: CAROLE

LOMBARD KILLED IN PLANE CRASH. I thought Jack was going to drop right there on the sidewalk.

"We rushed home, and Jack picked up the phone to call Clark. Someone answered and said Gable had already left for Las Vegas, which was the closest big city located near the mountain peak where the plane had crashed . . . the site from which a rescue mission was being launched.

"I'll never forget," Mary continued. "Jack and I sat up all night talking. Over and over again, he shook his head in disbelief. We especially talked about fate . . . How Carole shifted plans and had taken the plane instead of the train—because she was anxious to get home to her husband.

"It was so hard to believe that such a beautiful, funny, down-to-earth, full-of-life lady was lying someplace on the top of a mountain. It just didn't make any sense. We also had heard over the radio that, at the last minute, Carole almost didn't take the flight. She had been asked to give up her seat, along with her mother and Mr. Winkler, in order to make room for some soldiers on a priority flight. But at the last minute, Lombard, who had been out on a 'war mission' herself, was so eager to get to Clark that 'she'd pulled rank' and managed to talk herself and her party into retaining their seats. I've never seen Jack so sad. He felt so frustrated, wanting to do something, anything . . . and knowing there was really nothing he could do . . ."

That Sunday, for the first time, Jack was a little late arriving at NBC. The writers and production staff were waiting for him. Hickey predicted what Jack would say as soon as he arrived. "He won't do the show, believe me, I know Jack," Hickey had stated. But the others weren't so sure.

A few minutes later, Jack walked into the studio, and said simply, "I can't do the show. Notify the cast . . . Put together whatever you want . . . Make it an all-musical broadcast. You don't have to explain to the audience why I'm not doing the show. I think people will understand . . ."

Then, turning to his brother-in-law, Jack said, "C'mon, Hickey, I want to drive to Las Vegas. Please, come with me . . ."

As Hickey recalls, "I knew there was nothing Jack could do . . . Nothing anyone could do . . . By that time we'd had news that even Gable was just waiting in Las Vegas while men climbed the mountain looking for bodies . . . remnants . . . anything that was left after the crash. I knew Jack couldn't be of help, but I didn't argue with him.

"We drove slowly, with Jack just sitting beside me talking about Carole . . . how alive she was . . . how vibrant and vital . . . Then, finally, because he was so tired from not sleeping, he just put his head down. I had driven about eighty-five miles, to the outskirts of San Bernardino, California, when Jack shook himself awake. It was then I said, 'Look, Jack, there's absolutely nothing you can do. Even Clark is just waiting . . . We might be in the way . . .'

"Jack looked at me for a second, then shook his head. 'Okay, Hickey,' he agreed. 'Let's turn back . . .' "

That evening, Sunday, January 18, the show opened like this:

"Ladies and Gentlemen, this is Don Wilson. Jack Benny will not be with us tonight. He hopes that you will enjoy the program that we have prepared for you. Jack wants you to know he'll be back with us again next week. In the following half hour, you will hear Mahlon Merrick and his music . . . with Dennis Day."

Near the close of the show, Don came back and said, "Dennis Day and the mixed chorus will sing a hymn . . . a hymn of praise for our land of the free, 'America, the Beautiful.' "

There had been a sneak preview of *To Be or Not to Be* scheduled for that Monday. It was to be held at the Academy Theater in Inglewood, a suburb of Los Angeles, just a few miles south of Beverly Hills and Culver City, where Twentieth Century-Fox and M-G-M Studios were located. It was considered "an average audience" house, and several studios sneaked new pictures there in order to get spontaneous reaction . . . But the studio postponed the sneak until the following week. Still, Jack did not have the heart to go. Mary went and brought back glowing reports.

The audience had gasped when the title and Jack and Carole's names first came on the screen. That had been followed by tremendous applause which continued throughout the film. On screen, Carole Lombard was more beautiful and charming than she'd ever been, and Jack Benny was at his best. The studio waited two months to release the film, allowing time for the shock of Lombard's passing to sink in. Then *To Be or Not to Be* opened nationally.

Without a single exception, every review began with a reference to Lombard's death. A typical column, one written by critic William S. Cunningham in the Columbus, Ohio, paper of March 6, 1942, began:

> *Exit Laughing.* That's the way Carole Lombard would have pre-ferred, and that is what she does in "To Be or Not to Be" . . .
>
> The icy fingers of irony touched this picture in more ways than one and, at first, it is difficult to disassociate your recollection of the facts with what you are watching on the screen. However, the makebelieve world eventually does take over and you find yourself laughing freely, find your nerves tightening with some suspense in the melodramatic sequences.
>
> Remembering that Miss Lombard met her death in a plane crash following her appearance at a patriotic program, it does seem strange that her last film should be an anti-Nazi story, that planes should figure so prominently in the plot and dialogue, that even the title should have its ironic twist. Yet all of these things are necessary to the picture . . .
>
> The story concerns a troupe of Polish players in Warsaw. Jack Benny and Miss Lombard are the co-stars, and also man and wife. They are about to produce an anti-Nazi play when Hitler invades their country . . .

The critics uniformly raved about Lombard's final performance, as well as applauding Jack for his acting ability "as the actor, 'turned Nazi,' who outwits the Gestapo . . ."

To Be or Not to Be made money, but never lived up to its full-est potential because of Lombard's death. The film still plays today—in America, on late-night television—but in Europe, it is revived every year and run in a series of film classics.

Florence Fenchel remembers *To Be or Not to Be* very well. "In 1942," she recalls, "Dad and I were vacationing in Miami, Flor-ida, and we went to see the picture the day it opened. But the min-ute Jack came on screen wearing a Nazi uniform, Dad got up and walked out of the theater in a rage . . . I rushed after him.

"As soon as we got back to our hotel, I made an excuse and

went down to the lobby. I placed a call to Jack and told him of the incident . . .

"Later that evening, he called back to speak to Dad. It was almost impossible. Our father went on and on berating Jack for playing a Nazi . . . Finally when Jack got a word in edgewise, he managed to convey the *whole* plot of the picture to Dad. When he found out that Jack was only *pretending* to be a Nazi, he calmed down . . .

"The next day, he asked me to take him back to see the movie . . . And, for the rest of its engagement, he went back to see Jack every day . . . He loved the picture and cried every time he saw it . . ."

CHAPTER TWENTY-SEVEN

IT WAS A YEAR of mixed emotions for the Hollywood crowd. Lombard's death had intensified everyone's desire to pitch in and help the war effort. Every day, stars and bit players, movie executives and third assistant cameramen were leaving for basic training, boot camp, or volunteering their services to the Defense Department. War-bond drives were organized, and stars crisscrossed America, visiting hastily set up or recently reactivated military installations.

Close to home, Hickey left the Benny show to join the Air Force—and Jack, one of the original members of the Victory Committee, volunteered his services, and began taking his radio program on the road.

After a few months of this routine, Benny came to the conclusion, on his own, that his regular weekly format did *not* lend itself to GI audiences. He was, of course, well received wherever he appeared; but Benny's keen instinct told him a military audience would far more appreciate a looser structure . . . a less formalized show.

One of Jack's last remote radio broadcasts was from Camp Callen, La Jolla, California, 110 miles south of Hollywood.

Producer Murray Bolen remembers the occasion very well.

"Jack, Phil, and Don went down to the camp by car. The rest of us traveled on a chartered bus. During the middle of our show —unbeknownst to us—the Japanese dropped some bombs off the coast of Alaska . . . By the time Jack and the cast had signed autographs and chatted with the boys, a blackout alert had been imposed. Troop movements already had started.

"No one who didn't live in California at that time," Bolen continued, "could possibly visualize the special sense of urgency we all felt—especially since there were rumors every day that Japanese Zeros would soon be attacking the West Coast.

"We started to leave the camp, headed back to Los Angeles, only to discover that, while Jack still had his hired car, our bus had been commandeered. We finally dug up other transportation and started off . . .

"We had to travel the back roads, with only our parking lights on. Every ten minutes, we'd be stopped—either to let a convoy of troops drive by, or because we had lost our way and run into an orange grove . . .

"Jack was so funny, although he didn't mean to be. Every time the vehicles we were in stopped, Jack would jump out of his car and run back to see if we were okay. 'Don't worry, boys,' he'd say, like a protective mother hen, 'don't worry, we'll make it!' By then, the guys in the band as well as the rest of us had taken a few drinks—we weren't worried at all!"

It was shortly after the adventure in the orange groves that Jack made a firm decision, one he stuck to, with few exceptions, for the next three years. He would broadcast all season out of the regular NBC studios and, on weekends, he would take a few celebrities and visit nearby bases. But at the end of the 1942 season, he would devote thirteen weeks of his summer vacation touring bases. At his own expense, Jack left in July and traveled the length and breadth of America, doing special shows, bringing along guest stars, utilizing different material which he felt GI audiences would really appreciate. As usual, his instincts were right.

In May of 1942, the powers that be at General Foods decided

that, come fall, they would shift the sponsorship of Jack's show from Jell-O to another of their products—Grape Nuts. There were definite reasons for the change. Due largely to Benny's show, Jell-O had become a household staple—sales were at an all-time high. But with the war came shortages, and General Foods had only a certain amount of sugar allotted to it. Jell-O production was severely curtailed. Whatever they put on the shelves sold immediately—Jack Benny or no Jack Benny.

"When Jack's writers got wind of the change coming up," Murray Bolen explained, "they decided to put together the final show based on the premise: Jack's finally getting out of the kitchen with Jell-O, and going into the dining room with a breakfast food. Without even mentioning Grape Nuts by name, they came up with a funny, clever show . . .

"Everyone was pleased with the material. But five hours before air time, I received a wire from the vice-president, Charlie Mortimer, telling me we could *not* do the show as written. General Foods had *no* intention of tipping their plans . . .

"Logically, they were right," Bolen went on. "Jack's show was the number-one target of rival advertising agencies. For eight years with Jell-O, he had been counterprogramed as best as possible. But with a switch in products, those shows which aired opposite him would be given nearly three months to rethink their own advertising and talent formats. General Foods would not allow that to happen!

"We were really in a bind. There was absolutely no compromising. With only a few hours to air time, Jack and the writers pitched in and came up with an entirely new script. Fortunately, it went off smoothly. If it hadn't been for Jack's co-operation, I would really have been in big trouble!"

Being a Jack Benny producer meant sharing the privilege of a variety of experiences. Bolen recalls one memorable morning when Jack was at Paramount making *Love Thy Neighbor* with Fred Allen.

"I was working with the Benny writers in Jack's dressing room, when we decided to break for lunch . . . We walked out and bumped into Fred Allen. He was all done up in makeup, a Kleenex tucked into his shirt collar to prevent the pancake from staining it. He saw us and bellowed out. It seems he had been called to the studio at 6 A.M., and had been in full makeup since six-thirty. Now, here it was noon, and he had yet to shoot his scene.

"Right in the middle of the Paramount lot, Fred Allen gave a thirty-minute dissertation, at the top of his lungs, on the stupidity of the way they made movies—and he wondered how Jack took it. The angrier he got, the funnier he got, until we were all literally rolling on the lawn with laughter. No one was sharper than Fred Allen could be spontaneously. He turned the air blue. I only wish I had a tape of that diatribe!

"I'll never forget going back East with Jack and the gang for the premiere of the film. We had to do two radio shows from New York, so I was pretty busy while we were there . . .

"But on the train headed for home, we were all relaxed and happy. It was Christmastime. Mary had practically emptied the New York stores shopping for presents. Alice Faye was along with Phil Harris. Andy Devine's wife, Dorothy, was with us too.

"As we got on the train, Sherman Billingsley, a close friend of Jack and Mary's, and the man who owned the Stork Club, came to say bon voyage, and brought us a case of champagne . . . And, since we were scheduled to switch trains in Chicago, Rochester had wired ahead and asked some of his friends to meet the train and deliver a whole side of beef made up into barbecued spare ribs!

"Then, just before we left Grand Central Station, a man from Paramount's publicity department came running up to me. 'Murray,' he said, 'I was supposed to ride back to Hollywood with you, but I can't make it. Here's an envelope with the expense money for Jack and the gang. Be sure you spend it all . . . and Merry Christmas.'

"As the train pulled out, I casually opened the envelope. There was *six thousand dollars* inside! Needless to say, that was the most lavish train ride Benny and company ever took! But we still couldn't spend all the money. At Jack's insistence, we shared the cash with the porters and conductors all across country. It was the sweetest Christmas those guys on the Chief ever had . . ."

CHAPTER TWENTY-EIGHT

IN SEPTEMBER of 1942, *George Washington Slept Here* opened nationally, again bringing good reviews for Jack and the rest of the cast. Based on a Moss Hart-George S. Kaufman play, it told the story of a city lover who suddenly found himself in possession of a dilapidated country home purchased, without his knowledge, by his wife, played by Ann Sheridan.

On screen, the chemistry between Benny and Sheridan was very appealing to audiences, even if off camera his heart still belonged to Mary!

Simultaneously with the beginning of his fall radio shows, Jack went over to Twentieth Century-Fox to star in *The Meanest Man in the World,* along with Priscilla Lane, Edmund Gwenn, and Rochester. It was a pleasant comedy, very well received, and Benny gave his usual smooth performance.

In the summer of 1943, Jack spent a couple of miserable weeks being shot in both arms with every kind of immunization imaginable. He was getting ready to leave on a nine-week tour of Central Africa, North Africa, Egypt, the Persian Gulf, Tunisia, Ethiopia, Sicily, and Italy. Traveling with him were harmonica virtuoso Larry Adler, actress Anna Lee, and singer-actress Wini Shaw.

Both Mary and Jack's sister Florence were concerned about Jack's being so close to the front lines. But he never gave it a second thought, although, as Florence remembered, "I received a cable from my brother saying he had arrived safely in Africa . . . and, for the rest of the summer, he did keep in touch with Dad and me as often as he could just to reassure us . . ."

As Mary recalls, "Jack was really something. No matter where he was, he would write me a letter every other day. The trouble is, he was used to telling me *everything*—and he continued doing so. He forgot all about the fact that mail was censored. I'd receive these long letters with big sections either blacked out by ink or actually cut out with scissors . . .

"Whatever censors were reading Jack's mail obviously had a sense of humor. The third week he was away, I received a typical letter—half blacked out and cut up. At the bottom one of the censors had written: 'Dear Mary, Sorry for all we've had to take out. After the war's over, we'll send you the pieces!' "

When Jack returned, Mary was eager to "hear everything about the trip," so Jack surprised her by presenting Mary with a day-to-day diary of his trip. "After reading his words, it was as though I had been with him every step of the way. I learned all about his joys and fears and menus . . . and illnesses . . . It was beautiful!"

Here are some excerpts from Jack's diary just as he wrote them.

Tuesday—July 20th:
Left New York for Washington, D.C., by train. Stayed overnight and left the following morning on a C-75 transport plane for Miami. Had lunch, then flew on to Borengiron Field, Puerto Rico.

Thursday—July 22nd:
Next stop, Atkinson Field, British Guiana, South America, arrived in time for breakfast. By nightfall had reached Natal, Brazil.

Friday—July 23rd:
Visited Natal, a typical small South American town. Gave unexpected impromptu show for the soldiers, then left same night for Ascension Island in the middle of the South Atlantic.

Saturday—July 24th:
Arrived Ascension Field. Gave two shows for the boys . . . How they needed it! Left that afternoon for the Gold Coast of Africa, then on to Accra, British West Africa, same night. Met Yacht Club Boys who were playing their last engagement after an eight months' tour. We kept their accompanist—Jack Snyder.

Sunday—July 25th:
Visited Governor Burns Castle . . . also toured Accra, a real native city . . . Monday and Tuesday gave shows for American troops. Wednesday performed for British contingent . . .

Thursday—July 29th:

Left for Lagos, Nigeria. Gave show there for a small number of troops . . .

Friday—July 30th:

Arrived Kano, Nigeria. Visited walled city of Kano mentioned in the Bible. Gave a show for United States Army troops; second show for British soldiers.

Sunday—August 1st:

Arrived Maiduguri, Nigeria, in time for lunch. Heavy rain. Did our show in a warehouse for both U.S.A. and British. Wonderful dinner with surprise guest—General Stratemeyer, in charge of Air Force under General Hap Arnold (fine chap). Ice cream for dessert which was another surprise, plus a cake made in my honor! I named our plane—*5 Jerks to Cairo* and found it printed on both sides of the plane next morning. So, there we were, "the 5 Jerks to Cairo"—Anna Lee, Wini Shaw, Larry Adler, Jack Snyder, and Jack Benny. Forgot to mention we had the same two pilots assigned to us for our entire trip—Robert Jackson and George Crawford.

Monday—August 2nd:

Arrived in El Geteina, Egyptian Sudan. Did show for U.S.A. and British, plus some native Mohammedans all dressed in white robes and turbans . . . Coming over here, our pilots flew low part of the time so we could see a hippopotamus—we saw a lot of them. The soldiers around here buy beautiful Arabian horses for $20 or $30, including saddle and blanket! Got ten hours' sleep. Feel great.

Tuesday—August 3rd:

Arrived Khartoum, Egyptian Sudan. Was supposed to stop at El Fasher but, because of wash-out after heavy rain, our pilots were afraid to land. It was a big disappointment to the soldiers, so we spoke to the boys by phone from our plane as we passed overhead. Landed at Khartoum a few minutes before a terrific sandstorm. First warm weather and sun we had seen on trip. It's just like Palm Springs weather! Saw my first camel. Khartoum is situated on the Nile River . . .

Wednesday—August 4th:

Had wonderful morning shopping in Ondurman, native city just outside of Khartoum. Bought ivory and other gifts. Got a great kick listening to the bargaining and haggling that goes on continually. Streets filled with camels and little donkeys. Gave show that night for two thousand American and British boys.

Thursday—August 5th:

Arrived Asmara, Eritrea, a very small country taken over by Mussolini when he invaded Ethiopia. We are two hundred miles from Addis Ababa, and most of the natives look like Haile Selassie! Asmara is the first real sign of civilization we have seen so far —high mountains and very quaint. Mussolini made this his summer resort. Very cool. Taxis are horses and carts. Did show for American and British soldiers in local theater, and tomorrow will appear for Douglas Aircraft boys at Gura Airport, a thirty-mile drive from here. The roadside is beautiful . . . looks like the outskirts of Los Angeles . . . Saw a picture in Asmara with Barbara Stanwyck and Robert Young, all done in Italian. Spoke to New York yesterday and was only allowed to say "5" words . . .

Sunday—August 8th:

Left airport 11:30 A.M. for Aden, Saudi Arabia, Asia Minor, just across the Red Sea, not far from Mecca and by the Indian Ocean. Aden is the most interesting place we have been so far. Wonderful reception at airport. Met by American, British, and Arabian soldiers . . . Rode to our barracks on camels (my *first ride* on a camel). Very hot. Visited city of Aden with its beautiful harbor. Town as old-fashioned as it was years ago. Many Jews here. Funny little streets and shops filled with people, camels, goats, and mules. Arabian women must wear veils covering their faces *all the time* if they are married. Men can have many wives and change them whenever they want to. They seem to have no love for women and use them only for bearing children. Men find company in other men and walk down the streets hand in hand. Cain is supposedly buried here and Noah's Ark was built in this harbor. Did a show at night and left early the following morning.

Monday—August 9th:

Back in Gura for lunch and to pick up Larry Adler's clothes

142

which he had forgotten . . . On to Khartoum where we were given a reception and dinner. Stayed overnight. Colonel Yeomans was our host . . .

Tuesday—August 10th:

Arrived Cairo. Went right to Shepheard's Hotel. Received mail from Mary and Joanie which was the *biggest* thrill so far. Now I know what it means to soldiers to get mail from home! Met author John Gunther. Will rest here couple of days . . . Met General Brereton a week after his successful Ploesti raid on Rumanian oil fields . . .

Wednesday—August 11th:

Visited the pyramids, sphinx, and bazaar. Dinner that night with General Brereton, Frank Gervasi, war correspondent for *Collier's* magazine, and Thomas Mann's daughter, Erika—war correspondent for *Liberty*. Big celebration in our hotel complete with parade and band. Found out later it was in honor of the circumcision of a four-year-old boy . . .

Thursday—August 12th:

Gave surprise show this evening for convalescent American soldiers who were being entertained by H.M. King Farouk of Egypt at the Auberge des Pyramides . . .

Friday—August 13th:

Left for Benghazi, Libya. Flying over El Alamein battlefield where the fighting *was* rough. On this trip we'll be preparing to do a short-wave broadcast to U.S.A. when we get back to Cairo . . . Had first taste of army field ration food (oh! brother). Can see the road where Field Marshal General Rommel was chased from El Alamein to Benghazi. From a distance, can see trenches and battered Nazi tanks. Hard to imagine a war being fought on this desert. El Alamein and Tobruk practically all bombed. Arrived in Benghazi, Libya, staying at Red Cross headquarters (no accommodations—very tough), but we are in a *real war zone* . . .

Saturday—August 14th:

Did first show in this area at the 9th Bombardier Air Base. Got grand reception. Biggest thrill I ever had was at one o'clock that night when I was asked to do a short-wave broadcast to U.S.A.

with four flyers who had just returned from the raid over Vienna. I was really nervous and excited. Same night, as we were sitting in our headquarters, heard ack ack guns close by. Ran outside and saw them firing . . . It's hard to believe we are in a real war area.

Sunday—August 15th:

Benghazi. Gave second show to 389th Bomb Group, six miles away. Boys we played to were leaving the next morning for an important mission . . . Felt ill, guess I did too much swimming in the hot sun.

Monday—August 16th:

Larry Adler and I prepared our radio program which will be broadcast from Cairo. Larry a great help and very good writer. Did a show for 93rd Bomb Group who had just returned from a successful raid over Italy. Talked to the boys and they told me of their experiences. They called their raid "A Great Show." One of the boys (just a baby) brought down three planes. All of this group came back safe, but we lost eight planes from another division. Being right in a war zone I am learning things I would never know from reading papers or listening to radio. These fellows are *real heroes*. Three weeks ago, four of our boys in a raid knew they were sunk, so they dove their plane right into an enemy target, getting their objective, but in order to do so, they had to commit suicide.

Tuesday—August 17th:

Had pictures and movies taken christening a bomber they named *Buckshees Benny Rides Again*. (Buckshees is an Arabic word meaning "tip.") Also named a bomb *To Adolf with Love in Boom!!!* Going to double up on shows here so we can do extra one in Tripoli . . .

Wednesday—August 18th:

Swimming in the morning, visited hospital in the afternoon. Did show tonight for 376th Bombardier Air Corps. Living here tough, but am getting used to it. Mile away from a shower and I have to shine my own shoes. If Henrietta [note: the Bennys' maid] could only see me!

144

Thursday—August 19th:

Visited more hospitals in the afternoon. Am doing show tonight for 323rd Group. Saw bombers return from raid over southern point of Italy. Only one plane missing.

Friday—August 20th:

Terrific wind and sandstorm all day. Everything we have full of sand, including ourselves. Did our last show in this area for the 835th Group. Will leave Benghazi early tomorrow.

Saturday—August 21st:

Arrived in Tripoli, a beautiful city. Had room overlooking the harbor in a hotel just a block away from General Montgomery's point of victory.

Sunday—August 22nd:

Visited hospital wards in the morning. Met Toots Shor's cousin. Did one show for boys in the desert, and one at Red Cross quarters. We could have been the first bunch to go to Sicily and entertain. The boys there were expecting us, but our commanding officer in Cairo wouldn't permit us to leave. First time I have been angry about anything on this trip. (But when I found out the *real reason* later, I got over it—there was heavy enemy action where we wanted to go!)

Monday—August 23rd:

On our next trip to Cairo, had a nervous moment when another plane was flying too close to us. Arrived Cairo late in the afternoon. It's a great town, there's something exciting about it.

Tuesday—August 24th:

Visited wards and hospital at Huckstep about fifteen miles from Cairo. Did two shows for the patients. Most of these fellows banged up from recent raid over Sicily.

Wednesday—August 25th:

Did two shows in very large and modern theater at Huckstep. My picture *George Washington Slept Here* playing same theater at the time. Visited Sultan Hassan Mosque in the afternoon—six hundred years old and very interesting. Following day did two shows in Cairo's beautiful outdoor theater called the Empire . . .

145

Friday—August 27th:

Gave a show for New Zealand soldiers at Camp Neadi. There were seven thousand boys in audience, all sitting on a hill . . . one of the greatest sights of the trip. These boys did much to win the war in North Africa territory. The commanding officer, General Friberg, ran Rommel from Cairo to Tunis. After show, attended a party at General Brereton's home. Then said goodbye to war correspondent Frank Gervasi, who was leaving to join General Montgomery in Sicily . . .

Saturday—August 28th:

Left for Camp Devesoir, one hundred miles from Cairo. Did show that night, went swimming first in Suez Canal.

Sunday—August 29th:

Visited Ismailia, Egypt, fifteen miles away. Nice town. Had wonderful lunch at Jewish restaurant. Best gefüllte fish I ever tasted! Went swimming at French Beach Club. Came back to camp late, had dinner, then drove to Attika, fifty-five miles away, to do show. Passed through town of Suez.

Monday—August 30th:

Will do show tonight from Camp Kabritt. Just found out the plane they named after me in Benghazi was on a mission to Italy and got shot full of holes, but returned safely. Visited Port Said, a nice town.

Tuesday—August 31st:

Back to Cairo which is getting to be like coming back home. Nervous all day preparing for broadcast to the U.S.A. being done at 1 A.M. from auditorium with a large audience. Broadcast was a big success, but found out immediately afterwards that, on account of atmospheric conditions, it *did not* reach the States. Very disappointing.

Wednesday—September 1st:

Left at 2 A.M. for Tel Aviv, Palestine. Amazingly modern city —almost 100 per cent Jewish population. Complete blackout at night. Visited nightclub with Larry Adler and Erika Mann. Heard a fine violinist and a great five-piece orchestra.

Thursday—September 2nd:

Met Mayor Rokach of Tel Aviv. Very fine fellow. He took us all over the city. Wish we could spend a couple of weeks here, it's so fascinating! Gave show at Camp Telitvinsky, a rest camp for servicemen.

Friday—September 3rd:

Took auto trip to Jerusalem, also fine city (that is, the *new* Jerusalem). High-walled and nice *California* climate. Had lunch at King David Hotel. Very beautiful and modern. Right across the street is another beautiful building—the Y.M.C.A. From its tower you can see the entire city of Jerusalem (both new and old). Met Henrietta Szold, wonderful woman, eighty-two years old. Had very interesting talk with her. She comes from Baltimore, Maryland, and has lived in Jerusalem twenty-four years. At one time she was president of the Hadassah, but now takes care of thousands of refugees. Drove to Bethlehem, stopped at Rachel's tomb on the way. Visited Church of Nativity, approximately where Christ was born. Made a tour of old Jerusalem—walled city with narrow streets and many steps. Visited Church of the Holy Sepulcher where Christ was buried, also Calvary Hill, where He carried the cross. Visited the "Wailing Wall," saw many Jews in prayer. People live here as they did thousands of years ago. Came back to Tel Aviv and gave show for British troops at Camp Nathania on our night off.

Saturday—September 4th:

Left for the Persian Gulf, flying over Jerusalem, the Dead Sea, also Jericho and River Jordan. We still have our same plane *5 Jerks to Cairo* and same crew Our trip to the Persian Gulf is the toughest of all. Heat anywhere from 110 to 140 in the shade and this summer went as high as 187. Boys here doing a terrific job servicing Russia and need entertainment badly. We are the first—and probably only big show to reach them . . .

Sunday—September 5th:

Arrived Abadan. Had to circle airport one hour in sandstorm and even then we couldn't land (I was scared a little). We had to fly on to Basra, Iraq, fifty miles away, and land. *Very very hot.*

Took a nap in fan-cooled room, then flew back to Abadan. Gave two shows, one at Karrinshar for six thousand boys, and one at Abadan for five hundred. Abadan is the second largest oil center in the world . . . The boys here are marvelous, being able to function in the hottest place in the world! Impossible to work in the afternoon. All men, excluding those on guard duty, have to stay indoors from 1 to 4 P.M. Hard to realize we're so close to the Russian border . . .

Monday—September 6th:

One of our most interesting and exciting days, including a surprise visit and performance. Got up at 5 A.M., had breakfast and left by *freight train,* traveling in a boxcar with chairs in it! Went with Major General Connolly for Bandar Shahpur Post to be present for review and dedication of new Camp Clifford, which was named after a private killed on duty. Witnessed the awarding of medals for bravery to twelve soldiers who saved ammunition, lives, and supplies amounting to millions of dollars. Awards ordered by President Roosevelt, given by General Connolly, who commands entire Persian area. Immediately after awards ceremony, we gave a show at 10 A.M.—the temperature was 140! Next stop Teheran, largest city in Iran. Will live at General Connolly's home. No show tonight so did a little sight-seeing and wrote letters . . . Right now we are flying nineteen-thousand feet over the Luree mountains. It's very cold after leaving heat of desert (am a tiny bit nervous, but I guess everything is okay). Arrived Teheran, population 800,000 . . .

Tuesday—September 7th:

Saw the sights of Teheran. Everything very expensive here. For a 1937 Buick, you can get anywhere from $20,000 to $32,000 from the few rich, and anywhere from $4,000 to $7,000 for a set of tires! People here and in India will pay as high as $150 for a "Parker" pen. However, most of the people are very, very poor.

Gave a show for a great audience consisting of American and British troops and Russian officers—very colorful.

Wednesday—September 8th:

Went shopping, then left for Hamadan, Iran. Had wonderful

steak dinner here at Officers Mess—"gazelle" steak. Best food I've had since I left the U.S.! Gave show, then received a beautiful gift from the governor of this province, a Persian Kashan rug. Will take it with me and have it sent home first chance I get.

Thursday—September 9th:

Arrived Ahwaz, Iran, at noon. Temperature 110 in shade, 145 in the sun. Took a nap from 2 to 5 P.M. Gave a show that evening for five thousand boys. Slept on the roof on cots. It was cool and restful.

Friday—September 10th:

Did an early morning show at the hospital. Rested until 3:30 P.M. Left at four o'clock by car for hundred-mile drive to Andimeshk. Gave a show there, then drove right back to Ahwaz. Had extra car and two motorcycle escorts as they do have bandits in Persia. Found out today that Persia just declared war on Germany—also got word that Italy surrendered.

Saturday—September 11th:

Left for Cairo at 6 A.M. Am looking forward to mail. Arrived Cairo and received mail! Visited Alexandria the next day, a very nice city . . .

Monday—September 13th:

Broadcast to U.S. tonight (1 A.M. Tuesday). Show went over great!

Tuesday—September 14th:

Visited Egyptian movie studio—very, very interesting. Supposed to do show that night for R.A.F., but I couldn't appear due to cough on chest—it was an outdoor theater. Noel Coward was very happy to take my place as he knew I had entertained a lot of British boys . . .

Wednesday—September 15th:

Left for Tunis, stopping in Tripoli overnight. We are now starting to entertain in *North Africa* territory.

Thursday—September 16th:

Arrived Tunis, Tunisia. Did show for thirty-thousand boys.

Town badly bombed. Met Bruce Cabot and "Smiley," my caddie at Hillcrest. The Army made him a mailman!

Friday—September 17th:

Arrived Catania, Sicily, also badly bombed. Saw Mount Etna. Did show then went right to bed as I have a slight cold. Every place around hotel bombed, and millions of dollars' worth of airplanes smashed to pieces at airport.

Saturday—September 18th:

Did show at 6 P.M. in Lentini for the 12th Air Corps. Another one later that night for Canadians.

Sunday—September 19th:

Made surprise flight to Cretoni, Italy, to do a show for the 59th Fighters, part of the Seventh Army, who were just leaving for the Battle of Salerno. Big thrill playing for these boys as we missed them in Sicily. Returned to Sicily immediately after performance and gave show for seven thousand at San Antonio.

Monday—September 20th:

Arrived Palermo, Sicily. Still have my cold and was sent to 59th Evacuation Hospital. Hope to be out before my gang leaves town. Soldiers are playing all of *Fred Allen's* records in hospital—particularly those in which we worked together!

Tuesday—September 21st:

Still in hospital. Doctors and nurses wonderful, as they are in all the hospitals. Am in a ward with five others—three with malaria and two with yellow jaundice . . .

Wednesday—September 22nd:

Still in hospital.

Thursday—September 23rd:

Finally released, and permitted to drive around to see Palermo, which is really beautiful. Spent the afternoon at the pavilion on the beach. Very nice resort.

Friday—September 24th:

Spent two very interesting hours with General George Patton in his office—a very spectacular and emotional character.

150

Saturday—September 25th:

Left at 8 A.M. for Algiers. Did half a show in the rain, then a full show same night in a theater. Saw Adolphe Menjou here.

Sunday—September 26th:

Left early for Marrakech, Morocco—interesting town. Just received some bad news. Colonel Yeomans, our host at Khartoum, was killed in plane crash with twelve others . . . Visited the "Medina," the walled city, and native part of town. Did show tonight (our last one on African tour) to wonderful audience. Left immediately after show for *HOME* in bucket-seat plane via Scotland. Slept on floor of plane in Eskimo suit.

Monday—September 27th:

Arrived Prestwick, Scotland, in the morning. Visited the town of Ayr, and home of Robert Burns, the poet. Left shortly after noon for Iceland, arriving in time for dinner. Because of bad weather, had to remain overnight. Wini Shaw and I gave three shows that evening. Larry Adler and Anna Lee were not with us on the return trip. Anna remained in Algiers and Larry went to visit his folks in London.

Tuesday—September 28th:

Had very early breakfast and left for *home.* Stopped for lunch in Newfoundland, arrived New York City at 9 P.M. Imagine, having breakfast in Iceland and dinner in Reuben's restaurant in New York! Forgot to mention that all the way from Prestwick, Scotland, to New York, we had a German prisoner with us—a sixty-eight-year-old colonel. When we arrived in New York, no one met us as we were not permitted to tell of our arrival.

Came home fifteen pounds heavier. It was the most thrilling and memorable trip I have ever had in my life.

If the war continues, I hope to be leaving again . . .

CHAPTER TWENTY-NINE

EARLY IN THE SPRING OF 1944, Jack readily agreed to help the Canadian war effort by traveling to Vancouver, British Columbia, and taking his show with him. The "Benny Special" pulled into the Great Northern Railroad station in White Rock, Vancouver, a few minutes before midnight on Tuesday, April 18, 1944. It was pouring rain, still hundreds of loyal fans stood jammed in the depot, carrying signs welcoming Jack and his gang.

On the platform, a group of Mary's relatives stood waiting. Her uncle, Harry Wagner, Mary's mother's oldest brother, was out in front. Mary got off the train first and was literally pushed into his arms.

Jack came off the train and was surrounded by the press, but managed to greet Wagner and the rest of the family and remark: "Why haven't you relatives done a Jewish rain dance . . . *or something* . . . so the skies would have cleared!"

Don Wilson came off next, followed by Rochester, Phil Harris, and the Benny writers, who had just wound up a hot poker game as the train pulled in.

Jack and the gang were in Vancouver to kick off the city's Sixth Victory Loan Drive, in the hopes their collective efforts would help raise millions of dollars needed to bolster the Canadian war chest.

The following morning, thousands of people created a gigantic traffic jam at the corner of Hastings and Grandville, in front of the main post office, where a band shell had been erected from which Jack would fire the opening salvos of the fund-raising campaign.

The windows and rooftops of all the surrounding buildings were covered with spectators. One enterprising businessman, in a building a block away, placed his chair on a narrow ledge outside his third-floor window and sat, perched precariously, fifty-feet above the ground, watching the sights through a pair of binoculars!

The rain continued to fall. All Jack could see as he looked out were multi-colored umbrellas, water-streaked welcoming signs, and dozens of small boys perched on lampposts.

"We have weather like this in California, too," Benny quipped. "But down there, we call it dew."

For the Benny troop, it was a busy non-stop day, complete with a flag ceremony on an aircraft carrier and visits to defense plants. In the next five days, Jack and the group would make twenty separate appearances at bond rallies, shipyards, military bases, and hospitals, climaxing their stay with the broadcast of Jack's radio show.

Professionally, Jack was only doing what he had been doing for several years—traveling, at his own expense, to help the war effort wherever he was needed.

Personally, this particular trip had a sentimental meaning for Jack and Mary. Together, they were revisiting the town where they had met for the first time eighteen years before. To come back as top stars on the country's number-one radio show, to be so warmly greeted, and interviewed, and applauded by so many thousands of people was indeed very touching for both of them.

It was also a special moment for two other cast members, Phil Harris and Dennis Day. Back in Hollywood, Alice Faye, Phil's wife, was awaiting the birth of their second child. At her insistence, Phil had gone on the trip, hoping to get home in time for the birth. He didn't make it. On April 26, Alice was delivered of a six-pound baby girl.

As for Dennis, he had just enlisted in the Navy, and had been given permission to fly to Vancouver for one day to appear on Jack's show for the last time.

Jack and the writers had written Day's farewell into the script:

JACK: And now, ladies and gentlemen, Dennis Day will sing "Amour."

(Segue into Dennis's number)
(APPLAUSE)

JACK: That was "Amour" sung by Dennis Day . . . And

ladies and gentlemen, this is Dennis's last appearance on our program . . . And Dennis, all I can say is . . . if you were leaving for any other reason except to join the Armed Forces, I'd hate to lose you . . . But as soon as this war is over, I hope you'll be back with us again.

DENNIS: I sure will, Mr. Benny . . . and I'll be looking forward to it.

JACK: So will we.

DENNIS: You know, Mr. Benny, when I'm in the Navy, I hope people won't think I'm as dumb as I act on this program . . . because when I enlisted I took an intelligence test, and I got a mark of one hundred fifty-eight.

JACK: One hundred fifty-eight?

DENNIS: Sure, here's the card, and it also says that I have great powers of leadership and will be a great success because—

JACK: *Dennis, this is your weight and fortune* . . . You *weigh* one hundred fifty-eight pounds.

DENNIS: Oh . . .

There were nine thousand people packed into the floors and galleries of Hastings Park Forum for Jack's Sunday broadcast. When the show was over, Jack and the gang remained on stage. All eyes were on Dennis as Mary walked over and gave him a farewell kiss. He tried to remain in character, and joked: "Um'm . . . peppermint lipstick. Gee that tastes good . . ." Then emotion overcame him as Jack, Phil, Don, and Rochester formed a circle around him, patting him on the back, shaking hands, wishing him well.

For the audience, it was an equally tearful experience. Dennis could have been their own husband or son, their brother or boy friend saying a last farewell before going off to war.

When he regained his composure, Dennis stepped up to the mike and said, "The last five years have been the happiest of my life . . . I owe so much to Jack and Mary . . ."

Cheers and applause filled the hall. The orchestra began to play and Dennis sang one last song. Immediately afterward, he caught a plane for Tucson, Arizona, where he spent the next two months in training before receiving his assignment.

ack and Ingrid Bergman during a tour overseas. (Benny Family Personal Collec-
ion)

. to R. back row: Hickey Marks, George Balzar, Milt Josefsberg; front row:
ohn Tackaberry, Sam Perrin—Jack's radio writers, 1946. (Photo courtesy of the
Iational Broadcasting Company, Inc.)

Jack's footprints in Grauman's Chinese Theatre. (Benny Family Personal Collection)

Jack and Fred Allen clowning it up in *Love Thy Neighbor*, 1940. (© Universal Pictures)

Jack and Mary with Benita and Ronald Colman. (Photo courtesy of the National Broadcasting Company, Inc.)

Mary and Jack with the Bogarts. (Courtesy Department of Special Collections, University of California at Los Angeles)

Las Vegas: Jack's private slot machine put up by the hotel whenever Benny played there. The machine, which only took pennies, was installed as a gag. Only Jack could use it. A security guard was usually on duty in front of it. (Courtesy Las Vegas News Bureau)

Edgar Bergen and Charlie McCarthy meet Joanie, Jack, and Mary. (Photo courtesy of the National Broadcasting Company, Inc.)

. to R.: Jack, Frank Sinatra, Mary, Rosalind Russell, Gene Kelly, and Prince
Iike Romanoff, 1947. (Photo by Ed Braslaff, courtesy CBS)

.ck, Joan, Mary, Alice Faye, and Phil Harris off to Europe on the *Queen Eliza-*
th, 1948. (Keystone)

Jack and his father, Meyer Kubelsky. (Photo courtesy Waukegan *News-Sun*)

Illustrative of the caliber of guest stars *only* Benny was able to get week after week is this foursome shown during a rehearsal break for Jack's CBS radio show: George Burns, Frank Sinatra, Jack, Groucho Marx, and Danny Kaye. (Courtesy CBS)

Jack Benny and Isaac Stern from a Benny TV show. (Courtesy CBS)

L. to R.: Dennis Day, Hickey Marks, Mel Blanc, Mary, Milt Josefsberg; front row: Jack, Bob Hope, Don Wilson, Palm Springs, 1950. (Courtesy CBS)

Jack with Rochester and the famous Maxwell. (Courtesy CBS)

Guests on an early TV show of Jack's. L. to R.: Vincent Price, Dick Linkroum, Jack's first TV director, Jack, Claudette Colbert, and Hickey Marks, New York, 1951. (Courtesy CBS)

The first photo Johnny Carson ever took with Jack Benny at CBS in 1951. Carson was then doing a local five-minute-per-day radio show for KNX, the CBS Los Angeles station. (Courtesy CBS)

Jam session. L. to R.: Jack, Fred MacMurray, Tony Martin, Dick Powell, Dan Dailey, and Kirk Douglas, 1954. (Courtesy CBS)

Jack and Mary play eighteen holes at the Canyon Country Club in Palm Springs. (Benny Family Personal Collection)

Jack on violin, Richard Nixon on piano. Nixon was then Vice-President. (Benny Family Personal Collection)

Jack, Bing Crosby, and George Burns. (Courtesy CBS)

Jack and his sister Florence. (Benny Family Personal Collection)

1958 Emmy Awards ceremony. The year Hilliard Marks won an Emmy as Best Producer of the Year for "The Jack Benny Program." (Benny Family Personal Collection)

"It was really quite a farewell," Dennis remembers. "One of the most memorable days of my life. I still have the engraved gold watch Jack and Mary gave me . . . and the letter they wrote saying goodbye. Jack had slipped a check for a thousand dollars in the envelope as an added going-away present.

"Of course, the greatest gift was the way in which Jack said—both publicly, on the air, and personally, just to me—that my job would be waiting for me as soon as I got out of the service . . . *that* meant everything!"

Several days after the trip ended, an editorial appeared in one of Vancouver's newspapers:

WELL DONE, BENNY

Some Canadians are inclined to be critical of the participation in our Victory Loan Campaign of stars and starlets from Hollywood. They feel, and with some justification, that our cause is sufficiently worthy to appeal to our citizens and that it does not need the artificial stimulus of movie stars, charming though they may be. This is a high moral stand, but it is not entirely practical. The recent visit of Jack Benny and his troupe to Vancouver for the opening of the Sixth Victory Loan illustrates the point. First day applications in Vancouver's general canvas and payroll division nearly doubled, totaling $2,799,850 as compared with last year's first day total of $1,958,850. Campaign workers are quite convinced that the presence of these Hollywood stars gave the Loan a flying start by stimulating public interest. Incidentally, Benny did a notably good will job for the motion picture and radio industries on his visit here. His obvious sincerity, his pleasant personality and his willingness to do more than asked made a very favorable impression. Not all Canadian cities which have had entertainment celebrities as their guests have been as fortunate. There need be no criticism either on the question of expense. Certainly Canada's National War Finance Committee would not be justified in undertaking such expense in promotion. As it happens, Jack Benny himself paid all expenses including his party's transportation, hotel bills and wire charges for the broadcast. He has made a worthwhile contribution, not only to our entertainment but to our cause.

With Dennis gone, a decision had to be made about his replacement. Since there were only a half-dozen shows left before the summer break, Jack decided not to rush in finding a new singer. For the balance of the season, and six weeks into the new season, the search continued.

Meanwhile, everyone from opera star John Charles Thomas to Bob Crosby and Frank Sinatra made guest appearances. Then a young tenor named Larry Stevens was selected. Once that was done, a clever way had to be found to introduce him. After all, he was replacing Dennis, who in his five years on the Benny show had become extremely popular with Jack's audience.

A large portion of one show was devoted to establishing Stevens. On the program, Jack and Mary were going out for the evening to the Shrine Auditorium (actually a very large theater in Los Angeles, used for live shows and stage productions) to see a show starring Dunninger, the mind reader. On the way over, Jack and Mary discussed Dennis' replacement, and finding a new singer was weighing heavily on Jack's mind.

Dunninger began, putting on a display of his talents for the audience. Of course, as the Benny show unfolded, Dunninger selected Jack out of the audience . . . and Benny was a *very eager subject*. The following dialogue ensued:

DUNNINGER: You have a radio show . . . and you're looking for a singer, is that correct?

JACK: Yes, sir . . . and I've looked everywhere.

DUNNINGER: Well, Mr. Benny, I think I can help you.

JACK: Really?

DUNNINGER: Let me concentrate . . . I see . . . I see a gas station . . . It's on the corner of Third and La Cienega . . .

JACK: Third and La Cienega?

DUNNINGER: If you'll go to that gas station, you will be waited on by a young man with red hair by . . . I get the name of Stevens . . . Larry Stevens . . .

JACK: Larry Stevens?

DUNNINGER: Yes, this boy has never sung professionally. He has been working in this gas station for several months since he was honorably discharged from the Army Air Force . . .

JACK:	Gee!
DUNNINGER:	He is twenty-one years old . . . weighs one hundred sixty-five pounds and is a graduate of Fairfax High School . . .
JACK:	Larry Stevens, eh?
DUNNINGER:	He has a very nice voice and sings all the time, even when he's working.

The routine went on for a few more moments. Then, as dialogue and sound effects indicated, Jack and Mary were on their way home. Mary was driving. When she got to the corner of Third and La Cienega, she turned into a gas station. Jack thought she was being silly. But sure enough, the guy behind the gas pump *was* a young redhead, and fit the description Dunninger had given Jack. He began to pump gas and broke into song:

LARRY STEVENS SINGS: "I'll Be Seeing You" . . .

The sketch ended with Jack being very impressed, and inviting Stevens to appear on his broadcast the following Sunday.

So Larry Stevens had been integrated into the Benny show. By establishing the new tenor, supposedly the week *before* he started, Jack was giving his audience a chance to "discover" Larry on their own. The change in singers went smoothly—Larry stayed with the Benny show until Dennis was discharged from the Navy, two years later.

CHAPTER THIRTY

JACK'S FINAL SHOW for Grape Nuts aired on June 4, 1944. After he and Mary took a brief vacation, Jack left home again. He headed up USO Troupe 278, which included: Carole Landis, one of the most popular blue-eyed blond sex symbols of the day; Larry Adler, along for the second summer in a row; lovely song stylist Martha Tilton, and June Bruner, a pianist, accordion player, and singer. The group was enhanced by Captain Lanny Ross, who had been a guest singer on Jack's show ten years before, and who was now in the service, and assigned to accompany Jack.

The group's first landing spot was Port Moresby; from there, they went on to make a twenty-one-day tour of Australian bases. This was followed by five weeks of shows in New Guinea, the Marianas, the Marshalls, the Gilberts, the Solomons, the Kwajalein Atoll, and Hawaii.

As it had been the previous year, the schedule was rugged for all concerned. Doing several shows a day . . . visiting hospitals . . . getting four or five hours' sleep, then moving on again . . . entertaining in torrential jungle rains . . . wading in mud knee-deep . . . baking in the tropical sun . . . and eating GI food.

But Jack seemed to draw even more than his usual strength from his contact with the thousands of young men and women, all so far from home. He never complained, always did more at each show than had been planned, and spent endless hours talking to military personnel on a one-to-one basis.

Although his trips overseas were well publicized, including one to Germany, which he made with Ingrid Bergman, and one later on to Korea, which also "featured" Errol Flynn, much of what he did behind the scenes was *never* written about. Privately, Jack considered himself the personal ambassador from the GIs abroad to their families at home. Before each trip, he laid in a supply of small leather memo books, in which he jotted down the names, addresses, and phone numbers of people he met and talked with.

Because he could not call everyone's family, he concentrated on the wounded. Wherever he could, whenever he could visit hospitals, he'd walk from bed to bed, talk to each patient, and carefully jot down all the information on how to contact their families back home. After each name, he would make a personal notation so that when he did contact the families, he would have some special remembrance to pass on.

In addition to the wounded, he went out of his way to get identification on certain groups of service personnel stationed on remote islands in extremely small companies. These people suffered a very special kind of loneliness and privation, and Jack made an extra note of that.

As soon as he returned to Hollywood, he set the stacks of memo books in front of him on his desk. Carefully, he went over each entry, deciding whether to call or dictate a letter. As each decision was made and carried out, the name was carefully checked off. Even those closest to him were never fully aware of how meticulous he had been in following through on his promises.

After he passed away, among his personal effects Mary found literally thousands of letters from service personnel, as well as from their mothers, fathers, sisters, brothers, fiancées, and friends, all of whom he had either called or written. There were also thank-you notes from relatives of men and women who had themselves written home to say how much Jack Benny's appearance at their particular base had meant to their morale.

All of these letters were saved. Today, they form not only a priceless treasure store of World War II memorabilia, but another "special legacy" from Jack to Mary.

While Jack was still overseas, preparations had begun for the fall season of 1944, when he would be going on the air for a new sponsor, American Tobacco's Lucky Strike cigarettes. Ruthruff & Ryan, one of the top advertising agencies, handled the American Tobacco account, and over the summer, looked for the best producer they had to take on Benny's show.

At the time, Bob Ballin, an employee of Ruthruff & Ryan, was producing "Vox Pop," starring Parks Johnson and Warren Hull. While he was on vacation, he received a phone call from Don Stauffer, who headed up the agency's radio department, informing him that he was being removed from his current show to become producer of Jack Benny's broadcasts.

"I was very excited by the prospect of working with Jack," Ballin recalls. "I went to New York, checked in with the home office, then came back out to Hollywood. Jack was still not home from entertaining the troops . . . The man I made contact with was Myrt Blum, his business manager.

"'Let me tell you about the Benny show,' Blum said, 'It's already well grooved. What Jack needs is someone who can *help* him, not someone who is going to try and rearrange the show, or tell him what to do . . .'

"I understood perfectly. Jack had the number-one program. Obviously, it didn't need any tampering with . . . From the moment I got my new assignment, I thought to myself, this is going to be a million laughs. A few weeks later, Jack returned from his tour of the South Pacific, and the first time we met was at a writers' session in Jack's home on Roxbury Drive.

"When I arrived, Jack, his four writers, and his secretary, who took notes of script changes, were already hard at work. I sat down and listened as Jack read through the entire script aloud. Then, in turn, each of the writers tossed in ideas, and Jack made comments. It was an amazing scene. The material was funny— *very* funny—but none of them had as much as a snicker of expression on their faces. They were like five corporate executives sitting around discussing a special venture. It was then I learned firsthand that Jack Benny considered comedy a *business*—which he worked at very hard.

"My first show as producer aired on October 1, 1944. Jack's guest star was Fred Allen. To be honest, as experienced as I was at producing radio shows, I was scared to death . . .

"Allen had a reputation for ad-libbing, which would always break Jack up, or so I had been told. I knew this would make for a funny show, but it could sure play havoc with my main function, which was to get the program on and off the air, with *all* commercials heard, and not run overtime. I decided to level with Fred. I confessed that, since this was my first show with Jack, I was worried about his penchant for ad libs, and Jack's off-the-cuff responses. Fred stared at me.

" 'Your first show, eh? Well, in that case, you watch me and I'll watch you. Give me the standard signals . . . Don't worry, everything will be okay.'

"True to his word, Allen behaved. The show went off like clockwork. Oh, he *did* ad-lib a bit . . . and Jack *did* rise to the bait. But Allen knew *exactly* when to cut the clowning and return to the script. Jack loved the show. He was very pleased it had come off on schedule, which endeared me to him from then on . . .

"Working for American Tobacco was quite an experience. The president, George Washington Hill, had a reputation for being a really tough customer. I was amazed at his relationship with Jack. Benny was the *only* personality Hill ever liked well enough to become acquainted with. They even went fishing together a few times and, every so often, special boxes would arrive for Jack. Inside would be huge fresh salmon which Mr. Hill had caught, iced, and sent to Jack for his personal pleasure . . .

"To me, Jack was a brooding man . . . a very lonely man in some ways," Ballin continued. "That may sound strange, since he seemed almost constantly to be surrounded by Mary, his cast, and writers. In truth, he had so much energy, he wore everyone out . . . I discovered there were times when he wanted to do things, and found himself *alone,* doing them. But out of all of this came his great kindness and the sensitivity which made him the unique humorist he was. I never thought of him as a comedian, a joke-teller. He was a humorist pure and simple. Offstage, he would say funny things, but with such a straight face, most often you did a double-take as you realized some witty or philosophical remark had just whizzed by you—undetected, at first . . .

"One time Jack agreed to speak to a woman's club group and asked me to go with him. On the way back, he spotted an ice cream parlor and said he'd like to stop. We went in, sat at the counter, and Jack ordered a chocolate soda with two straws. He knew *I* knew he wasn't supposed to have such sweets. After making me promise not to tell Mary, he drank the soda with such glee, draining the glass just like a little boy, making sounds through the straws when he hit bottom. After he'd finished every drop, he said, 'Bob, that was good . . . I sure wish my shows were that good!'

"Actually, all of Jack's programs turned out well. At the beginning, I had a habit of complimenting him after every show, saying, 'Jack, today's program was great. Did you like it as well as the one we did last week?' Invariably, Jack would reply, 'I don't know. How can you compare them? How can I top myself? I

161

can't. I just do my very best every time I go on . . .' After a while, I stopped asking.

"Because Jack was such a perfectionist, I expected he would be quite temperamental. He rarely was. But every so often, he would blow his stack. The first time he jumped on me happened on our last show of the season. For years, Jack traditionally had the writers save him enough time at the end of the final show so he could thank everyone who had contributed to the program during the year. He also wanted extra time to say goodbye to his audience as he went off for the summer.

"On this particular show, we had a guest who was very wordy. Before we went on the air, he asked if, at the end of the program, he could have fifteen or twenty seconds to make a brief statement to the radio audience—and it had been okayed. Everything went fine until the guest began talking . . . and talking . . . and talking. I stood there frantically signaling him to speed up, to wind up, to get off. But he kept on going until we ran out of time and went off without Jack being able to say anything.

"As soon as we left the air," Ballin remembers, "Jack came looking for me. He was angry. 'What happened?' he demanded to know. 'What went wrong? I didn't have a chance to say thank you and goodbye!' While I stood there not knowing what to say, searching for the words to tell him that it was his guest who had inadvertently fouled him up, Jack just turned around and walked out. The whole cast disbanded and we went our separate ways.

"I felt awful. When you come to know a man like Jack, it's a terrible personal blow if you disappoint him in any way, even if it isn't your fault. I drove straight home, feeling very down. I hadn't been there five minutes when the phone rang.

" 'Hello, Bob?'

" 'Yes.'

" 'This is Jack . . .'

" 'Yes, I know . . .'

" 'What can I say, Bob, except that I apologize for my behavior . . .'

" 'That's not necessary, Jack,' I replied.

" 'But the whole thing wasn't your fault. I found out . . .'

" 'Jack, that doesn't make any difference. I understood why you were upset. I'm just sorry things didn't work out for you on your last show of the season . . .'

" 'Please, Bob, will you forgive me for the way I acted?'

"I came up with a corny cliché response. 'Jack, never explain. Your friends don't need it, your enemies won't believe it. Please, forget what happened . . .'

"I hung up and couldn't believe the conversation. For a star of Jack's caliber to be so humble, so apologetic . . . It may not sound like much, but if you're in *our* business, you find out quickly that a great percentage of big stars, no matter what they do or say, are *never* wrong in their own minds. Rarely does anyone in Benny's category take the time to say I'm sorry. Jack was a very special man . . . No matter who you were, if you worked for him, he made you feel important . . . needed.

"Jack was always doing the unexpected," Ballin went on. "One season, we did our last broadcast from New York, and we all went back to California by train. It was a special time in my life. My fiancée was with me. We planned to be married in Hollywood as soon as we got home. On the ride west, I noticed that Jack seemed extremely pleased about something. I couldn't figure out what it was . . .

"When our train stopped at Denver, we all got off to take the obligatory stretch. Only then did I discover that Jack had told someone on his staff about my impending wedding plans. Special arrangements had been made for a surprise ceremony in Denver. We were whisked away by limousine to the governor's mansion. There, in the study, we were married, with Jack as my best man and Mary as matron of honor. The event, because it involved them, made news all across America. It was a highlight in my life —and I owe it to the Bennys. That they would have gone out of their way to make such a gesture touched me—deeply . . .

"There are so many memories I have of him," Ballin added. "He liked to come over to my house every once in a while and just chat. He'd always call first and say, 'Hello, Bob, this is Jack. What are you doing tonight?' And if I said nothing special, he'd ask if he could come over. Of course, he was always welcome . . .

One evening, he came to my house, and we were going to sit in the living room and talk. He walked across the room, headed for a footstool I had in front of the fireplace. Before I knew what happened, he'd missed the stool and had fallen flat on his ass into my fireplace—thank God it wasn't lit.

"He just sat there and laughed. 'I knew someday I'd be a flop, Bob, but I never thought it would be in your living room!' That was Jack!

"Sometimes I would visit him at home. Invariably, I'd go upstairs and find him in the bathroom, practicing the fiddle. He'd always say, 'Sit right over there,' pointing to the john. I'd put the lid down and sit, entranced as he'd go on and on. I loved listening to him. Every time, I'd think to myself, here I am in the presence of Jack Benny, this big star . . . I'm sitting in his bathroom, listening to him play Mendelssohn. Those private concerts were my favorite form of entertainment!

"I was also involved with Jack when he came back from a trip overseas and told me he'd met a young GI comic there who he would like to try out as a possible summer replacement for his show. The man's name was Jack Paar. I made arrangements for Paar to do a tape which was brought to Hollywood for the agency to listen to . . . The next thing I knew, Paar arrived in person to work with Jack's writers. Never had such an unknown been given the opportunity Benny gave Paar. It was yet another example of Jack's generosity and concern for helping others . . ."

CHAPTER THIRTY-ONE

IN JULY OF 1945, when Hickey Marks got out of the service, he did not resume his position on the Benny show. Jack already had a staff of writers: Sam Perrin, George Balzer, Milt Josefsberg, and John Tackaberry. They had been hired in 1942, after Bill Morrow went into the service and Ed Beloin became a screenplay writer.

Instead, Marks went to work on Ann Sothern's radio show, "Maisie," along with Lee Loeb and the show's creator, Mary McCall, Jr., who had written the "Maisie" films for Metro-Goldwyn-Mayer. Frequently, when they worked together at Miss McCall's house, Hickey felt a touch of nostalgia. It was the former Lita Grey Chaplin place, the first real home Jack and Mary rented when they originally settled down in Beverly Hills.

Early in January 1946, Perrin and Balzer, who had written a show—*Are You with It?*—got the go-ahead on a Broadway production. They took a leave of absence from Benny's staff to go to New York. It was then Jack called and asked Marks to come back and be a part of his writing team again.

"Then, in April," producer Ballin recalls, "just a couple of months before we were to go off the air for the summer, I informed Jack I was being made vice-president of Ruthruff & Ryan. I also said I'd heard rumors the Lucky Strike account was moving to another agency, Foote, Cone and Belding, although nothing was definite yet.

"Jack understood how important the advancement was to my career. He congratulated me on the promotion, then asked if that meant he would have to find someone else to produce his show. Reluctantly, I said that was correct.

"Jack asked if I could recommend a successor with whom he would be compatible. My immediate reply was, 'Yes, Hickey. He knows as much about the production as I do.' Jack seemed pleased. He admitted that having Hickey produce his show was something he had wanted and had thought about for quite a while . . ."

In midsummer 1946, the Benny program did move to Foote, Cone and Belding, with a new producer—Hilliard Marks. There was also one other change—in singers. Dennis Day had been mustered out of the Navy in April of 1946, and as Jack had promised, he was rehired to go back on the show that fall.

As Dennis related, "I never realized that my association with Jack would become almost a lifetime career! Everyone welcomed me back with open arms—I was a member of the Benny 'family' again.

"In 1948, when I got married, Jack and Mary gave Peggy and me our wedding reception. And, over the years, as my children were born, the Bennys showered us with baby gifts . . . 'Who knew you'd wind up having *ten kids,*' Jack always joked . . . 'And I thought you were so naïve! Would you believe this kid has six sons and four daughters . . . I'll go broke buying gifts if he doesn't stop, already!'"

Dennis remained with Jack right through to his final radio show in 1954. Then he went on to do Benny's television show for the next ten years. After that, he appeared on several of Jack's TV specials. If ever there was a display of show-business loyalty, it was Jack's to Dennis Day.

"September 29, 1946, was *my* D day," Hickey remembers. "That was the date on which Jack's first show of the new season went on the air. For me, it was a nightmare! I held the stopwatch in my hands, which were damp with perspiration. All I kept thinking of was how Jack told me he had dripped with perspiration during his early days in vaudeville, before he had attained self-confidence . . . before he had experienced the warmth of the audiences' response. Now it was my turn. Although I knew the routine of Jack's program backward and forward, I was extremely nervous having the actual responsibility for producing the show. I wanted very much to do well . . . to please Jack. For *me,* it was *his* reaction which counted.

"Let me digress a moment. Jack, as we've said many times before, was a perfectionist when it came to his craft. He was the undisputed master of comic timing. For years, his show had been number one, yet he never rested on his laurels. Week after week, year in and year out, he wanted his programs to be the very best.

"Still, knowing Jack as well as I did, I understood that he never had any real concept of the *technical* side of his show. Therefore, he always surrounded himself with first-rate people, and he expected them to do their jobs correctly. Now I found myself in *that* spot. I had to prove to Jack, the agency, and the sponsor that I knew what the hell I was doing.

"Today, such shows are prerecorded or, in television, either filmed or taped. If you make a mistake, you can correct it. But thirty years ago, all of the Benny shows were done live. Once I gave Don Wilson the signal—*that was it*—we were on the air. There was no chance to redo anything. We had to be right the *first* time. I had twenty-nine minutes and thirty seconds to deliver the Jack Benny show, complete with commercials, dialogue, and music.

"As close as Jack and I were offstage," Hickey continued, "as much as we were good friends and devoted brothers-in-law, I knew if I did not do my job correctly, Jack would fire me. He was the softest touch in the world about everything—except his show!

"As producer, I had the responsibility of working during the week with Jack, the cast, and the writers. On Saturdays, prior to Sunday's air time, all of us would meet at ten in the morning.

"Everyone came to these rehearsals except the orchestra. Jack insisted that the guys in the band not hear any of the material prior to the show. He wanted their reaction to be spontaneous. Once the script run-through was timed, I would tell Jack whether we were running too long or too short. At this point, time had already been allotted for laughter, the three commercials, the public service announcement, and Jack's 'tag'—his closing words following the last commercial—after Don said, 'Jack will be back in just a minute . . . but first . . .'

"When the reading was over, the cast was dismissed. Then Jack, the writers, and I would go through and make any necessary cuts, or additions and changes . . .

"On Sundays, I would get to the NBC studios at Sunset and Vine by ten o'clock. We always broadcast from Studio B—for Benny. At ten-thirty, Dennis Day and the orchestra, with Mahlon Merrick conducting, would rehearse their musical number. Jack and the rest of the cast came in between eleven-thirty and noon—with Jack invariably arriving earlier than everybody else. As soon as we were assembled, there was another reading with the revised script.

"In radio, the allowance for laughter is referred to as 'the spread.' Here is the way the actual timing sheet for Jack's half-hour radio show looked. This was the same basic formula we used when we went into television.

		Minutes	Time Elapsed
COMMERCIALS:	Opening	1:05	1:05
	Middle(comedy-integrated)	:50	1:55
	Closing	1:05	3:00
	Dennis Day Song	2:30	5:30
	Jack's Tag	1:30	7:00
	Public Announcement	:30	7:30
	Spread	7:00	14:30
	Credits	:30	15:00
	Benny Show Dialogue	14:30	29:30

"Despite all the advance preparation, very rarely did a show go off exactly on schedule. With Jack, there were so many variables! By having the timing written on the top of each page of script, I always knew—minute by minute—if we were running short or long. 'Short' was no problem. We could compensate for that merely by giving Jack a signal to stretch . . . to slow down the pace of the dialogue. If we were running long, I could always delete Jack's tag, the public service announcement and the closing credits. Whenever that happened, Jack would just come in, following the closing commercial, and say, 'We're a little late—so good night, folks . . .'

"I must add here that, in addition to the co-operation from the cast, I always had marvelous help from our engineer, George Foster, who could perform miracles in the control room—and frequently was called upon to do so. George, along with the rest of the behind-the-scenes crew, was magnificent. Jack's shows were always a product of dedicated, efficient teamwork.

"By thirty seconds to air time, everyone on stage had been given the 'stand by' signal. Then it was time for the opening commercial, which originated from another studio. I'm sure you all remember those Lucky Strike commercials where the tobacco auctioneers chanted, then wound up by saying: 'SOLD—AMERICAN!'

"After the opening commercial, I would give Don Wilson a hand signal to go ahead. At the same time, I pushed a button that caused the 'On the Air' sign to light up, alerting everyone in Studio B that the Benny show was now in progress.

"So it was on that Sunday in September 1946 when I gave Don his signal, pushed the button, and Jack's show went on. Up until the middle comedy commercial, everything went just fine. However, my first program was also the debut show for the Sportsmen Quartet.

"I thought I had allowed enough time for laughs, but I had not fully anticipated the prolonged reaction which the quartet received from the studio audience. Here's the exact dialogue from the point in the show where we started to run over.

DON: Oh, Jack, Jack . . . Can we do the commercial now? The quartet is ready.

JACK: Oh, good, good. Mary, I want you to hear this. This is a new commercial Don thought up with a quartet behind it. I've got them tied up for eight weeks at five hundred dollars a week. Go ahead, Don, let's hear it.

DON: Okay. Ready, boys. Let's go . . . LS/MFT. LS/MFT. Yes, sir, you bet, Lucky Strike Means Fine Tobacco . . . Yes . . . Lucky Strike Means *Fine* Tobacco.

QUARTET: (hums one note)

DON: Yes, ladies and gentlemen, in a cigarette it's the tobacco that counts.

QUARTET: (hums one note a little higher)

DON: So smoke that smoke of fine tobacco, *Lucky Strike.*

QUARTET: (hums two notes)

JACK: For this I'm paying five hundred dollars?

DON: Yes, Ladies and gentlemen, quality of product is essential to continuing success.

QUARTET: (hums five notes)

JACK: (yells) Wait a minute . . . wait a minute . . . Don . . . is that all?

DON: Yes.

JACK: For that I'm paying five hundred dollars . . . for eight weeks? Stand aside, Don. I want to talk to this quartet. Listen, fellows, if you think I'm gonna pay you five hundred dollars a week just for that, you're crazy.

QUARTET: (hums two notes)

JACK: *Now cut that out* . . . and get out of here.

"Jack's standard method of getting a laugh from this kind of situation was to say nothing . . . fold his arms . . . and stare out into the audience. The longer Jack remained silent, the bigger the laughs grew . . . This is what threw me.

"During Dennis' song, I rushed out of the control booth and whispered to Jack that we were running much too long. He said, 'Don't worry, kid, we'll make it. Just relax.' Well, I *didn't* relax. I couldn't. Still, we managed to get off the air exactly on time. To this day, I don't know how we did it.

"Afterward, Jack walked over to me, saw me wiping my forehead, and looked surprised. 'What were you so nervous about? Everything went like clockwork.' Then Mary and the rest of the cast came over to congratulate me on a successful first show. As I walked back into the booth, Emerson Foote, head of the agency, shook my wet hand and said, 'Well, now you're a full-fledged producer of the Jack Benny show.' I was very relieved. For the next thirteen years that I served as both Jack's radio and television producer, I tried hard to anticipate any and all emergencies—but of course that was not always possible.

"During our radio days, there were many funny moments. For instance, on one program, Jack had Edgar Bergen and Charlie McCarthy as guests. During the show, we came to a place in the script where Jack was supposed to be talking to Edgar, with Charlie throwing in his usual kibitzing remarks . . .

"I saw Jack walking across the stage to the microphone Edgar was using. Bergen was standing up, and had Charlie seated on a chair. Jack walked in front of Edgar and began to turn the mike toward Charlie—*while Edgar was still talking*. I came out of the booth and switched the mike back to the proper position. I couldn't say anything, so I stood there pointing until Jack became aware of what *I* had done to compensate for what *he* had done. I mean, after all, Charlie was *the dummy*. The audience was aware of what had happened and literally screamed with laughter . . ."

After each program, Jack always called home and talked to Florence and his dad. Meyer, now seventy-seven, had had a heart condition for many years, but was still his son's number-one fan. Besides, Edgar Bergen was one of Kubelsky's favorite comedians and Jack was sure the show had pleased him.

But when he phoned, Florence told him they had not listened to the program because their dad was very ill and the doctor had been there. From the tone of her voice, Jack sensed the situation. He left for Chicago immediately. The following day, October 14, 1946, Meyer Kubelsky passed away.

CHAPTER THIRTY-TWO

OVER THE YEARS, the question asked Benny most frequently was, "What were the biggest, longest laughs you ever received on radio or television?" It was never easy to answer—there were so many. But there is no doubt that Jack's *most publicized* laugh was the one which followed the ". . . money or your life" bit.

"Jack originally did that on his radio show," Hickey recalls. "Later, it was repeated on television. As frequently happened, the fantastic punch line came about accidentally. Jack, the writers, and I were at a rewrite session. A situation had already been established. Jack was supposed to be right outside of Don Wilson's house when a holdup man was to stick a gun in his back and say, 'Your money or your life . . .'

"The writers had gone around but had not yet come up with Jack's reaction line. Suddenly, Milt Josefsberg turned to John Tackaberry and said, 'Come on, how do we finish this thing?' To which Tackaberry replied, 'I'm thinking it over . . .'

"Instantly, Jack slapped the table and said, 'That's it.' Tackaberry hadn't meant it to be *the* line . . . It was Jack who had immediately recognized its potential . . ."

There were also Jack's trips to his vault, which became a running gag Benny used for years. It was first established on radio through a series of sound effects. Footsteps . . . chains rattling . . . iron doors clanging . . . whistles sounding the alarm . . . with Jack finally arriving at his underground vault.

The man in charge of the strongbox (actor Joe Kearns) always said, "Who goes there?" To which Jack always replied, "It's me, Ed."

The guard would then respond, "Oh, it's you, Mr. Benny . . ." and the rest of the particular routine would follow. On one occasion, when Jack entered the vault, the guard asked, "What's new?"

"The war's over," Jack answered.

To which Ed responded, "Oh, good . . . Who won? The North or the South?"

It was during the long pause which followed, when Jack looked out at the audience, that the laughter would begin to build . . . and build.

Over the years, Mary was also responsible for some of the Benny show's biggest laughs. On one program, they were doing a drugstore routine. Jack and Mary walked in, sat down at the counter, and started to order. Mary's line was supposed to be, "Waiter, I'd like a swiss cheese sandwich on rye bread." What slipped out, however, was "Waiter, I'd like a chis sweeze sandwich . . ." The audience howled.

That's a good example of how an accident became a running gag on Jack's shows. Someone would make an inadvertent mistake . . . The audience would laugh . . . The mistake would become part of Benny's repertoire, until he sensed that it had run its course. So, for weeks after Mary's initial slip of the tongue, whenever anyone else made a mistake, Jack would turn to her and say, "Well, chis sweeze, you certainly started something!"

Then there was the program with opera star Dorothy Kirsten as Jack's guest. She and Don Wilson were discussing various operas in front of Mary and Jack. It was a long involved intellectual conversation. Finally, Dorothy said to Don, "Don't you think, in the aria 'Un Bel Dì Vedremo,' that the strings played the con moto exceptionally fine . . . ?" At that point, Jack was unable to contain himself any longer. As befitting his know-it-all character, he interrupted: "Well . . . I thought . . ."

That was as far as he got when Mary looked at him and said, "OH SHUT UP," in her unique tone. The audience roared. Jack always thought that was one of the biggest laughs the show ever had.

During this period they also did numerous broadcasts from Palm Springs, California. Jack and Mary loved spending time in the desert, especially when the weather turned a little cold in Los Angeles. On one of these occasions, Jack and Hickey decided to drive down to the Springs early. Mary was coming down later in the week. Jack had just purchased a new Cadillac convertible and wanted to try it out on the road.

"He picked me up and we started out—with *me* in the driver's seat. Jack was a very bad driver, although he loved being behind the wheel. But invariably, when we went places together, I did the driving and Jack did the complaining. This time was no different. 'It's *my* car,' he said. 'How come I never get to drive it?' I just smiled and slid behind the wheel.

"Palm Springs was close to a three-hour drive then—before the freeways were built. As we rode along, discussing that week's show, I noticed the gas gauge was almost at empty and pulled into a station at the next small town. I asked the attendant to fill it up, then Jack and I sat, engrossed in our discussion about the show. Easily twenty minutes had passed when I looked up and saw the attendant walking around the car, a perplexed expression on his face. 'How much do we owe you?' I asked. 'Nothing, so far,' he replied. 'I can't figure out where your gas tank is . . .'

"I turned to Jack. 'Where does the gas go?' He shrugged his shoulders. '*You're* the damn genius that wanted to drive . . . you figure it out!' I got out and circled the car. As far as I could see, there was no gas tank. We wound up calling the Cadillac agency in Beverly Hills, and it turned out that this was the first model which had the tank *under* the taillight!

"Our shows originated from the Palm Springs Legion Hall. That week, we were having Al Jolson as our guest star. Al had been on Jack's show once before while I was producing. He was about the only star I was in awe of . . .

"At the last rehearsal, we were running two and a half minutes long. I explained the predicament to Jack and told him we couldn't cut any more of the dialogue. He suggested I ask Jolson to cut one of his songs.

"I looked at him. 'Jack,' I said, 'it's *your* show . . . Why don't *you* ask him?'

"He smiled, 'Not *me,* you're the producer. You talk to him!' Jack was a little in awe of Jolson, too! He loved Al, so when I seemed hesitant, Jack really rubbed it in. 'Now, go ahead and do your job.'

" 'Suddenly, *I'm* the big man?' I replied. Jack wasn't going to budge—so I went to find Al.

" 'Mr. Jolson,' I began . . .

" 'Please, I've told you before, call me Al . . .'

" 'Well, Al . . . we're two and a half minutes long and . . .'

"He interrupted me. 'Then I'll cut one of my songs,' he volunteered. I just stood there. It was like discussing taking one of the Psalms out of the Bible!

" 'Listen,' Al went on, 'maybe we'd better plan to cut a chorus from my *second* number, too . . .' I told Al that wasn't necessary. Jolson was marvelous on the show, and it went off without a hitch.

"A short while later, I went with Jack to the Shrine Auditorium in Los Angeles, where he was to make a benefit appearance. Jolson was also on the bill. On the way over, I mentioned to Jack that I had never seen Al perform in blackface, and he began to talk about the old days in New York.

"He told me that every Sunday night there were shows at the Winter Garden. All the performers in town who could make it appeared for the benefit of the Actor's Fund. Jack said Jolson had always been the standout. No one ever tired of his blackface routine. Each time, it had been a new thrill to see him perform.

"When we reached the Auditorium, we went directly backstage and bumped into Al. Jack told Jolson I had never seen him do blackface. He asked if Al intended to do the routine.

"Jolson shook his head. 'Jack, it's so much trouble putting all that stuff on.' But as he talked, he walked over to his makeup case. He had his blackface paraphernalia with him—it was like a good luck charm he carried everywhere.

" 'Please Al,' I said, 'do your blackface. I made you cut one song in Palm Springs and it tore my heart out . . . If you don't do your blackface tonight, it will tear me up even more!' Al knew I was sincere in my admiration for him . . . He excused himself and we left the dressing room. Ten minutes later, Jolson reap-

174

peared, in blackface, with the white gloves and scarf, wearing the dark suit he always put on for that routine.

"When it was time for Al to go on, Jack and I stood in the wings watching. Jolson strutted on stage and began his whole medley: 'Swanee' . . . 'Waiting for the Robert E. Lee' . . . 'Dixie' . . . and 'Mammy,' sung on bended knee. Midway through, I looked at Jack and he looked at me. Both of us had tears streaming down our cheeks. It was a moment I'll never forget . . .

"When we did our radio shows from Palm Springs, one of Jack and Mary's favorite guests was Charlie Farrell, who owned the Racquet Club, a popular mecca for show-business greats. Every time Charlie was on, Jack kept building him up as the star of *Seventh Heaven*—a film which he had made with Janet Gaynor.

"One week, from the Springs, we had Sam Goldwyn as a guest. He was also a favorite of Jack's. He had been on our program from Los Angeles several times, including one memorable show when we also had Hoagy Carmichael as a guest. Mr. Goldwyn kept calling him 'Hugo,' another funny bit which Jack revived from time to time. Goldwyn, of course, was famous for his malaprops.

"This particular week, the writers had come up with a very funny line for Sam. Jack was to say, 'Tell me, Mr. Goldwyn, what was the biggest mistake in your life?' Sam's reply was to be, 'That I never produced *Seventh Heaven*.'

"The night of the show came and we went on the air—live. But when Jack said, 'Tell me, Mr. Goldwyn, what was the greatest mistake you ever made?' Goldwyn announced, 'That I never produced *Gone with the Wind*.' There was total silence from the audience. Somehow, they sensed it was a wrong line, and they didn't understand what the hell Goldwyn was talking about.

"Jack looked up from his script, speechless. Mary laughed so hard, she practically fell down on stage. Recovering his poise, Jack said, 'Sam, read the line *that's written*.'

"Goldwyn answered, 'I *can't* say that line.'

" 'Well!' Jack came back. 'At least *tell* the audience what it says in your script!'

"Goldwyn looked out at the people. 'It says here my biggest

175

mistake was I never produced *Seventh Heaven*—but that isn't right. My biggest mistake is I never produced *Gone with the Wind*.'

"Now the audience screamed with laughter. We damn near ran overtime. It was one of those shows where I had to cut everything after the end commercial. Jack came on and just said, 'We're a little late—so good night, folks.'

"In truth, Goldwyn had been accurate. David O. Selznick had offered *Gone with the Wind* to him first, but Sam couldn't see it as a film and had let it slip through his fingers. Subconsciously, it was on his mind—and he *had* to articulate it! . . .

"Over the years, I always had been able to tell when my sister Mary was about to faint. You know, she has low blood sugar, and every once in a while, she gets a certain funny look on her face. Well, we were still on the air with Goldwyn, and had only a few minutes to go, when I looked out of the booth and saw Mary— with *that* expression. I watched as she rushed out of the studio. I couldn't leave the booth. Jack couldn't leave the stage. A few minutes later, we ran after her. By the time we got outside, Mary had fainted and was stretched flat out on the ground. I always carried an ammonia pellet to put under her nose to revive her. But before I could bend over and break the capsule, a woman fan came running up, stepped right over Mary, and asked Jack for his autograph. You had to be there. *That* was a funny scene!

"Producing Jack's shows was never dull—I have thirteen years of memories to prove it!"

CHAPTER THIRTY-THREE

LATE IN THE FALL OF 1948, Jack Benny made headlines. After fifteen years with the National Broadcasting Company, he was changing networks. "Amos 'n' Andy," Burns and Allen, Edgar Bergen, and Red Skelton were also involved in the move. Perhaps because Jack was so readily identifiable as "the owner of the seven o'clock Sunday spot on NBC," his was the name which headlined the story of the massive switch to CBS in the Hollywood trade papers.

William Paley, president of the Columbia Broadcasting System, had instigated the move. In anticipation of television's vast future, he had accomplished the single biggest talent coup in the history of radio. By hiring this block of comedic giants, Paley had assured himself that, when TV became a household word, the word—and the stars—would belong to CBS.

As always before Jack made any key decision, he discussed the network change with Mary. She was all for it. However, there was something on *her* mind which she *did not* discuss with him, not until the end of Jack's first CBS season.

As Mary explains it, "In the beginning, my appearances on Jack's radio show were fun. I actually enjoyed working once a week. But ironically, the more shows I did, the more nervous I became. I still can't figure it out logically. All I know is that every Sunday wound up being the most tortuous day of my week.

"I waited until we were off on our summer holiday. When the 'right' moment came, I told Jack that, after seventeen years of doing the show, it was just taking too much out of me. I ended by saying that I would *not* be on his program any more. I just couldn't do it . . .

"Jack was surprised, to put it mildly, but he was also very understanding. He realized that while being in front of an audience was the happiest part of *his* life, I never felt that way. He was so sweet about it. He just looked at me and said, 'Okay, doll, if that's the way you want it, that's the way it will be . . .'

"Naturally," Mary went on, "Jack had to discuss my decision with Hickey, who was producing the show. The week we came back from vacation, Jack and my brother had lunch. I knew nothing about their talk until Jack came home that afternoon, very excited.

" 'Doll, everything is going to work out fine. Hickey's been talking to Bing Crosby about how they *tape* his radio show. That gave him an idea. He says you can still be on the show without appearing before the audience. You can stay home—and do your part right from the den . . .'

"I didn't have the slightest idea what Jack was talking about. I don't think he really knew either. The next day, Hickey came over and explained it to us.

" 'Look, Mary, it's very exciting. You'll be the only radio star to appear on a weekly show—*without really appearing!*' Sometimes my brother got overly enthusiastic about things . . . I was always the practical one in our family. But he seemed so sincerely happy at 'the solution' that Jack and I listened while he went into further detail.

" 'I've been over talking to Bing at the "Kraft Music Hall." He and Murdo MacKenzie [producer-engineer] have been pre-recording their shows on tape. It's fantastic. If you make a mistake, you can stop and do it over again. If we apply this technique with you, no one will know that you're not in the studio . . .'

"I must admit," Mary continued, "we were getting more and more curious, until finally, Jack saw it as a real possibility. 'Okay,' he said. 'Tell us, just how in the hell are you *actually* going to do it?'

" 'Tomorrow I'll take one of the recordings from a program we've already done and transfer it to tape—just to show you how the process works. I'll delete Mary's lines from that tape and have my secretary type up a page with her original dialogue. I'll come over here with George Foster and bring all the necessary equipment,' Hickey explained.

" 'If you're around, Jack, you can feed Mary her cue lines. If not, I'll do it. In response to the cues, Mary will deliver her lines and they will be recorded on the tape. I'll go back to the studio and integrate Mary's lines wherever they come in the show. You'll see, it will sound exactly as if Mary had been in the studio with the rest of the cast . . .' "

"They looked at me like I had two heads, but they agreed to let me try. I'm afraid it would get too technical if I went into further detail. Let's just say we tried it—and it worked!"

Mary agreed. "Every week," she recalls, "my brother and our engineer came to the house. They fed me my cues, and I did my part with the tape recorder going. I'm still not sure I understand how it worked. All I know is for the remainder of the Jack Benny radio shows, when you heard me every Sunday night coming over the air from the studio, what you *really* heard was me—coming from my own den!"

Mary may have become an "absentee" radio actress, but she was right by Jack's side when yet another major career decision had to be made. It was during this same period that Jack and Hickey traveled to New York for an important meeting with Mr. Paley; Vincent Riggio, chairman of the board of American Tobacco; Paul Hahn, president of American Tobacco; and Ben Duffy of Batten, Barton, Durstine and Osborn, who had taken over the account from Foote, Cone and Belding.

The topic under discussion was the possibility of Benny's going into television. A decision was reached that Jack should do a test show first. The executives needed some questions answered. For instance, how would Jack look on the small screen? What format should he follow? Could he successfully transfer his assets from radio to a *visual* medium? Should he perhaps revert to the type of show he had done in earlier times—namely with him acting as m.c.—or should he try to keep his radio family intact?

"As soon as we returned to Hollywood," Hickey said, "Jack and I sat down to discuss the pros and cons with Mary. Now that he had agreed to the test, how would he pull it off? Jack was fifty-four years old, and frankly concerned about his appearance on the tube.

"At that point, Mary took the initiative. 'Jack, I'll work on the production of the show very closely. I'll be with you every day and we'll take it step by step . . . And, believe me, doll, I'll tell you honestly how I feel you look, and if the show *works* . . .'"

Preparations began for the program, which was scheduled to air on May 8, 1949, from the old CBS Radio Studio A on Sunset and Gower. The facilities had been taken over by Channel 11, a local television station owned by CBS.

During those "primitive" days, the Columbia Broadcasting System did their shows via "kinescope." Early on, certain key decisions were made jointly by Jack and Mary. There were to be no TV cameras on stage—then the normal procedure. Instead, special lenses would be utilized and the cameras were to be placed halfway back in the studio, in front of which the audience would be seated. The use of studio monitors would be eliminated. Jack wanted complete access to his audience unhampered by the usual technical equipment.

As promised, Mary was at the studio constantly during the days of rehearsal. She sat in the audience, "directing" the proceedings, making sure all of Jack's decisions were carried out to the letter.

Isaac Stern, Bob Crosby, Margaret Whiting, the Andrews Sisters, Lum and Abner, and Rochester had been signed to guest-star. The writers came up with a top-notch script. And when the day of the show arrived, Mary selected Jack's wardrobe, a neat dark suit, blue shirt, and tie.

Everything had been done that could be done. Now it was all up to Jack. Just before he went on, he confessed to Mary that he felt unusually nervous. She gave him a reassuring hug and took her place in the audience.

What happened next was remarkable. Jack sauntered on stage simulating his usual breezy manner, and instantly his instinctive inner confidence took over. He looked very handsome. He appeared extremely at ease. He was a dynamic man, looking at least fifteen years younger than his actual age.

The applause which greeted him was overwhelming. From the moment he began his opening monologue, it was clear Jack Benny would be a natural in this new medium!

JACK: Ladies and gentleman, I want to introduce myself . . . I'm appearing here tonight through the courtesy of a ten-inch tube . . . However, I do want to apologize for my appearance here this evening as I know that most of you prefer wrestling. Had I known that wrestling was going to be so popular on television, I would've stuck to it . . . because that used to be my business, and I was very good at it, too. As a matter of fact, Gorgeous George got his idea from me. I was known as "The Body Beautiful Benny" . . . When I stepped into the ring and took off my robe . . . . WELL! . . . I made Frank Sinatra look like a nickel . . . But I'm really crazy about television. I could sit home for hours and just look at the test patterns . . . And one thing I must say in all seriousness . . . that is that I'm not a bit nervous. I know that most comedians are nervous about television . . . like Bob Hope . . . Eddie Cantor . . . Red Skelton . . . but not me. I figure this way . . . If

I'm a success tonight, all right . . . If not, I'll kill myself . . . Of course, there's one comedian I'm sure will have a little trouble on television . . . and that's Fred Allen . . . I don't know whether you've seen him in person or not . . . but with those bags under his eyes, he looks like a short butcher peeping over two pounds of liver . . . Incidentally, I'm not getting paid for my appearance here tonight . . . and I don't mind working for nothing . . . but I wonder who I have to see about this parking lot ticket . . . You know, after the first hour it's seventy-five cents . . . You know how it is . . . seventy-five cents here . . . seventy-five cents there . . . it amounts to a dollar and a half . . .

The years that Jack Benny had spent performing in vaudeville, the techniques that he had perfected on stage, in radio, now became responsible for his tremendous success on television. Jack's usage of the pause . . . the way he stared at the audience . . . the gestures he made which became part of him were even more effective *visually*. The characteristics which had become Jack's stock in trade provided him with a tremendous advantage. His unique delivery enabled him to use less material, thereby making it easier for him to memorize his lines. It was almost twelve years before Jack even got around to using cue cards.

And, on that night, in 1949, before anyone else had ever seen Jack on the small screen, it was Mary who was the first to realize his enormous potential—and tell him. When the show was over, she came up on stage, kissed Jack, and said, "Doll face, you'll just be sensational on television . . ."

It was Mary's enthusiastic praise that helped Jack make the decision to go on TV as early as he did—with his "radio family" intact.

CHAPTER THIRTY-FOUR

JACK'S FIRST regular television show originated from the Lincoln Square Theater at Sixty-fifth and Broadway in New York City on Saturday, October 28, 1950. It was forty-five minutes in length, and Dinah Shore and Ken Murray were the guest stars. The program had to be done back East because facilities for coast-to-coast transmission had not yet been perfected. As a matter of fact, Jack's first show was seen live in the eastern states—but wasn't viewed until a few weeks later by audiences west of the Mississippi.

Every six weeks, the Benny company went east to do the television program. During this period, the weekly radio show continued. By employing the taping device Hickey had first tried out with Mary, Jack and the cast were able to tape in advance the program that would be heard while they were in New York.

In preparation for the debut television show, Marks flew to New York two days before Jack and Mary in order to make final arrangements. Once there, he went over to see Fred Allen, whose own TV program had been on for several months.

"I watched Fred's show, then I went back to his dressing room. I'll never forget my first sight of him. He came walking in, dripping wet, and the valet handed him a terrycloth robe and a large bath towel. Fred dried out while we were talking. He looked terribly tired, and his first words confirmed my impression . . .

" 'Don't ever let Jack do television, Hickey. It will kill him.' I didn't want to disagree with Fred, so I just told him Jack's setup would be entirely different . . .

" 'How different can it be?' Fred inquired.

"I explained that Jack would have his cameras out front, in the middle of the theater. It would be just as if Jack were doing a vaudeville show . . . and much easier than the setup Allen was using.

"Fred still looked skeptical, but he didn't say anything else about warning Jack. We went on talking and I asked Fred how much time he allowed for laughter. He said between three and a half and four minutes. I knew that wouldn't be enough for Jack. I decided to allot at least *ten minutes* for laughs.

"A couple of days later, I was to meet with Jack at the Lincoln Square Theater. I also had to have an important talk with the head of the CBS engineering staff. Before Jack arrived, I explained our physical setup to the head of the department. I told him where we wanted the cameras, in relation to both the stage and the audience. I detailed basically the same setup we had used in Los Angeles when Jack had done his test show.

"The engineer said he didn't see how that arrangement would work, even though I told him we had already used the format successfully. He couldn't see it and started giving me an argument. Unbeknownst to me, Mr. Paley had come into the theater to meet Jack, and was standing directly behind us. He broke up the argument. 'Whatever Mr. Marks wants, give him. He is speaking for Mr. Benny,' Paley said. That ended the discussion.

"Following our meeting, Mary, Jack, and I had an early dinner, then we split up. I dropped them off at their hotel, the Sherry-Netherland, and went back to my hotel, the Warwick. I left word at the desk that the only calls I would take were from my family or Mr. Benny.

"At 4:30 A.M., my phone rang. It was Jack. 'Have you heard the news?' he asked.

" 'Jack, it's the middle of the night . . . what news?'

"He told me . . . Al Jolson had passed away the previous evening. He was in San Francisco to do a 'Bing Crosby Show,' had finished rehearsing, and had gone back to his hotel when he had a heart attack and died . . .

"Then Jack said, 'I'll have to go back for the funeral . . .' I told him to sit tight, I'd be right over. When I arrived, he was pacing up and down, and Mary was sitting on the couch. The whole scene was very reminiscent of the Carole Lombard tragedy when

183

Jack had wanted to rush right to Las Vegas, near where Carole's plane had crashed.

"At first, Jack was still adamant. He insisted we cancel the program. That didn't surprise me. Jack was never a proponent of that 'show must go on' tradition. But this time, I explained to him, we were involved with a completely different setup.

"Publicity about the opening show had already gone out nationwide. The guest stars and the cast members, Don, Rochester, Mel Blanc, Artie Auerbach (Mr. Kitzel), and the Sportsmen Quartet, were all in New York. Special facilities had been tied up for the Benny show. The client had already bought and paid for the time . . .

"No matter what I said, Jack was determined to fly home for the funeral. It was really Mary who kept her cool through the entire discussion. Then, she just looked at him and said, 'Doll, Al, of all people, would have wanted you to do your show . . .' Finally, Jack agreed . . ."

But one year later, on September 23, 1951, when, according to Jewish tradition, the monument—a magnificent statue of Al, bending on one knee, exactly the way he performed when he sang "Mammy"—was formally unveiled, it was Jack who delivered the memorial address:

Today there is something new under the sun . . . For under this California sun has risen a monument of unmatched beauty which stands as a memorial to the World's Greatest Entertainer, one of its greatest benefactors . . . and our friend.

As I looked upon this glorious shrine, I was struck by two thoughts—what it meant to Mrs. Jolson and to Al's many friends. And then there was the thought of the generation not yet born who will visit here. I was heartened by the realization that they will not ask why an edifice of this magnitude was built. For this shrine, in all its magnificence, is only proper and fitting to the man in whose memory it was erected.

I consider it a high tribute that I was asked to speak at this dedication. I feel the choice was governed largely by the fact that I have recently returned from Korea, where Al gave his last full effort to his fellow man.

Before I left Tokyo for Korea, I was told, I think as a warning for my personal feelings, that I would hear Al's records being played everywhere I went. Truthfully, I was apprehensive. I was almost prepared for a prolonged emotional depression. But when I got to Korea, this foreboding vanished. Al's voice was everywhere. Wherever I went, Jolson was singing again. His voice rose from the rear areas, the grouping points, the front lines . . . Indeed it seemed at times to spring from those rugged hills. On the faces of the thousands of boys who listened was no sadness, but rather a look of rapture and of gratitude for what had been left them.

To bring laughter and entertainment to the world during one's lifetime is a wonderful and gratifying thing. Those who, during their span of years, have brought happiness to countless millions can find a purpose to their lives enjoyed by a relative few. But to be able to leave behind so much—so much of one's self . . . so much of one's heart . . . is a far greater recompense. Thus was Al Jolson doubly blessed.

It is more or less accepted that memory is a fickle thing—that it fades in proportion to time—made necessary by the press of day-to-day events. To us whom Al has left behind, time has been unusually kind. It has helped erase the sorrow of his passing, yet has left his memory a bright and living thing. His great gift to mankind, his voice, is with us now and forever.

Before I finish, I'd like you to know that this isn't the only shrine to Al Jolson. Eight thousand miles from here, nestled in the hills of Korea, is an outdoor amphitheater where our troops are entertained. This amphitheater is within a few miles of the disputed Thirty-eighth Parallel . . . and it is called the Al Jolson Bowl. To those boys eight thousand miles away who gather there every day, the memory of Al Jolson, as with us, will never die.

"The night of our television debut," Hickey went on, "I stood in the control booth looking like Fred Allen—dripping wet. I had allowed ten minutes for audience reaction, and it *wasn't enough!* With all of Jack's stares and 'hmmmmms' and pauses, the laughter came closer to fifteen minutes . . . and we still had a very funny routine to get to . . .

"At the very end of the show, Jack was to look out at the audience and say, 'Ladies and gentlemen, our time is just about up, and I don't think you'd want to leave without hearing me play my theme song, 'Love in Bloom' on my violin. So, with your permission, I'll play now . . .'

"By prearrangement, as soon as Jack struck up the first few

bars, the entire audience was to get up and start walking out. When we came to that part of the show, we were so late that I literally held my breath as Jack delivered his lines, picked up his fiddle, and began to play. Exactly on cue, the entire audience got up and started to leave . . . The cameras caught it all. We *had* made it . . . and our reviews were very exciting."

Jack's next three television programs were done in New York. But the following season, beginning on November 4, 1951, the Benny show moved into the newly constructed CBS Studios on Beverly and Fairfax in Hollywood.

For years, Jack had demonstrated his unique ability to attract top guest stars for his radio shows. Now, he was able to repeat the feat by bringing the most important celebrities onto his television show—much to the concern of the film studios, who had not yet acknowledged TV's role in the media and looked upon the tube as a direct threat to box-office profits.

One of those top stars, Claudette Colbert, recalls the initial program she did with Benny:

"I was the first legitimate actress to do a TV show with Jack. Every one of us was scared to death of television—including me. But I trusted Jack implicitly. I went on with him April 1, 1951—his third show. When he asked me to appear, I couldn't turn him down . . . to know Jack was to both love and trust him.

"I know it sounds silly now when you talk about stars being scared of TV . . . Today, everyone's doing it," Claudette went on. "But back then, twenty-five years ago, the studios we were under contract to were not all that pleased at the prospect of 'their' talent exposing themselves on a tiny screen. Yet I went on with Jack—and, because of him, it was a very happy experience . . ."

She reminisced further about the Bennys:

"Mary and Jack both had been patients of my husband, Dr. Joel Pressman, long before I knew them. I didn't meet them until after I'd married Joel in 1935. From the moment we were introduced, we hit it off, and became very dear and intimate friends.

"I've been going over in my mind the reasons why Jack was so successful," Claudette continued, "because he was *not* a funny man by himself. Jack always had an appreciation of other people's humor. He had a terrific sense of humor himself, but he was *not* a joke teller. When he was given a script, he did a lot of editing. He knew what was funny for himself, his cast, his guests—but that did not make him necessarily a 'funny man.'

"I've known a lot of the terribly funny and very successful comics. So many of them always feel compelled to tell a joke a minute—even *offstage*. Obviously, more often than not, most of them laid eggs. But it was impossible for Jack to lay an egg. Of course, it was that magnificent timing he had . . . And, instinctively, Jack knew when to be 'on' and when to be 'off.'

"He had the the the most endearing qualities . . . Don't misunderstand, there *were* times *offstage* when he could be hysterically funny . . . I was out on a personal appearance tour one time when a writer came to interview me. During the course of our conversation, Fred Allen's name came up. I told the reporter I thought Fred was sensational . . .

"When the interview broke in print, and Jack read it, he interpreted it to mean that I had said Allen was my favorite comedian —which I hadn't meant at all. The next thing I knew, I received this long handwritten letter from Jack. In part, what he said was: 'Dear Claudette, It's pretty revolting . . . I'm very insulted. Here we are such great friends and you go on and on in print about Fred Allen . . . How could you???'

"I answered him back with some facetious comments . . . This began the exchange of a long series of notes between us. Jack's letters proceeded to get funnier and funnier with his pretended rage. Like one of the Benny show's running gags on radio, we kept writing back and forth until we'd exhausted funny, insulting things to say to each other . . .

"The year following my appearance on Jack's television show," Claudette added, "I was in Paris when I ran into Jack by accident. I hadn't known he was coming over. Mary wasn't with him— which usually made him unhappy—but on this occasion he was beaming.

"It seems he had met Queen Juliana and Prince Bernhard of the Netherlands. They were enchanted with him and had invited Jack to visit them at the palace. He was due to leave Paris the following morning for Holland. Jack was like a little kid—so happy at the thought of going someplace new. I told him he was going to be in *rare* company . . . I couldn't think of anyone else in our circle who had been invited to house-guest—or palace-guest—with the Queen!

"Jack went off . . . I didn't see him for a few days. When he came back to Paris, he phoned and we arranged to meet for lunch. Over our meal, Jack went on and on.

" 'Claudette,' he said. 'I had such a marvelous time. I mean, it really was just me and the Queen and the Prince. It was so intimate, I couldn't believe it!'

"Jack described the palace, the magnificent grounds, and all the other beautiful sights he'd seen. Then he began to laugh and I asked him what was so funny.

" 'Well, my second evening,' Jack explained, 'there were just four of us for dinner: the Queen, the Prince, the royal family physician, and me. Between the first and second courses, the Queen and her doctor got into an argument—*in Dutch*. They went on and on, until Prince Bernhard finally apologized to me and offered a translation. It seems the Queen wanted to get a motor trailer and go on a camping trip. The doctor explained to her that camping along the public roadside was just not something a Queen could do . . . Juliana became furious and kept bringing up reasons why she should be able to . . . That's how relaxed she felt in front of me,' Jack continued, shaking his head in wonder. 'Isn't that something!'

"Jack was not really awed by where he had been. Oh sure, all of us are awed, in a way, by meeting any member of any royal family. But after Jack got over the initial idea of sleeping at the palace, instead of *playing* it, he slipped into that situation without being rattled. He always had that marvelous inner calm . . .

"Still, I do remember him saying that Queen Juliana's palace was sure a long way from Waukegan! What made Jack so especially dear to all of us is that no matter how far he traveled, no matter how high his own star rose, there was always a part of him, one corner of himself, that was forever back in Waukegan—and he never forgot it!"

CHAPTER THIRTY-FIVE

WHILE JACK was involved with the exciting new facets of his career, at home, his daughter Joan had grown into a young lady. Physically, she had turned into a beauty. Scholastically, she was a brilliant, straight "A" student. With all these assets, she was still a typically adventurous teen-ager. And, as in earlier years, George and Gracie's daughter Sandra was one of her closest friends.

"Sandy Burns and I always had a special relationship because our fathers and mothers were so very close. We didn't go to the same schools when we were little. Sandy went to a parochial school, Marymount, and I went to El Rodeo, the Beverly Hills public grammar school. But we spent a great deal of time together. Often, I'd sleep over at her house on Saturdays, or she would spend the night with me.

"Ronnie Burns is two years younger than Sandy and I. When we were growing up, he and his friends used to get us in all sorts of trouble. Whenever anything happened, and Gracie asked who did it, Ronnie would turn to us and say, 'They did.' He always had such an angelic look, so Gracie believed him. Sandy looked angelic, too, but her mother knew she wasn't!

"When we were ready for high school, both our parents enrolled us at Chadwick, a private school in Rolling Hills, California. By that time, I had skipped a grade and began making friends among my own classmates. Sandy tended to stay with the girls on her grade level. But even though we had different friends, we remained very close.

"During that period," Joan recalls, "Sandy and I were different in other respects, too. She already had a steady boy friend. Her big idea of a fun weekend was to cook for him and then listen to records. To the contrary, I preferred going out to the glamour spots, to nightclubs, like Ciro's or the Mocambo, when my parents let me! Today, I've reversed all that, but in my teens, I loved the excitement of a night on the town.

"One day, during the summer after we graduated, I was at Sandy's house swimming. Her steady, Jim Wilhoite, was there, too, along with a friend of his. George and Gracie were gone for the day, and we were just relaxing, when Sandy and Jim suddenly decided to elope to Las Vegas. They asked us to go along. Jim's buddy and I both said sure. At that stage in life, I was ready for anything!

"We drove to Vegas and Sandy and Jim were married in one of those dumpy little wedding chapels with us as their witnesses. Then it was time for Sandy to call home and break the news. There was a lot of hemming and hawing. Should *she* call George and Gracie *cold* and tell them, or should I call and tell my parents first and let *them* break the news?

"Finally, Sandy decided she had to make the call. It was then we discovered we were all broke. Fortunately, we had seen a sign on the Flamingo Hotel when we first drove in, advertising that Tony Martin was playing there. Sandy and I both knew Tony and his wife, Cyd Charisse, very well. We arrived at the hotel, and went up to the Martins' suite. They must have been asleep . . . We knocked for quite a while before Tony finally came to the door and let us in. After we explained the situation, Sandy placed the call.

"George Burns was absolutely beside himself. In fact, he was furious. Subsequently, we found out that George and Gracie had immediately phoned my parents—who rushed over to console them. Later that day, when I spoke to them, they were equally furious at me for being a party to this 'whole terrible scene.'

"Sandy and Jim Wilhoite had two girls together . . . They were divorced, she remarried, and had two more daughters. In fact, her oldest is already married!

"Today, although our lives have taken different paths, we remain close. In the last twenty years, I've seen Sandy a total of maybe two dozen times, because she lives out of town. Still, there is an unbreakable bond between us. The last time I saw her was at my father's funeral . . .

"I'll never forget something Sandy did. When I married Seth

190

Baker, we went to Maui, Hawaii, for our honeymoon. While I was there, I received a letter. It was the kind of thing I never expected from Sandy. We were both really still such kids. But her letter was very serious. She wished me happiness. She wrote that we'd always be close friends no matter what . . . Then she told me how much she loved me . . .

"As far as my *own* first marriage is concerned," Joan reflected, "it's so hard to explain. I had very frivolously met this man in New York. It was during Christmas vacation of 1953. I was in my junior year at Stanford University. A girl friend of mine was getting married, and I had gone East to be her bridesmaid.

"I met Seth at the wedding. We went out the following night. To be frank, I was swept away with the glamour of the whole situation. That may sound odd coming from my background, where I was constantly exposed to that type of life. But it's quite different —*seeing* things as somebody's child—or *being* grown up and going with a *date* to places like the Stork Club and El Morocco. I was awed by the whole scene.

"At the end of ten days of a whirlwind romance, of being wined and dined, Seth and I decided to get married . . ."

Mary's memories of this momentous occasion in her daughter's life are equally as vivid.

"Jack and I were spending the holidays in Palm Springs," Mary began. "Jack was out playing golf, when the phone rang. It was Joanie, telling me that she was in love and was planning to get married. Quite obviously, the announcement took me by surprise. I told Joan she wasn't to do anything until she talked to her father. A few hours later, when Jack came in, he called New York . . .

" 'Daddy, I'm going to get married . . .'

" 'No, you're not . . . Come home first and let's talk things over,' Jack insisted.

"So," Mary continued, "Joan flew home—engaged to a man she hardly knew. She was so young, still at school, and naturally we discussed the whole situation thoroughly. Above and beyond every other consideration, Jack and I wanted only what would make Joan happy. At first, frankly, neither of us were too thrilled, but she *seemed* to be so in love. Finally, both her father and I

191

agreed, if marriage was what she wanted, she had our blessings . . ."

The decision having been made, Mary entered into the spirit of the occasion in true Benny style.

Joan remembers *everything* in exquisite detail . . .

"Mother and I began planning for the wedding. At that time, I thought a ceremony with fifty or a hundred guests would be an enormous event . . . but things got out of hand. The guests list kept being expanded. Before I turned around, one thousand invitations had been sent! My dress had been ordered from Don Loper. The flowers had been selected. The Crystal Room of the Beverly Hills Hotel had been reserved. *The whole thing became panicky.*

"Seth arrived in California five weeks before the wedding. We hadn't seen each other since our engagement. I took one look and thought: 'What have I done? I don't want to marry this man . . . I hardly know him!'

"We spent a great deal of time together. Three days after his arrival, I decided that not only didn't I know him, I didn't *like* him. Looking back, I recognize how young and naïve I was at nineteen. It didn't occur to me I could just go to my parents and say, 'Please, call the whole thing off.' They already had spent so much money. I kept thinking, 'If I say anything, I'll get killed.' I figured it was easier to go ahead with the marriage—and then get divorced. I was terrified of just saying, 'I can't go through with this.' Besides, we already had received seven hundred presents!

"It was overwhelming. Too much for me to handle. When my wedding day actually arrived, I steeled myself and put on my beautiful gown. I only vividly remember a terrible few moments. As I took Daddy's arm, and we got ready to march down the aisle, my knees suddenly turned to water. But I kept saying to myself, 'You've got to go through with it.'

"Then, going down the aisle, I thought, 'Why can't I turn around and run?' But I put *that* out of my mind pretty fast . . . It was the most terrible experience of my life. We spent our wedding night at the Beverly Hills Hotel . . . and I cried until morning came.

"After our Hawaiian honeymoon, Seth and I moved to New

York. I loved living there. As for our marriage, I regarded every day as making the best of a bad thing. I just decided to enjoy New York. Nine months after we were married, I became pregnant, which meant staying together another nine months . . . When they knew my time was near, my parents came East, along with George and Gracie."

Mary recalls the scene. "We were asleep at our hotel," she began. "Seth called to say he was taking Joanie to the hospital. I woke Jack, and George and Gracie, and we all rushed over to the hospital. By the time we arrived, Joanie's son, Michael, had already been born. It was a tearfully joyous moment for Jack and me . . . He was an enormously proud grandfather . . ."

Six weeks after the birth of her son, Joan came out to California to "show him off." Seth came along, too, but only stayed a few weeks. By then, the young couple had already decided they couldn't make it together. Seth returned to New York, and Joan started divorce proceedings. The marriage had lasted two years.

Subsequently, Joan married successful businessman Buddy Rudolph. He legally adopted Michael, then he and Joan had a child together, Maria. Some years later, he passed away.

"Joan married film producer Robert Blumofe," Mary went on, "and became pregnant with her third child. Once again, the moment we knew she'd gone to the hospital, Jack and I rushed over. As with her first and second children, by the time we got there, the baby had been born . . .

"Just as we arrived, Joanie was being wheeled out of delivery. She opened her eyes, looked up at me, and said, 'Happy birthday, Mom, I gave you a wonderful present . . .' Then she went back to sleep. Indeed, she had given me the *greatest gift*. My grandson Bobby was born on my birthday, June 23. The following year, Joan had her fourth child, a beautiful baby girl, Joanna. She arrived on June 29, which is not only Hickey's birthday, but our mother and father's anniversary as well. Such lovely coincidences!"

CHAPTER THIRTY-SIX

DURING THE SUMMER OF 1956, Jack decided to combine work with pleasure and film four television programs abroad—in London, Paris, Venice, and Rome.

The only regular members of the Benny show who went along were Hickey, Ralph Levy, the director, writers Sam Perrin and George Balzer, and script girl Jeanette Eyman. They left ten days before the Bennys in order to check the facilities at London's Shepperton Studios, and also to make preparations for a live TV show to be done for the British Broadcasting Company.

Many people close to Jack have commented that he was constantly focused in on his career . . . his show. The first question he asked when Hickey went to meet the Bennys at the airport helps to confirm this:

"Jack knew I was a tourist at heart, but instead of asking me about the changing of the guard at Buckingham Palace, or the jewels in the Tower of London, or other historical points of interest, his opening line, after hello was, 'Have you been to the Palladium yet?' *That* was Jack!"

Before they started to film their television program at Shepperton, they did a live show from the Palladium. It was on this occasion that Jack received one of the biggest laughs of his career—again, accidentally. In the script, a member of the cast insulted him. As usual, Jack looked out at the audience . . . glanced back at the character actor . . . then stared out at the audience again. It was at this point—the laughter having just about died down—when a Cockney voice from the balcony called out, 'For God's sakes—*say something!*' Jack broke up. His own reaction was as great as that of the audience. Fortunately, time was not of the essence on the BBC. It was at least fifteen minutes before Jack could continue the show! Later, when someone suggested he put a plant in the audience and use this line again, he refused. Jack knew that the perfect timing—created spontaneously—could never be successfully repeated again—by design.

A similar thing happened several years later, while Jack was appearing for a week of outdoor performances at the Greek Theater in Los Angeles. He was on stage when a low-flying helicopter circled overhead. Jack stopped talking and stared up at the chopper until it finally flew off. Then he looked at the audience and said, "I don't mind planes flying overhead . . . but I hate it when they stop to see the show for nothing!"

The audience reaction was so great that, after the performance, James Doolittle, who produced all the shows from the theater, suggested Jack use the line again during the rest of his engagement. Jack refused.

"Everything is a matter of timing," he said. "It would drive me nuts waiting every night for a helicopter to fly over."

Doolittle said that was no problem. He could make arrangements to rent one . . . But Jack replied, "I won't do the line again, Jimmy—even if you do pay for it!"

"At any rate," Hickey recalls, "after the show for the BBC, we started to film at Shepperton. Because the studio was a forty-five-minute drive, we left our hotel at six every morning in order to be ready to film by nine. The British crew was very meticulous. Before the cameras were set up, it would be ten, at which point everything stopped for a tea break. We worked until noon, then the crew took a two-hour lunch. We would resume shooting and, at precisely four, everything stopped again for high tea.

"This went on for a few days—until I just couldn't take it any longer. Not only were we behind schedule, but it was costing Jack a fortune. I finally shook my head and just walked off the sound stage. Jack saw me leave and followed. When we got outside, he asked what was wrong. I told him the difficulty we were having. Then I said, 'Jack, if Paul Revere had known how slow the British were, he could have walked!'

"The following week, Jack was invited by producer Mike Frankovich to attend a Variety Club luncheon. During the meal, Jack was asked to get up and make a few remarks . . . and he included my Paul Revere line. Everybody thought it was very funny.

But the following morning, when we arrived at the studio, none of the crew was there. They had read what appeared to be Jack's insulting remark in one of the evening newspapers, and refused to work. We had to appeal to Douglas Fairbanks, Jr., for help. Fortunately, he was able to explain that Jack hadn't meant to be critical, and things were smoothed over."

Mary's birthday coincided with the Bennys' stay in London. As always, Jack wanted to do something special for her. He confided in close friends Merle Oberon and Ty Power, who happened to be in London, and together they decided to arrange a surprise party.

Mary remembers that birthday very vividly. "Merle called and said, 'I've got the biggest surprise . . . I've arranged for you and Jack to meet the Queen! Get all dressed . . . Ty Power's going, too . . . We'll pick you and Jack up at the Dorchester . . .' Naturally, I was thrilled. Merle was such a dear friend. The thought that she had gone to all that trouble meant a great deal . . . Seeing Ty, another close friend, was a special bonus.

"I was really excited, and Jack seemed pleased as a kid at my anticipation," Mary continued. "The big night arrived. Right on the dot, Merle and Ty came up to our suite. All the way down in the elevator, Merle kept chattering on about last-minute details and protocol . . .

"When we got down to the lobby, Deborah Kerr was walking by, and I stopped to say hello. But Merle seemed edgy. 'Come on, Mary,' she said, 'we've got to go . . .'

" 'But Merle,' I said, 'I at least have time to say a few words to Deborah . . .'

" 'No, you don't,' Merle insisted. 'Let's go . . .'

"Just then, Ingrid Bergman walked into the lobby, saw us, and came over. Naturally, I stopped to chat with her.

" 'Mary!' Merle said again. 'Come on . . .'

. " 'But Merle, I have time to at least say a few words to Ingrid . . .'

" 'No, you don't, Mary,' Merle said, this time propelling me by the arm, she on one side, Ty on the other. *'You can't keep the Queen waiting!'*

"Merle really meant business! We made our way to the outside of the hotel, then she said we had to walk around the block . . . it was something to do with protocol . . . we had to use a special side entrance in order to meet the car that was taking us to the palace.

"We walked and walked. By this time, I was letting them do the leading. Then Ty opened a side door, and I found myself inside the Dorchester's Grand Ballroom. There was a huge banner stretched clear across the room which said, 'Happy Birthday, Mary' . . . All around me, people began to sing the birthday song.

"Suddenly, I realized what the frantic maneuvering had been about. I'm not an easy person to surprise, and I was really flabbergasted at all the effort and trouble that had gone into planning a big party on such short notice.

"Everywhere I looked, there were friends of mine, including Ingrid Bergman and Deborah Kerr, whom I had been so anxious to talk to in the lobby! There was Noel Coward, Rex Harrison, who was with his wife at the time, Lilli Palmer. Sir Alec Guinness was there . . . as was producer Lew Grade, now Lord Lew Grade of Elstree . . . In fact, every top British star in town was there.

"By the time they wheeled in the huge cake, which had 'Happy Birthday, Doll' written in icing across the top, the evening was already a huge success. After I kissed Jack, I walked over and hugged Ty, then I kissed Merle and said, 'I loved being Queen for a Day—even if I *didn't* wind up at Buckingham Palace!' "

The next stop was Paris, where Maurice Chevalier was to be the guest star. They were very good friends and Mary and Jack spent a lot of time with Chevalier socially. They were his guests for lunch at his home in Marnes-la-Coquette, a lovely suburb outside of Paris.

"One of the highlights of our Paris stay was the dinner Jack hosted at Maxim's just before we left for Venice," Marks recalls. "Mary invited Maurice, Sylvia Fine, Danny Kaye's wife, Freddie Kohlmar, who was producing a film in Paris, and Dr. Paul Emile Seidmann and his wife, Ginette Spanier, the head of Pierre Balmain's, the famous dress designing empire.

"It was a very lavish affair. But Jack, no matter how many

times he had been abroad, could never figure out the rate of exchange . . . nor how much to tip. When they presented him with the dinner check, it was in francs. Jack just sat there staring at the bill, simultaneously pulling a wad of traveler's checks from his pocket. All the guests were aware of Jack's frustration—but, as a gag, no one came to his immediate aid.

"This went on for quite a while, until finally Maurice broke down and told Jack how much he owed. After he had converted his traveler's checks to francs, he began to tip very lavishly. When Jack noticed a man pass our table in a dinner jacket, he thought it was the maître d' and pressed a few hundred francs in his palm. The man stopped for a moment, handed Jack back the money, then walked over and sat down at a nearby table! Everyone laughed—but Jack. Finally, I said, 'Don't forget to leave a tip for the florist . . . After all, he *did* put the centerpiece on the table.' Jack just glowered at me. By that time, he was in no mood for jokes.

"The next morning, just before we left by plane for Venice, a telegram arrived at the George V Hotel. It was from the previous evening's dinner guests, and read: DEAR JACK . . . DON'T FORGET TO TIP THE PILOT!

"We arrived in Venice and took a car to the spot where everything was transferred to a motorboat which would take us across the canal to the island of Lido. We passed St. Mark's Square . . . the Bridge of Sighs . . . Everything was just magnificent.

"It was our first trip to Venice—and we all agreed it was everything we'd heard—and more. As we were crossing the canal, we passed Barbara Hutton's villa just in time to see her step out of her private gondola . . . Finally, we arrived at our hotel, the Excelsior Lido, and got settled in.

"We spent a little over a week filming the show," Hickey went on, "and, in our spare time, there were a great many things to see and do. One night, Jack, Mary, and I, along with Cyd Charisse, who had come with us, headed for the island's gambling club. Cyd's husband, Tony Martin, was finishing up a film in London, and was scheduled to join us when we reached Rome.

"We went inside the casino, which very much resembled the

sporting club in Monaco. Mary and I spotted a group of people around a table, and walked over to see what they were playing. It looked something like *chemin de fer,* the card game. Mary loves to gamble, but when we asked a few people what the game was, everyone was either too busy or else they didn't speak English.

"Mary just can't stand *watching.* She has to gamble, even when she doesn't know what it is she's gambling for. We decided to go into partnership . . . Each of us put up twenty-five dollars and began to play. We decided to put our money down and just let the chips fall where they may, so to speak. To our amazement, we won . . . and won. The croupier kept giving us stacks of lire . . .

"While the other players were standing around the table meticulously making notes in little leather books—I suppose it was some sort of system—Mary and I kept raking in the money. By the time Jack and Cyd joined us, after taking a tour of the casino, Mary and I were ready to pick up our loot and leave. As we walked away, we heard a few people comment: 'Those crazy Americans!' I guess they were right. We had won over six hundred dollars, and we still didn't know what game we had played!

"When we finished filming in Venice, we were to leave by train for Rome. But, unbeknownst to us, the railroads had gone on strike the previous evening. So, at the last moment, it seemed we would be forced to drive. Jack wanted to wait until the rail strike was over, but we had a schedule to meet, and we had already stayed in Venice three days longer than planned.

"Jack didn't want to fly on a charter plane, so there was no alternative. We hired two limousines and prepared to drive to Rome. Suddenly, Jack became very apprehensive. He remembered what his friend producer-director Mervyn LeRoy had told him some years before. In 1950, LeRoy had been in Italy directing *Quo Vadis,* and Jack and Mary had visited him. Mervyn obviously had had some bad experiences, because he admonished Jack, 'Whatever you do, *never* travel any distance in Italy by car.'

"As always, it took Mary to calm Jack down. 'Look, doll face, Cyd and I will take the lead car. If you get into any trouble, have your driver blow his horn, and we'll stop . . . Believe me, *nothing* is going to happen!'

"We loaded the cars with luggage. It was ten o'clock in the morning when we started off on what was to be an eight-hour drive. Jack and I could see Mary and Cyd through the back window of their car. They were engaged in animated conversation. We laughed. They must be talking about clothes!

"Suddenly, going up a steep mountain road, our car developed vapor lock. As soon as we started to stall, Jack yelled to the driver, 'Blow the horn . . . Blow the horn.' But those of you who have traveled through Italy know that is the way they *always* drive over there—*everyone* blows his horn.

"It was obvious, when they kept on going, that Mary's driver hadn't heard us . . . Our car came to a dead stop, and we got out. It was very hot and humid. I've seen Jack mad—but *never* that mad. He kept pounding on the car fender and repeating, 'If Mervyn told me once, he told me a million times, don't drive in Italy!'

"Our driver stopped the first car he spotted—a small Fiat—and went over to talk to the man and woman inside. He came back a few minutes later. There was nothing they could do to help, he said. Even if they did have a rope, their car was too small to tow us.

"Then Jack walked over to the little car, leaned in, and repeated, 'If Mervyn LeRoy told me once, he told me a million times, never travel by car in Italy!' The people didn't recognize Jack. The poor man kept shrugging his shoulders and saying over and over in Italian, 'I don't understand . . .'

"We were really stuck and Jack kept fuming. About forty-five minutes later, we saw Mary's car coming toward us. They had finally realized we weren't behind them, and had doubled back. I started to laugh and suggested to Jack that this adventure would make a great premise for one of our television shows. For one of the rare times in his life, he had *completely* lost his sense of humor!"

Mervyn LeRoy was one of Jack's closest friends. In his own biography, *Take One,* LeRoy related another travel incident which was as typical of Jack's constant concern over his "image" as was his inability to comprehend that the man in the Fiat hadn't understood a word he'd said!

LeRoy, telling an anecdote about a certain trip he and his wife once took, related: "We made a tour of the Orient with Mary and Jack Benny, and visited such places as Japan, Thailand, and Hong Kong . . . Jack had to fly back from Hong Kong on short notice, and was unable to get a first-class booking on the plane. He was very unhappy at the prospect of flying tourist class.

" 'My God, Mervyn,' he said. 'Mary and I *can't* fly tourist. The public thinks I'm cheap now. What will they say if they see me in the tourist section?'

"He did manage to get first class from Honolulu to Los Angeles, but he was in the tourist section—trying to sink low down in his seat so nobody would notice him—from Hong Kong to Honolulu . . ."

"It wasn't until one o'clock the next morning that we finally arrived in Rome," Hickey continued. "Jack and Mary got off at their hotel, the Excelsior, and Cyd and I went on to the Grand, where Tony Martin was already registered. I was exhausted and went right to bed. At 3:30 A.M., my phone rang. It was Jack. The suite they had reserved was still occupied. The people in it had been scheduled to leave by train, but were held up due to the strike. Jack said, 'Please, call your front desk and see if you can get us a suite.'

"This further complication led me to believe even more so that our Venice-to-Rome saga would make a good TV show—but I wasn't going to bring *that* up to Jack again . . ."

Mary also recalled another event of the Bennys' fabulous summer:

"Tony Martin was scheduled to make a benefit appearance in Monte Carlo and, impulsively, we went along. When they found out Jack was coming, they asked if he would appear, too, and naturally, my husband said yes. We had a marvelous time there, and also another opportunity to gamble.

"After the benefit, we were the guests of Aristotle Onassis. He invited us on his yacht for cocktails, then escorted us to his own private gambling casino. Capucine, the French actress, joined us. Once there, Onassis handed Cyd and me a big stack of large, rectangular-shaped chips, and told us to enjoy ourselves.

"We didn't need any encouragement. Both of us kept betting the chips as if they were Monopoly money. Then Capucine came up to us and wondered why we were wagering so much. 'The chips are worth twenty-five dollars each,' she informed us. But it was too late. By the time she came over, Cyd and I each had won several hundred dollars . . . Onassis was a very generous host!"

CHAPTER THIRTY-SEVEN

ON SEPTEMBER 23, 1956, Jack did his first television program after returning from Europe. It was the start of another season— and a most singular event. Alfred Wallenstein, the famous symphony conductor, was the guest star.

On the show, there was much talk about Jack's forthcoming debut as a violin soloist at Carnegie Hall. The dialogue began like this:

REPORTER: Mr. Benny, I know that Carnegie Hall is in serious financial straits . . . But do you honestly feel that your violin playing will save it?

JACK: Well, let me put it this way. When a drowning man is going down for the third time, he doesn't care whether Heifetz or I throw him a rope . . . So, right after the show, I'm leaving for New York, where, on October 2, I'm giving a violin concert in Carnegie Hall accompanied by the New York Philharmonic which will be conducted by Alfred Wallenstein . . . Isn't that right, Wally?

(WALLENSTEIN—A PAINED EXPRESSION ON HIS FACE —NODS)

On Tuesday evening, October 2, 1956, at nine o'clock, the program began. Carnegie Hall was completely packed by the time the seventy members of the New York Philharmonic Symphony Or-

President Harry S. Truman and Jack. (Francis Miller, *Life* magazine, © Time Inc.)

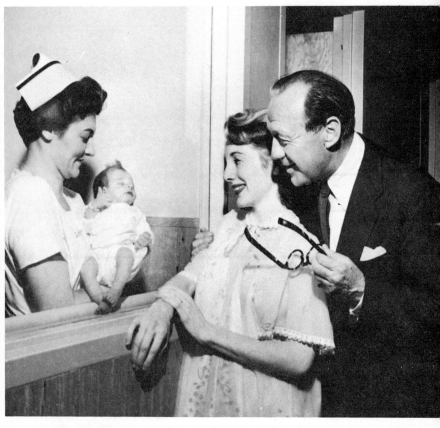

New mother Joan and Jack visit baby Michael, Jack's first grand-child. (Benny Family Personal Collection)

Jack riding in the Waukegan parade, 1959. (Photo courtesy Waukegan *News-Sun*)

Jack in front of his junior high in Waukegan. (Photo courtesy Waukegan *News-Sun*)

Jack dressed up, impersonating Gracie, with George Burns. (Courtesy Las Vegas News Bureau)

Jack and Jimmy Durante. (Leonard McCombe, *Life* magazine,
© Time Inc.)

Jack's two violins, the Stradivarius and the Pressenda, which he willed to the Los Angeles Philharmonic. (Photo by Bud Berman/Benny Family Personal Collection)

Jack, President Lyndon B. Johnson, Hickey Marks in the Oval Office, 196 (Courtesy LBJ Library)

Jack and Marilyn Monroe. (Courtesy CBS)

Jack and Ed Sullivan. (Photo by Walt Davis, courtesy CBS)

chestra took up their instruments and conductor Alfred Wallenstein raised his baton.

After they played the *Roman Carnival Overture* by Berlioz, mezzo-soprano Jennie Tourel sang. Following intermission, the "star" of the evening walked on stage.

He was wearing white tie and tails, and carrying his Stradivarius. After prolonged applause, Jack tucked the fiddle beneath his chin, turned to the orchestra, and said, "Can I have an A, please?" Suddenly, with a mock expression of embarrassment, Benny looked at the audience and shrugged his shoulders—he had neglected to bring his violin bow!

As the bejeweled and bedazzled audience howled, Benny walked off, retrieved his bow, and once more took stage center as the crowd clapped and shouted "Bravo!"

His first selection, *Gypsy Airs* by Sarasate, was an extremely intricate piece. As he progressed, and the music became more difficult, the concertmaster arose and, *unasked,* took over. Jack gave him a withering stare. The musician sat down. As the selection ended, Benny walked over and whispered into Wallenstein's ear. In turn, the conductor whispered into the concertmaster's ear, whereupon the latter slunk offstage—while Jack smiled a know-it-all smirk and, once again, the audience cheered. The fact that, midway in the piece, he had integrated sixteen bars of "Love in Bloom" served only to intensify Jack's air of pride—and the audience's amusement.

Preceding his second selection, Mendelssohn's *Concerto for Violin and Orchestra,* Jack informed his audience that he required sheet music for this tune, and requested a stagehand to provide same, forthwith. A man walked on with the music and placed it on a stand which barely reached Jack's knees. Then, taking the violin from Benny's grasp, the stagehand tuned it . . . and returned it to Jack.

Dripping with confidence, Benny tackled Mendelssohn—this time being aided midway by the *assistant* concertmaster, who was also summarily banished!

Following his solos, Jack did a monologue. It ran about fifteen minutes, after which he took a seat in the concertmaster's chair and joined the orchestra in their concluding number.

Writing in the New York *Times,* the next day, music critic
Harold C. Schonberg commented:

> . . . Mr. Benny is a very funny man and he makes very funny
> music. As for matters of intonation and technique, he was fine; it
> merely was that last night the Philharmonic was unfortunately out
> of time with him.
>
>   But he put on quite a show and made a rather charming speech
> afterward, and two worthy causes benefited—the Committee to
> Save Carnegie Hall and the National Association for Retarded
> Children. Last night, music was not the food of love, but the food
> of laughter, and Mr. Benny dished it out in great, heaping doses.
> Nobody was the loser but Sarasate and Mendelssohn.

During an interview a couple of days later, Jack was still full of
the wonder and awe at the thought of having *really* played Carnegie Hall.

". . . there's nothing as funny as humor against a classy background," he said. "The laughs come from the fact that I'm so
damn highbrow, so haughty and lofty—and so lousy. In other
words, the laughs don't come from my bum playing, but from the
spot I find myself in . . ."

The reporter followed that answer with another question: "But
do you really mean to play your best, Mr. Benny?"

"Seriously, I really do, though it doesn't help," Jack answered.
"Still, why shouldn't I try? Comedy or no comedy, I honestly love
music."

Jack had given the columnist a perfectly straight answer. He *did*
love music and, whenever he played with professional musicians
on a concert stage, he *did* try his best.

Joan Benny Blumofe, commenting recently on Jack's passion
for the violin, recalled a period, many years before, when her father had first resumed playing in earnest:

"I was in my early teens—but reasonably adult—when Daddy
decided to go back to the violin. He started practicing again, and I
was very much a part of that. I had been studying classical music
and piano for years, so he would come to me and ask, 'What records do you have?'

"I'd say, 'Daddy, you should listen to the Milstein and Heifetz recordings of Mendelssohn. There are two *different* inter-pretations.' He would listen, then we would discuss it . . .

"My bedroom was right next to the bathroom where he prac-ticed. I would stop him when I thought he wasn't playing a certain phrase right . . . He would *always listen* to my opinion. That was a wonderful period—the very first time we could *totally* share an experience as equals. Before that, it had always been a father-daughter kind of thing. But when it came to music, he went out of his way to let me know I was actually contributing something to him . . .

"The violin meant so much to Daddy . . . He loved it. But, to be perfectly honest, he didn't exactly play well. Or, let's just say, there are degrees *and degrees* of expertise. The majority of the public, not technically attuned to music, thought Daddy sounded fine. The bulk of his audiences, who loved Daddy as Jack Benny, comic, were actually surprised he played as well as he did. The real musicians respected him for how hard he tried.

"The violin is the most difficult instrument. It's the only one that *doesn't* have built-in indications, like guitars have frets, and a piano has a keyboard—and either you hit a C, or you don't. With the violin, you have to *hear* it in your ears. If your finger is off the string even one sixteenth of an inch, you're in the crack—and therefore, off key. Daddy never realized when he was playing off pitch—and it was *not* something you could just come right out and tell him. Although, at first, I did try! It's interesting that as a child violinist, he was considered a prodigy. But that facility, and perfect pitch, is something you *can lose* over the years if you don't keep working at your instrument.

"When he seriously took up playing again, he shut himself up in the bathroom and practiced for hours every day. Sometimes, he used to drive me up the wall! In desperation, I'd knock on the door. 'Daddy, why don't you *really* practice the scales?' He hated doing that. But once in a while, to please me, he *would* run up and down the notes.

"Then I'd say, 'Daddy, that last note was a little too sharp,' so he'd play it again. Before I had a chance to comment, he'd say, 'Well, *that* time it was perfect . . .'

"It wasn't! I'd say, 'Daddy . . . please, try it once more.' He would, and was *always* the same degree off pitch. But he'd look at me and say, 'Now, Joanie, *that* note was perfect.' I'd just smile—and retreat!

"When he played concerts with the most famous symphony orchestras, they covered for him—made him sound really good. When he did even fairly well, the audience loved it. They were so surprised! When he played badly, everyone thought he was *deliberately* going off key. I attended many such concerts, and got such a kick out of it when people said to me, 'Wasn't he funny? He played off key with a *perfectly straight face!*' I would just nod. I never dared tell anyone Daddy hadn't meant to be off!

"He began every concert by coming out on stage and being funny for a few minutes before he picked up his violin only to discover he had forgotten his bow. He would stare at the audience and they would roar. Immediately, he had established himself as Jack Benny, comedian—everything after that was uphill!"

Among his concert engagements, one of Jack's favorite appearances was the very first "confrontation" between Benny and former President Harry S. Truman, when they appeared together in concert in Kansas City, on March 22, 1958. Weeks before Jack's arrival in Missouri, the two-thousand-five-hundred-seat Municipal Auditorium was sold out. Before Benny had fiddled one note, $55,000 had been raised, wiping out the orchestra's complete deficit.

From the moment the former President met Jack at the airport, the quips began—and continued hot and heavy all during Benny's stay. First, Mr. Truman made it clear that, even though he was a well-known pianist, he *would not* be playing any duets with Jack.

"I'll be m.c., and conduct the orchestra in 'Stars and Stripes Forever,'" the former President said. "After all, we don't want to run the risk of having to return all the money!"

However, during rehearsals, the duo of "Harry and Jack" *was* heard by those privileged to be around the auditorium. On the program, Jack performed *Gypsy Airs* and the first movement of Mendelssohn's concerto. By this time, he had added another selection to his repertoire—*Capriccio Espagnol* by Rimsky-Korsakov. All during that number, he kept shouting to the conductor, "Not so fast—not so fast!"

Once again, the audience alternated between laughter and shouts of "Bravo"—and, when it was over, not one person asked for his money back!

When Jack returned to Hollywood, there was a letter waiting for him:

HARRY S. TRUMAN
Independence, Missouri
March 31, 1958

Dear Jack:

You do not know how very much Mrs. Truman and I appreciated your letter of the 25th. Everyone in Kansas City was pleased with your contribution in behalf of our orchestra.

Mrs. Truman and I enjoyed having you at the house but regretted that the lack of a cook kept us from giving you luncheon there.

I hope I will never miss an opportunity to see you whenever I am in Los Angeles, and I expect you to let me know in advance if you plan to be in this neighborhood again.

Sincerely yours,
Harry S. Truman

What Jack started in 1956 with his debut at Carnegie Hall became a most important part of his life for the next eighteen years. During that span of time, he raised close to $6 million for the benefit of musicians' pension funds, as well as singlehandedly "rescuing" several symphonies from going under because of financial problems.

The violin, which as a boy he played well but hated to practice, became in his later years a constant source of joy . . . a special therapy for him. Once he had reached the age when no one forced him to practice, he began, on his own, working every day, playing for hours—the most difficult pieces.

Jack appeared as soloist with nearly every major symphony orchestra in America and Canada, as well as abroad. Among his performances were those with: the New York Philharmonic, the National Symphony of Washington, the New Orleans Philharmonic, the Denver Symphony, the Honolulu Symphony, the Chicago Symphony, and the San Francisco Symphony. Two of the orchestras which Jack especially enjoyed playing with were the

Los Angeles Philharmonic and the Israel Philharmonic—both conducted by Zubin Mehta.

Mehta, known the world over for his brilliant musical interpretations, is currently in his fifteenth season with the Los Angeles Philharmonic. He will become musical director of the New York Philharmonic in 1978. In addition to his concert duties in Los Angeles, he is musical director of the Israel Philharmonic and travels between California and Israel several times each year.

Between Mehta and Benny an extraordinary mutual admiration society existed. Mehta recently recalled, with deep affection, their relationship:

"Many people have asked me how good a musician Jack really was. First, let me say I was one of those who *did not* know—until the last years of his life—Jack's real age. When I found out, and realized he could play *that* much, I was astounded!

"He wasn't just doing simple pieces. He was playing difficult violin concertos. He would play them a little slower . . . and they would be slightly out of tune . . . But for a man of his age to have the *physical dexterity,* the courage to even *attempt* those pieces was quite something. Especially for someone who hadn't touched a violin seriously for long periods in his life—not until he was already over fifty. I only knew him the last ten years of his life. He was already over seventy. But when we met, I just assumed he was in his early sixties. He *never* looked older than that to me.

"When Jack played—in his own unique style—he did very well . . . My wife Nancy [Kovack] and I observed, and would laugh *quietly* about the fact that, during his later years, when he performed with every major orchestra in the United States—*he really thought he was appearing with those orchestras*. He would talk to us privately about his 'concert engagements'—with absolutely no intention of being humorous. It became like a second career for him.

"Jack was Walter Mitty playing the symphony circuit. He came to *believe* he was a legitimate performer in the concert world. He would say, with a straight face, 'Last week, I played a concert with Lenny Bernstein . . . Next month, I'm appearing with Eugene Ormandy . . .' Then he would go on and tell us about his most recent concert experiences. He never joked about his music.

But he *did* keep repeating one regret . . . 'If only I could bear down . . .'

"You see, his arm *was* a little weak. Whenever he heard those incredible orchestral sounds behind him—and he *couldn't* produce a sound to match them—it was frustrating for him. I think he was secretly angry with himself because he hadn't kept up playing all his life. A really great violinist is capable of making the sound of one hundred people—without a mike . . . So Jack was obsessed with his bow arm. He was always talking about it . . . saying how sorry he was that he had come to a time in life when he couldn't bear down.

"In addition to playing, Jack was a completely dedicated music fan. Whenever he was free, he would come to our rehearsals at the Music Center. He loved to follow 'his fellow violinists around,' especially Isaac Stern, who was Jack's unofficial concert booker, Pinchas 'Pinky' Zukerman, and Itzhak Perlman. Even when I'd call and tell him a new young fiddle player was joining our symphony, he'd come right down, listen to him, and go into raves.

"Jack, personally, favored romantic concertos. He didn't go much for modern music. But he loved being around the orchestra so much, he'd sit in on rehearsals, no matter what we were playing. Naturally, his favorite musicians were the violinists. He would take them all out for a bite to eat. He was not *the* Jack Benny when he came to visit us—he was just Jack, the music fan . . .

"Once, he came to the Music Center to watch us rehearse, then drove back home with me. I had a very short time to get ready for our evening performance. Jack came upstairs and we continued to talk as I got ready. He was absolutely amazed to see me shave with *all my clothes on*. 'How do you live at this pace?' he asked, not realizing that his own life was equally as fast-paced!

"Jack and I were together on many occasions . . . In Montreal, we both appeared in 1967 at the Expo. I was doing a number of performances, and Jack came to see me conduct the opera *Otello*. It was obviously a little too long for his tastes. Afterward, I took him to get a bite at Ben's, a big delicatessen. We ordered, then Jack leaned over and said something that absolutely sends shivers up the spine of any serious musician . . .

" 'Couldn't you make a few *cuts* in the opera?"

"In 1972, Jack came to Israel to play with their symphony orchestra. The whole trip was quite a rare experience . . . and, for Jack, a little bit of a shock. When he walked down the street, most people didn't know him! In English-speaking countries—Canada, England, Australia—where they had heard him for years on radio and television, he was a household word. But as soon as he stepped out of that sphere, not being as much in the movies as some of his other colleagues, nobody knew him.

"Where we stayed, at the Tel Aviv Hilton, which is only occupied by American tourists, he couldn't even get out of the elevator without being mobbed. For him, the Hilton lobby was the same as being in Beverly Hills, or New York. But when he left the hotel, it was as if he were incognito. After so many years of stardom, it was a strange sensation for him, and he kept mentioning it. He had never really experienced it to quite the same extent before. Suddenly, to be almost anonymous—it was incomprehensible . . .

"Once, he went for a walk alone on Dizengoff Street, which is Tel Aviv's main boulevard. When he came back to the hotel, he said, 'I never had any idea what it was like—*just being another tourist.*'

"Because he *was* this great star, and because I knew very few Israelis—except those educated abroad—would recognize him, I had made doubly sure, before his arrival, that we built up his concert with enormous publicity. I also insisted that a good portion of the audience be American tourists because, on the whole, Israelites don't really quite understand American humor. Consequently, we sold tickets to all the people at the Hilton—which wasn't difficult. When they found out 'their Jack Benny' was going to appear, they grabbed for the tickets.

"The Israeli orchestra took to him immediately—it was the same way wherever he played. A lot of the fiddle players in the Israel Philharmonic were trained in America, so they knew him well. But none of the musicians took Jack, or his efforts, to be those of a comic. They could see how serious he was about his playing.

"The night of our concert, the Mann Auditorium was packed—and Jack had them rolling in the aisles. In addition to *his* countrymen, there *were* many native Israelis and immigrants in the audience. Even though they *couldn't* understand English, and did not really know of Jack's fame, his humorous manner and sincere effort to play the fiddle charmed and enchanted them.

"While we were in Israel, I drove Jack to Caesarea, overlooking the Mediterranean Sea, where I play concerts in the summer. I explained that the ruins of the outdoor theater remained from Roman times, while other relics were from the Byzantine period. At first, he didn't connect the continuity of it all. Once he understood the chronological sequence, that one area was two thousand years old, while another part came four hundred years later, and so forth, he was thrilled like a little boy suddenly discovering the world. He said, 'You know, I've spent so much of my life going from the studio to home to my office. I've missed out on so much . . .' He was very humble about things he didn't know . . .

"Afterward, Jack went alone to meet Golda Meir . . . and to touch the Wailing Wall in Jerusalem. He found both experiences very moving . . . Jack was the simplest, kindest person, not possessed of the super-ego you associate with Hollywood celebrities of his caliber. He had such a positive attitude all the time. Everything he said and did and felt about the world was an expression of joy . . .

"I was scheduled to be a guest star, along with the Gregory Pecks, on Jack's 'Third Farewell Special.' We were due to go into rehearsals early in January 1975, and to tape the show on the tenth, eleventh, and twelfth. But before that, I had a commitment to fill in Israel. However, during the first weeks in December, Jack and I talked by phone frequently.

"He personally wanted to discuss the music I would play . . . He asked how many musicians I needed . . . We even discussed my fee. Jack was so eager about doing the special, and he seemed happy handling the details himself . . .

"We spoke together the day before I flew to Israel for the week of Christmas to conduct Handel's *Messiah*. It was the first time it had ever been performed in Israel, and we played to packed houses. After a performance, I was driving back from the Auditorium when I heard a BBC bulletin that Jack had passed away . . ."

CHAPTER THIRTY-EIGHT

DURING THE THIRD WEEK in June 1957 Jack Benny set out to conquer yet another facet of show business—Las Vegas. For years, he had been resisting gigantic financial offers to make his club debut playing the desert gambling resort. Actually, once or twice, he had been tempted. But it was Mary who felt that the "environment" might not be the most ideal place for him to perform.

"Then," Mary explained, "Noel Coward came from England and made a smashing debut in Las Vegas. It was at that time I told Jack to seriously consider the offers he had received. I figured if it was classy enough for Noel, it was good enough for Jack!"

In April of that year, once Jack's television show had gone off for the season, he and his writers concentrated on putting together an act. As usual, Benny was the consummate performer, unwilling to play Vegas unless he could present a smash "package." After weeks of preparation, Jack opened at the Flamingo Hotel.

Playing Las Vegas was, and still is, a very special challenge for the performer. While thousands of people flock there daily, unless an entertainer is top drawer, he comes out second best in competition with the gaming tables. Jack, acutely aware of this, found himself somewhat nervous during the early days of rehearsal.

In radio and television, his shows came into people's homes—and were listened to and watched by millions. In films, people plunked down their money at box offices and went into theaters because they *wanted* to see the particular film and stage show. Concerts were attended by people who *had paid* for their tickets in advance. But Las Vegas—that was a whole new ball game! Especially for Jack Benny, whose reputation for good taste and "clean humor" was already legendary.

Could he make it? That was the key question—and it wasn't

too long before he found out. His first two shows played to packed houses. For the entire three weeks of his engagement, literally thousands were turned away. Jack's "package" offered complete entertainment. Those who came out of devotion to a comic they'd grown up with found themselves applauding and shouting "Bravo" until their voices were hoarse.

On Monday, June 24, the "trade reviews" came out. Both were unanimous raves, the likes of which very few stars ever see.

Daily Variety said:

Jack Benny, a talking fiddle player, has been around for some years, but this is his first time, by his own claim, and to anybody's knowledge, as an entertainer in a so-called nightclub. To nobody's surprise, except possibly his own, he's as glove-fit for the bistro medium as he has been everywhere else in show business.

To put it simply, the past master of the long take and the milked laugh is a smash in this large supper room, no cinch for a polite comedian in view of the fact that there are more people sitting to the sides of the stage than there are in front . . . The audience was very receptive to his two shows opening night (June 20) . . . it was a capacity crowd which seemed as though it were prepared to laugh at Benny even if he took out his handkerchief . . .

The Hollywood Reporter, echoing the same sentiments, went on to analyze his act, as *Variety* had:

. . . Jack Benny's appearance . . . was a glistening and distinguished and memorable moment in the history of the contemporary American theatre . . . Mr. Benny has a flawless triumph . . . It was an evening in which every moment was a highlight . . .

In essence, what Jack did was not only to have a monologue of superior quality, but also to surround himself with other extraordinary performers. The show began with the Flamingo Girls, all long-stemmed beauties, exquisitely gowned, appearing in a spectacular production number.

They were followed by dancers Chiquita and Johnson, acrobatic specialists capable of performing breathtaking, intricate maneuvers.

Next came talented and lovely Giselle MacKenzie, then a popular star on television, who sang like a bird and played the violin like a virtuoso. After Giselle's numbers, Jack came on and delivered such fresh and funny material, the crowd was in a state of continuous laughter.

". . . I'm proud to play here," he told the audience. "After all, if it's good enough for Noel Coward, it's good enough for me . . . Besides, I love to gamble like Nick the Greek. Only they call me Jack the Welsher. I stayed up all night gambling until eight in the morning. I only lost four dollars, but I saved the price of a hotel room . . ."

The most hilarious part of the show came when Jack went off stage, only to return in tattered trousers and a straw hat, clutching his fiddle. Accompanying him was an equally ragged bunch, the "Beverly Hillbillys." Surrounded by five male hayseeds and a deadpan eleven-year-old, Jack began with "You Are My Sunshine," and had the crowd rolling in the aisles. The little girl, whom Jack introduced specially, was Valerie Scott, the daughter of Jack's secretary, Bert, making her debut. She was terrific.

Hank Greenspun, editor of the *Las Vegas Sun,* a well-known writer who could be a tough critic when necessary, went into absolute raves:

> . . . Jack Benny played the Palace—in vaudeville, radio, television, and almost every medium of show business.
>
> Jack Benny helped make the Palace.
>
> Jack Benny chose Las Vegas for his nightclub debut.
>
> It isn't necessary for Mr. Benny to sit up half the night waiting anxiously for local critics to write of his success.
>
> After his performance opening night, all the critics could write is: "Jack Benny opened at the Flamingo Hotel last night. Las Vegas is a success."
>
> Las Vegas has had one new entertainment high after another.
>
> But where do you go after you reach the top? After Jack Benny, what next?

Meanwhile, back in Hollywood, the Television Academy obviously agreed Benny *was* tops. His show was voted the best comedy series of 1958, bringing an Emmy to Producer Hilliard Marks. Four additional Emmys were won by Benny writers Sam Perrin, George Balzer, Hal Goldman, and Al Gordon.

CHAPTER THIRTY-NINE

IN JUNE OF 1959, Benny's last program before the summer break originated from New York.

"Jack and I were at the Sherry-Netherland Hotel," Mary recalls, "when Hickey came over to talk to us about leaving the show. We had discussed this before . . . I knew exactly how my brother felt. He had been working with Jack for twenty-one years, first as a writer, then as a producer. All during this period, he had been investing in real estate. He now felt as if he wanted to pursue that full time.

"Jack was reluctant to see him go. But he understood completely, and told Hickey he could always return to the show, as either his producer, or as one of the writers . . . and he did return, as a writer, in 1965.

"For the next two seasons, Seymour Berns became Jack's producer-director. Then our close friend, Freddie de Cordova, who is now producing Johnny Carson's show, took over . . ."

There are few people in Hollywood who were as close to Jack, both personally and professionally, as de Cordova. His memories span a thirty-eight-year period.

"For me, careerwise, every step along the way, Jack and Mary were involved," he began. "That even goes for my association now with Johnny—I'm in my seventh year. My first meeting with Carson came about when I did some specials with Jack in which Carson was the guest star. It was directly due to my relationship with Johnny from the Benny shows which gave Carson the belief I might be the right person to handle his program . . . that opened this great opportunity for me.

"I originally met the Bennys in 1936, while I was still in New York, working as stage manager for a show called *High Kickers*. Mary had come into town first, and we had been introduced by mutual friends. One evening, after my show, I joined Mary and a group at the El Morocco nightclub. A few hours later, Jack arrived in town, and came over to join us.

"It was really a thrill meeting him. As far back as I go, he was already a superstar. When he walked in that night, he was as debonair, charming, and delightful as I imagined him to be.

"Our friendship began that first evening and, over the years, we kept in touch. I moved to Hollywood in 1943, and went to work at Warner Brothers as a dialogue director, later as a director of films. One of the first things I did when I came here was to call Mary. I think I had been pinpointing my arrival as much on Jack and Mary as I had been in terms of a career . . .

"Almost immediately, the Bennys took me into their social life —their house was the *palace* of Beverly Hills—which meant the beginning of my meeting everybody in Hollywood. Although Mary was the social boss of their lives, it was Jack who first suggested 'we have Freddie around.' Because Jack included me, a comparatively unknown newcomer, I was automatically treated as nicely by his friends as he treated me. This meant I had entree into everything going on in town—which was very unusual. I couldn't do *anything* for him, while he was number one in everything!

"We did not work together until after I left motion pictures and got involved with television—because of Jack and Mary. In 1953, they talked to George and Gracie about me. Ralph Levy was leaving their show and, at the Bennys' suggestion, I replaced him as Burns' director—a job which became the springboard for whatever success I've subsequently had.

"Mary and Jack could always send you in to see somebody with authority. Nobody took their advice lightly . . . Eventually, I went to work for Jack. Once again, I replaced Ralph Levy, who had been the Bennys' director.

"At that time, I was producing and directing 'The George Gobel Show,' which ran opposite Benny on alternate weeks. Jack was on NBC, Gobel was on CBS. In 1960, when Jack's show was picked up, and Gobel's wasn't, Mary asked me if I would like to produce and direct Jack's show. It was a fantastic offer which began my seven years of day-in, day-out association with Jack and Mary . . .

"The longer I knew Jack, the more his uniqueness amazed me. Personally, he was the epitome of a major star for whom—in some respects—life always remained a pleasant, enjoyable mystery. He *knew* he was a big star, but he didn't act like any other celebrity I've ever known. He appreciated things *more* than others. He was always *more* surprised. He was *happier* at someone else's success. Somehow, he managed to retain a kind of boyish, naïve enthusiasm, and a special joy for day-by-day living.

"When it came to his career, however, he was as articulate, demanding, and as aware of what was going on as anybody I've ever met. He was never rude or crude, never mean or difficult. Professionally, he just wanted the very best he could get. People always said Jack was a great editor, that he instinctively seemed to know what was best for him and his show. That's true, but also *oversimplified*.

"Jack worked very hard to make what he did seem so casual and spontaneous. In truth, he was enormously concerned, *line by line,* with whatever he did. He had an ear for a wrong sentence, a bad reading, an off character. And, while it was true that Jack was perpetually generous in seeing to it other people got the laughs when they worked with him, that *wasn't* Jack being darling, that was his *professional evaluation* of what worked best for him . . .

"When we were together, I was able to separate business from our personal friendship. Whenever I walked into Jack's office, he and I were there to work. He expected *all* of his people to work hard, too. At the same time, he was more grateful to the cast and crew surrounding him. He never failed to thank us . . . unlike many other stars who merely accept things and just walk away.

"Jack's show had to be well organized. His material had to be good. When I directed him, I needed a *valid* reason for asking him to stand a certain place . . . or to move over. If you were stalling—if you hadn't done your homework—you always knew that *Jack knew*. At work, he often had an impatience with people who weren't trying their best. He knew what he wanted. If he got less, he was displeased.

"I'll give you a perfect example. Mary and Jack had gone to

Palm Springs for a few days of rest, but Jack had taken along that week's script to read. After going over it, he was very unhappy. He called Hickey and me and told us to come down to the Springs to work on the show with him. He felt he had not been given first-rate material, and he was upset.

"It was *not* to be a social weekend. We were to sit with him and listen to what he thought was wrong. We were to take his ideas, evaluate them, and fix that script—or he wasn't going to do it. Jack was very capable of saying, 'If this isn't right, I'm not doing the show.' It was not a petulant, big star act. He simply balked at appearing before the public unless he could do as good a show as possible.

"Sure, Jack was interested in ratings. All stars are. But for him, the key was *not* whether a show was highly rated, but whether the program was good in *his* eyes and among those whose opinions he highly respected, especially Mary.

"Jack demanded a show presented intelligently, as well as humorously, even absurdly, if it were skillfully done. A joke, even if it got a lot of laughs in rehearsal, but didn't belong in the context of the show, was the first thing to be thrown out.

"That weekend, the three of us completely rewrote the script, and Jack finally said, 'That's it. *Now* we have a show.' Then he turned to Mary and asked her to look over what we had rewritten. She read it and agreed. When we brought the script back to town, the other writers weren't too pleased. But Jack said, 'I'm happy, and that's the way it's going to be!' He could get very firm. He wasn't vitriolic or nasty. But we were working for a star who definitely was the boss!

"Away from work, he was as undemanding a person as I've ever known. Still, Jack always knew if and when anyone treated him in a cavalier fashion. On the other hand, you *didn't* pick on Jack . . . And no one ignored him. He often said the only great thing about being a star was you didn't have to stand in line at the airport . . . Yet, he never threw his weight around. He took life in stride. He was remarkably complacent about things. When we traveled, if one suite was better or larger than the other, he would always ask, 'Which one would you prefer?' He always gave *you* the choice. As a result, those of us he was with invariably saw to it that *he* wound up with the best. You couldn't help it, he was so dear about things.

"I'm not particularly a naïve person, and, in *my* eyes, Jack and Mary were the most in love couple I ever knew. Together, they were true romantics. They *thought* in terms of each other. *Saw* in terms of each other. When he called her 'doll,' and she called him 'doll face,' those were not mere words. They lived their love for each other constantly.

"If Jack was away from Mary, he would call home maybe five times a day, either with something to say, or *nothing* more than, 'Hello, doll . . . How are you? I just had lunch . . .'

"Invariably, Mary, who has a wonderful sense of humor, would reply, 'You called me from Australia (or Canada, or New York) just to tell me you had lunch?'

"Jack would break up at that. He found her enormously amusing, one of the funniest, most perceptive women he'd ever known. He believed that, in Mary, he had just about the number-one woman in the world.

"I never saw that attitude vary. I never saw Jack lose his intensity of admiration for Mary. He always respected her professional opinions, and trusted in her talent for *picking* talent. In fact, his belief in her evaluation of just about anything in the world was absolute. She was, far and away, businesswise and socially, the outstanding arbiter of Jack's feelings. That never changed or diminished.

"There were so many little, special things Jack did out of his love for Mary. For instance, she had acquired this large collection of open-mouthed frogs which were in both their homes in Beverly Hills and Palm Springs. Some of them were enormously expensive, others not so. But over the years, those open-mouths were the recipients of lots of money and a great many gifts—all of which Jack would secretly leave for Mary to find.

"He would see something he thought Mary would like. He'd buy it, have it wrapped, and quietly place it in some frog's mouth. Or, before he went out to play golf, he would reach in his pocket, pull out a twenty- or a hundred-dollar bill, and put it in one of the frogs. Sometimes, days would go by before Mary passed the *right* frog and saw her surprise present. Jack always loved being there whenever Mary discovered her latest love gift. He was like a child in the way he adored giving her pleasure . . .

"Jack was a ladies' man. I first noticed it when I came to California with my mother—and Jack went out of his way to be darling to her. It wasn't a one-time thing. For as long as she lived, my mother could count on special attention from Jack . . .

"But his way with women went much further than that. Jack was an enormously complimentary man around women. It wasn't bullshit either. He would *really* notice, for instance, what my wife Janet wore. He liked her very much. In all fairness, if Jack wasn't mad about you, he didn't spend a lot of time with you. He had too many other places to be.

"But Jack adored Janet. He thought she was 'a little Mary.' Both were demanding, perceptive, had grand taste, etc. Whenever he saw Janet looking particularly pretty, maybe a day or two would go by until he would see her again, then he'd say, 'That was a lovely blue outfit you were wearing . . .' If Jack had asked *me* what color my wife had worn a few days before, I wouldn't have known.

"Women adored him. Men adored him, too. I know it sounds incongruous—not the adoration, but the fact that, at the same time, he was also a man who *never* knew where the buttons were to put on the heat in his house—and he lived there for twenty-five years! He ate dinner a thousand times at his dining room table and *never* missed the chandelier hanging overhead—until eight years *after* it had been removed. Yet this very preoccupied man could remember, down to the last detail, if my wife wore a particular necklace with a certain outfit . . . or if she had been dressed in pink the week before!

"Whenever Jack went to a party, he was perfectly groomed, wearing a simple-styled but elegant suit. Being very good-looking, he was completely charming and captivating. I don't know whether much has ever been said about how terribly attractive he was to women. They all considered him handsome. Not pushy or aggressive, but enormously charming. Women were enchanted by him—and I'm talking about some of the great beauties of the world like Ann Sheridan, Barbara Stanwyck, Irene Dunne, Claudette Colbert, Marilyn Monroe. Women who were themselves much fawned over. If there was a social gathering, and Mary wasn't feeling well but insisted Jack go, he would invariably escort one of these women, and they loved it!

"Jack was, quite simply, a ladies' man without making it a business. He was attentive. Willing to sit and talk with women. At some Hollywood parties, the minute you arrived, the men and women would separate. Jack noticed that and, frequently, he'd say, 'Well, I've had enough of this . . . I'm going over to talk to the *pretty people* . . .'

"Then he would go and talk with the ladies—and *really* be interested in what they had to say. That was an underrated facet of Jack's personality. He actually enjoyed being with the ladies. It was never an effort for him . . . As a man, he was an absolute delight.

"I always saw a great deal of him at work, as well as in the evenings. Every day, we talked at length over the phone. *That* was another facet of Jack's. Personally, if something pleased him, he couldn't wait to get on the phone and share whatever it was with his friends. He was just unbelievable in his goodness.

"Jack had a quaint, darling wit. His favorite saying was: 'Kiss my ass . . .' which represented the naughty-boy quality in him. He never really talked dirty, either at home or out with the boys.

"I have a big barrel that came from Jurgenson's Gift Shop in Beverly Hills which has a very special place in my home. Originally, it had been filled with liquor, plus all sorts of imported canned goods, fruit and cheeses. On the outside, there is a gold plaque which reads: 'Kiss my Ass.' It was a Christmas present Jack sent me . . .

"If you're lucky, maybe once or twice in a lifetime a person has a job that, if you could afford to, you'd gladly *pay* them, because it's such fun. Well, that's the way I felt about working for Jack. In every sense, he was such a very special person . . ."

CHAPTER FORTY

JACK WAS NEVER a gambler. Early on in his career, he and Phil Baker did go out once in a while and play cards or shoot dice. But from the time he first started playing Las Vegas and Lake Tahoe, he had a philosophy which made a lot of sense.

"Entertainers who play Vegas shouldn't gamble," Jack said. "Let's say the guy is making a thousand dollars a week. One day, he walks over to the crap table and gets lucky. In five minutes, he wins a thousand dollars. He says to himself, 'Jesus, I have to work a whole week for a thousand bucks and here I've won it in only a few minutes' . . . On the other hand, if the entertainer *loses* a thousand, with the income tax he has to pay, he would need to work maybe fifteen weeks to earn back a thousand he could *keep* . . ."

"In some ways, Jack *was* very practical," Hickey Marks said. "But he *did* have a weakness—he loved to play slot machines. Somehow, he didn't consider *that* gambling.

"One evening, when he was working at the Sahara Hotel in Vegas, he came walking into the dressing room just before show time. I took one look at him and panicked. He was all bent over . . .

" 'Jack, my God, what's wrong with you?'

" 'Nothing,' he grinned.

" 'Well, why are you walking like *that?* You're all hunched over like an old Jew . . .'

"His smile widened. 'I just hit *twelve* jackpots!'

"Both coat pockets were loaded with half dollars. After the first show, he changed his clothes and was sitting in his dressing room. When I walked in, I saw him carefully counting his fifty-cent pieces. My opening line was, 'Honest to God, Jack, I haven't taken *even one* from you.'

"We used a similar situation later on a television show. There was a scene where a telegram arrived. Rochester went into Jack's room, found his trousers, removed a quarter, and gave the Western Union boy a tip. Minutes later, Jack walked into the room to change his clothes. He picked up his trousers, weighed them, then said, 'Rochester, who took twenty-five cents out of my pants?'

"Most often, Jack played the half-dollar machines. At Harrah's, the owners loved to humor him. Whenever the staff saw Jack heading for the slots, one of them would casually saunter over 'to watch.' Jack would become so involved, he never noticed someone standing *behind* the machine triggering the back of it so he couldn't lose!

"Eventually, as a gag, the hotel brought in a special machine which only took pennies. Whenever Jack was appearing there, they would wheel out the penny slot, put a rope up around it, and hang a sign on it: For Jack Benny's Use Only."

The mention of Harrah's leads to yet another example of Jack's generosity to fellow performers. In 1963, Benny flew to Australia to appear in both Melbourne and Sydney. While he was in the latter city, he went to see a young performer he had heard about.

At that time, Wayne Newton was a talented twenty-one-year-old, who sang and played various musical instruments, including the fiddle. He already had scored a couple of hits on Capitol, his two best-known records being "Danke Schoen" and "Red Roses for a Blue Lady." But at this point, he had yet to make it really big.

Recently, Wayne talked with deep emotion about the impact Jack had on his life:

"When we first met, in Sydney, I was playing a small club, the Chevron Hilton. Mr. Benny heard about our show and came to see it. Then he invited us to see his show. Afterward, we went backstage and he just said straight out, 'Why don't we work together?'

"Naturally, I said I'd love to. He told me he was playing Harrah's early in 1964, and wanted me to be his opening act.

"I explained that I already had played Harrah's *lounge* on and off for several years, and that, as much as I wanted a chance to play the main room, I had been *turned down* by everybody in the

223

state. I was considered a lounge act—not important enough for the main room . . .

"From an entertainer's point of view, the difference between working the lounge and headlining the main room is the difference between starring in a good-quality low-budget film as opposed to being the lead in a fifteen-million-dollar extravaganza. Even a low-budget star is expected to perform well. But he's *not* considered to have the drawing power of a performer whose name on a marquee *automatically* brings people to the box office.

"Only the biggest stars are booked into main rooms, and they are given the right to select their opening acts. Shows run about an hour and a half, with the opening acts doing twenty to twenty-five minutes before the top star appears. Normally, all performers do two shows each night . . .

"When I told Mr. Benny the truth about my own situation, he said, 'Look, it's *my* package. I'll do the show the way I want to . . .'

"When Harrah's found out Jack was bringing me, they screamed. But he said, 'Either you take the kid or you don't accept me . . .' I wound up playing Harrah's three times as Jack's supporting act. The fourth time, I went in alone—*as the headliner.*

"It's funny . . . I have and had such a great deal of respect for him, I could never bring myself to call him by his first name. After four years of working together, I finally came up with a compromise. It came about one day when we passed each other in Harrah's parking lot. I said, 'Hello, Mr. Benny . . .'

"He said, 'Hello, schmuck!'

"I was still in shock when he walked up to me, his blue eyes sparkling, and said, 'Listen, Wayne, if I can call you schmuck, you can call me Jack!'

"It was then I gave in—and called him *Uncle Jack.*

"I've always credited him with 'discovering me' once I'd reached that point in my career where those in charge of hiring talent felt I had gone as far as I could go. But Uncle Jack never wanted any credit. He said, 'Wayne, if I hadn't given your career a boost, someone else would have. There was just no stopping you.' I thank God I never had to find out if that was true or not!"

Mary remembers this period very well:

"Jack called me from Sydney, and told me he had just come from listening to a young boy appearing in a club down there. I rarely remember Jack being so enthusiastic about a talent. Since Jack was *always* praising other artists, I could tell he was exceptionally excited about Wayne.

"He raved on and on, then said, 'Doll, I've asked him to appear with me when I go into Harrah's. We'll be sensational together . . .'

"What Jack wanted, he got—even though the people at Harrah's weren't too thrilled at first about Wayne being on the bill . . .

"It's funny, thinking back to that incident. Today Wayne has a multi-million-dollar contract with the Hughes' Hotels Summa Corporation. He plays Las Vegas *forty weeks* a year as a headliner. No other star in the business has ever accomplished this feat. But originally Jack had to fight to get him on the bill!"

Newton credits Mary for her help in his career too.

"I was much heavier when I first went with Uncle Jack. Then, one night, I walked into his dressing room while Mary was there. She said, 'Wayne, when are you going to lose weight? It doesn't look good. It's not healthy for you . . .'

"Uncle Jack interrupted. 'Ah, Mary, leave the kid alone . . .'

" 'No, Jack, what's right is right . . . Wayne *is* too heavy.'

"So I took off *one hundred pounds.* It was Mary who gave me the incentive. After I lost the weight, she advised me about what clothes to buy. I learned, early on, how much respect Uncle Jack had for her opinions. How he listened to her. The last time we played the Tropicana together, Jack and I were sitting in his dressing room when Mary came in. She looked at him and said, 'Jack, *you're sitting in your stage pants . . .'*

"There must have been twenty people in the room, but he just smiled and said, 'You are so right, doll!' And he took his pants off!

"He had the most fantastic ability to concentrate. Some people say he was continually preoccupied, but I call it having *tunnel vi-*

sion about his performance. To me, that means being intensely involved in trying to work out something new, or in wondering why something he had tried hadn't worked in the way he thought it would. Jack was a very special kind of perfectionist. When we met, he had already been a top star for close to forty years. Still, he never tapered off in his desire to work hard at being the very best. He never rested on his laurels . . . *That's part* of what made him so extraordinary!

"Uncle Jack was a totally decent, nice man. I never remember seeing him angry . . . and I was with him at times when people did things to him that made me shudder. Once, we were together in a restaurant while on the road. Jack had invited the whole cast —there must have been thirteen of us—to be his guests for breakfast. Suddenly, this stranger walked up to our table, shoved his check in Uncle Jack's face, and said, 'You're so cheap . . . I'd like to know one time if you'd ever pick up some one else's bill . . .'

"Mr. Benny just took the check out of his hand and said, 'Thank you . . .' The guy left in total shock.

"I was present another time in Las Vegas when a woman came up to him and asked: 'Are you Jack Benny?'

"He said, 'Yes, ma'am . . .'

"Then she said, 'Well, good luck, *anyway!*'

"Whenever I'm asked what my most embarrassing moment on stage was, I always say it happened the night I was appearing with Mr. Benny in Lake Tahoe, and Phil Harris was in the audience. It was one of those evenings when we could do no wrong. The audience was screaming with laughter . . . applauding loudly . . . I got a standing ovation. Incidentally, whenever that happened, Jack would pretend to be mad and whisper a dirty name to me under his breath . . .

"Anyway, I did my act and the audience was extremely responsive. Then I left the stage and Mr. Benny came on for forty-five minutes. Afterward, I always came back on and we would close the show together.

"That particular evening, while I was waiting in the wings, I heard Uncle Jack introduce Phil from the audience. Harris stood up, and said, 'Jack . . .'

"Mr. Benny answered, 'Yes?'

"Then Phil said, *'Do you really think you need that kid?'*

"The audience started to roar at the way Phil was sort of putting Jack down . . .

"At that moment, I walked back on stage and Mr. Benny turned to me and said, 'Would you like to sing our song now?'

"I replied—and I die a million times whenever I think of it—something which, inadvertently, sounded fairly smart-alecky, such as, 'Would you like to try it without me?'

"What I meant was, 'Look, you've had your whole career *without me* regardless of what Phil Harris thinks.' I said it as a compliment—but it *didn't* sound that way.

"Uncle Jack picked up and went right on as if I hadn't said a word. I went offstage in tears. I was distraught thinking that I could have said something so dumb to a man I loved so much. After the show, I waited for Phil Harris to leave Jack's dressing room. Then I went over, knocked on his door, and asked if I could talk to him. He said sure.

"I told him how sorry I was. I apologized with tears running down my face.

"He just looked at me. 'What's the matter with you?'

"I told him how awful I felt because of what I'd said on stage.

" 'What did you say?'

" 'That stupid remark . . . but I meant it as a compliment . . .'

"He interrupted me. 'Well, *that's* how I took it, you dumb son-of-a-bitch. Now get out of here!'

"That's the kind of gentleman Jack was . . .

"When I became a headliner on my own, Jack was as thrilled for me as if I had been his son. Whenever he could, he'd surprise me by showing up where I was playing. He'd just walk on stage, unannounced, grab my fiddle, play it, and walk off.

"A few years ago, the very last time Jack appeared at the Tropicana, I went over to visit him. That same night Pearl Bailey, who opened his show, suddenly got sick, and Jack phoned and asked me to go on with him. It was a total conflict of interest because of my contract with the Hughes' Hotels. But I knew Walter Kane, entertainment director for the Summa Corporation, would understand. I made a quick call to tell him I was going to appear with Uncle Jack . . . that it was something I just *had* to do. Walter immediately gave me the go-ahead.

"Uncle Jack also asked if I could do the next night's show with him if Pearl still wasn't well enough to go on. Without hesitation, I said yes. I would have gone to hell and back for him . . .

"The following day, I flew to Los Angeles to rehearse a 'Dean Martin Show.' I was also scheduled to do 'The Tonight Show.' Early that evening, while I was at NBC taping with Johnny Carson, Jack called and told me Pearl would not be able to perform.

" 'What time can you be back here?' he asked.

" 'What time do you want me?'

" 'The show goes on at eight . . .'

"I told him I'd be there. I had my crew with me, plus all my music charts. When I got back to the Tropicana, I not only had Walter Kane's blessing again, but he came with me.

"I arrived just in the nick of time, took over Pearl's dressing room, changed, then went and knocked on his door.

" 'Uncle Jack, how much time do you want me to do?'

" 'Oh, well, *like you always do*—about twenty–twenty-five minutes . . .'

"I stood there in total shock. I hadn't done twenty-five minutes in *thirteen* years! I started to laugh, and he had no idea why. I went back to my crew and told them to throw away three quarters of my routine . . .

"Actually, it was a kick for me . . . being totally lifted up and carried *back in time*. To show you what kind of a man Jack was, when I begin my act, I always put my fiddle on the piano. When I get ready to use it, one of the guys hands it to me. Well, that night, I got to the place where someone handed me the violin, and I realized it wasn't mine. But I had no alternative, so I played. It turned out to be a magnificent instrument. Then I realized Jack had taken my fiddle and replaced it with *his* Stradivarius . . .

"Show business is the only profession in the world where a kid of twenty-one could have been in a position to become a co-worker and a friend to a man like Mr. Benny. Being with him, watching him, talking to him, I learned more about performing than I ever knew before . . .

"Even after we no longer worked together, he would write to

me, send me cards and letters. Once, he even sent me a clipping from Omaha which read: 'Jack Benny gets standing ovation.' His letter said, 'You see, *I get them, too!*'

"A couple of months before he passed away, I was in Beverly Hills with my agent. While he went to do some business, I took a walk. I was waiting for the light to change when I saw Mr. Benny, but he didn't see me. When I got right up to him, I said, 'Uncle Jack . . .' He just stood there for a moment.

"Then he said, 'Wayne, I'm so sorry . . . I'm so embarrassed . . . I'll make it up to you . . . I'll come to Vegas and go on stage with you and take your fiddle and do a whole routine . . . You've got to forgive me . . .'

" 'For what?'

" 'I *really tried* to help you with that show—but I was tied up . . .'

" 'Don't worry about it,' I said, and we parted.

"I realized he had been referring to something specific, but I had no idea what. It bothered me, so I asked my manager what it was all about.

"He groaned, and explained that Jack was obviously referring to a show I'd done a few months before. It was my own television special with Burt Reynolds, Robert Goulet, Carol Lawrence, and Lee Majors. Only, at the last minute, Carol broke her foot, and couldn't do the show. Unbeknownst to me, my manager had called Jack and asked him if he could do a walk-on. Jack had been unable to do it. Only, no one ever told me. And that's the thing that was on *his* mind the very last time I talked to him—*that he had let me down!*

"The night Mr. Benny passed away, I was on stage in Las Vegas . . . Naturally, I flew down for the funeral, but I had to go right back. When I reached the airport, there was a call for me. Bob Goulet had taken ill and couldn't work. My manager said they wanted me to go on for Bob, then do my own regular shows. What that amounted to was me doing four shows in one night . . . running back and forth between hotels.

"Then he said, 'Look, knowing how you felt about Jack, I think both hotels should go dark [cancel performances] out of respect to him . . .'

"I said, 'No . . . we would be doing the greatest injustice you could ever pay a man like Uncle Jack . . . Why, I've seen him go on stage in the rain . . . perform when he was ill . . . I want to do it—for Goulet—but especially for Jack.'

"Jack Benny represented the epitome of what I hope one day I can become. He had true class . . . He was a total genius . . ."

CHAPTER FORTY-ONE

IN FEBRUARY 1963, Jack, celebrating his sixty-ninth birthday, told a newspaper columnist, "I'm getting old enough to do just what I want to do, see only people I enjoy seeing. I'm too old to waste my time being bored . . ."

For Jack, avoiding boredom meant *doubling* his work schedule! He put together a stage show and, prior to opening on Broadway at the Ziegfeld Theatre, took the company to Toronto, Canada. For Jack, it was a momentary throwback to the "old days." Forty years before, he had played in Canada, on stage at the Orpheum Theatre, sharing the bill with the great magician Harry Houdini. When he opened in New York with his vaudeville-type revue show, it marked his first appearance as a star on the legitimate stage in New York after a thirty-two-year absence, when he had left *Earl Carroll's Vanities* to go into radio.

The New York engagement lasted six weeks, played to capacity audiences, and meant that Benny had to work day and night in order to keep up with his commitments. As usual, Jack thrived on the pace, the excitement. His was an exhilaration of spirit, buoyed up constantly by the warmth of his reception.

Speaking about this period in her husband's life, Mary said, "It reminds me of a line they once used on Jack's show. Rochester was talking to somebody about him . . . 'What a man, Benny! He lives like a lamb and dreams like a wolf . . .'

"In a way, that summed up Jack's life. He did *live* like a lamb

. . . and he did *dream* like a wolf. But his dream, first, last, and always, was show business. I should know. I married them both, the man and the dream.

"You have no idea how happy Jack was at the prospect of picking up and moving the whole television show to New York while he appeared at the Ziegfeld Theatre. He was as excited as I've ever seen him. And, as always, he was able to communicate his own sense of joy to the thousands of people who came to see him every night . . ."

Benny's stage show was a huge success, perhaps best measured by the glowing tribute he received from the distinguished New York critic Walter Kerr. The review had to be *read* by Kerr over the radio. When Jack opened, on Wednesday night, March 6, 1963, there was a newspaper strike, which meant a total blackout of all the usual New York daily papers . . .

And Walter Kerr's review, which he gave in a broadcast over CBS, began:

This seems most unlikely, but it may have been William Shakespeare who described Jack Benny best. In one of his plays, Shakespeare speaks of a character who waits "like patience on a monument, smiling, at grief." That's Mr. Benny, all right, except that he somehow manages to become both patience AND the monument all primped into one . . .

His dignity of course is monumental. No waving hello, no little hop, skip, and jump to the footlights, no mighty flourish from the brass to bring him on. He simply enters like a floorwalker who has just been promoted to the best floor, and he has come, basically, to keep an eye on you. He clasps his hands together as though to say, "What can I do for you?" or perhaps "Who stole my muff?" He is languid and lethal and rueful and baleful and at all times ready to bite his lip in embarrassment, should anything untoward turn up . . .

On the bill with Jack in his semi-vaudeville type revue were the Clara Ward Gospel Singers and sexy nightclub vocalist Jane Morgan, with whom Jack did a Robert Goulet-type number, kissing her romantically—then reverting to character when, in mid-kiss, he pulled out a jeweler's glass and began appraising the diamond she was wearing! In addition, Jack did his famous violin bit, "Getting to Know You," accompanied by still another remarkable child, Toni Marcus.

A couple of days after Jack opened, Mary recalls coming back to their suite at the Hotel Pierre after shopping with Sylvia Sullivan, Ed's wife.

"The moment I walked into the room," Mary began, "and I saw Jack pacing up and down, I knew something was wrong. As we've said before, Jack, on occasion, could have quite a temper, but I can't ever remember seeing him in such a rage.

" 'What's wrong, doll face? What's happened?' I asked.

"He told me he was having lunch at the Friars Club when someone came up to his table and said, 'I hear they're splitting you and Skelton . . .'

"At that time, and for several years previously," Mary continued, "Red and Jack's shows had aired back to back, on Tuesdays, with Skelton on from eight to nine, followed by Jack from nine to nine-thirty. It had been and still was a winning combination. Now CBS planned to program an intervening show, 'Petticoat Junction.'

" 'What's the big deal, Jack? So you go on a half hour later. If the new show is successful won't that be good for you?'

" 'You're missing the whole goddamn point,' Jack answered, suddenly directing his anger *at me*. 'I hope the new show *is* successful. But why didn't they call me *first*? After all the years I've been with CBS, and what I've done for them, at least they could have discussed with me what they had in mind, instead of me having to hear about it from someone at the club . . .'

" 'Doll,' I said, 'please, take it easy. Sit down . . . Relax . . . Let's just talk it over . . .'

" 'There's *nothing* to talk about,' Jack said, still fuming. 'I've already called Taft Schreiber [Jack's agent at MCA] and told him to get me out of my contract . . .'

"That was the very first time Jack had ever impulsively acted on his own about a major decision without first discussing it with me. I realized the depth of his hurt . . .

"I continued talking, trying to calm him down, while I simultaneously tried to weigh the consequences of the situation. 'How can you get out of your contract?' I asked. 'Besides, what would you do?'

" 'Mary, my show at the Ziegfeld is a success. I can take it to Boston, Philadelphia, Detroit . . . maybe even London. I could give my concerts . . . Look, next year I'll be *seventy* years old. Damn it, I want to be free to do just what *I want to do.*'

"At that moment, the telephone rang. Jack told me to answer it. As I walked toward the phone, he said, 'If it's Bill Paley, tell him I'm not in . . .'

"It wasn't Paley, but Taft Schreiber. Jack took the call and I got on the extension. Taft explained that, according to the terms of Jack's CBS contract, he still had one more year to go. He advised Jack to at least wait until the new season started and the ratings came in . . .

"Adamantly, Jack told Taft that if he *had* to do one more full season for CBS, then he would. But he also said that, since Taft had previously told him NBC wanted him, at the end of the year he was through with CBS and would make the move back to NBC.

" 'Okay, Jack, if that's what you want,' Taft said. 'But Bill Paley has been trying to call you and hasn't been able to reach you . . .'

" 'I know,' Jack replied. 'I was here all the time . . . I just couldn't take his calls. I couldn't speak to him. You know how many years Bill and I have been close friends. Besides, I found out the decision to switch my time slot wasn't his. Look, I just don't have the heart to talk to him while I'm in this kind of a mood. I might say something to hurt *his* feelings, and I just can't do it . . .' "

Upon completion of Jack's New York run at the Ziegfeld, he returned to California, and continued on his weekly TV program. Later in the year, he did a cameo in Stanley Kramer's film *It's a Mad, Mad, Mad, Mad World.*

Even though "Petticoat Junction" turned out to be a big success, one which *helped* Jack's ratings, at the end of the season, he *did* leave CBS. Early in 1964, Jack returned to his original network, NBC, where he did a series of shows which still rank among the very best ever done on television. Among his guests were Lucille Ball, Mr. and Mrs. Edgar Bergen, Bob Hope, Paul Lynde, the Marquis Chimps, the Smothers Brothers, Mr. and Mrs. Jimmy Stewart, and Andy Williams.

Recently, Edgar Bergen sat reminiscing about Benny:

"Back in vaudeville, Jack and I appeared together occasionally on the same bill, and we did play many of the same towns in the late 1920s. However, we really didn't become close friends until later, when I got my own show, and we started broadcasting from adjoining studios.

"Originally, I went into radio a few years after Jack. I started in December of 1936, on the Rudy Vallee show . . . I'll never forget the time Jack came to a rehearsal and watched me perform after I had begun using Charlie McCarthy. I walked into the studio carrying Charlie in a small black suitcase. As I opened the case, I noticed Jack staring at me in amazement. I couldn't understand why . . .

"The following week, Jack and a few other comics came to me —at Jack's insistence, I later learned! 'How can you keep Charlie like that? It's horrible!' They *really* bawled me out. Jack didn't say it in so many words, but I could tell by his expression, he thought I was being perfectly awful to Charlie!

"In their minds, Charlie was *so real,* which, of course, was a great compliment to me. But leave it to Jack to get so incensed he'd formed a 'delegation' to tell me! I immediately went out and bought a *full-length* suitcase in which Charlie could stand up! Inside, there was a mirror, a clothes brush and rack. The case was lined in green velvet and also had a velvet cushion. When I showed it off, Jack and the others felt better about Charlie's 'living conditions!'

"One of the most memorable guest appearances I ever made was on a *live* television show with Jack. On the program, Jack visited my house, but I wasn't home yet. My real-life wife, Frances, playing herself, made him welcome . . .

"They were sitting and talking, when a midget, dressed like Charlie, and wearing an identical facial mask, walked into the living room. Jack was astounded. The three of them played a scene, then Charlie left, and another midget came in wearing a Mortimer Snerd mask. Jack was flabbergasted, while Frances played it perfectly straight. Just as the show ended, I came walking in the front door. Jack, who was just leaving, said, 'Hello,' shook his head in disbelief . . . and exited.

"Doing that live, in front of a studio audience, was very tricky business. It took more courage than I would have had. There were just too many possibilities for things to get sloppy and go wrong. The Charlie and Mortimer masks the midget wore could have slipped (Billy Barty played both parts).

"It really took guts. But Jack thought we could pull it off—and we did—with me standing offstage in the wings doing the voices, and Billy Barty on stage, moving his lips in perfect synchronization. He always said that was among his own personal all-time favorite shows.

"Jack was a very dear friend. In fact, Frances and I felt so close that we asked him to be our son Christopher's godfather. At the christening, the baby pinched Jack's nose. It was quite a sight. We all had difficulty keeping straight faces.

"Over the years, Jack was a marvelous godfather. He'd drop in often, always bringing the baby a present. He loved visiting the nursery, where he and Chris would be alone together. He really enjoyed spending time with the boy.

"The funny thing is it wasn't until later on that I realized a godfather is supposed to be a baby's *religious* 'father.' It had never occurred to me—that's how close we were. That's how *unidentified* Jack was with any one ethnic group. Of course, I knew Jack was Jewish. It just never crossed my mind to ask anyone else.

"Throughout his entire career, Jack had the best timing of any comic I ever knew. He would often compliment me on my timing and delivery, but I never had the nerve to pause as boldly as he did . . .

"He called me one day and said he'd heard me use a line where Charlie was talking to a guest star and said, 'Could I see you home this evening after the broadcast? And we could have a little fun . . .'

"She answered, 'Well, I don't see any harm in that . . .'

"Then Charlie said, 'Oh, gee, I wish you could . . .'

"When Jack asked if he could use that line, I said, 'Why I'd steal lines from you and *never ask*. Of course you can use it . . .'

235

"The whole point is, Jack was such a *gentle*-man . . . and his goodness transcended age and the generation gap. He could spend hours with young Chris, and he loved my daughter, Candy—and she him. They used to have this running routine between them. She loved to bug him . . . especially on the telephone. Whenever she called, and Jack answered, she'd say, 'Hello, Mr. *Bernie* . . .'

"He would reply, 'No, this is Mr. *Benny* . . .'

"Then Candy would repeat, 'Mr. *Bernie* . . .'

"Jack always, going along with the gag, would say, 'It's Mr. Benny, *Sandy!*'

"He was the best we had. The very best . . ."

CHAPTER FORTY-TWO

WHEN JACK turned seventy-one, not only his friends, but the press thought he might finally start to take life easy. Jack had other plans.

It was at this time Hickey Marks returned to work for Jack as his head writer. "During the next nine years," Marks commented, "I never traveled so much in my life. Jack was tireless. Each season, we did one or two hour-long television specials on NBC, and in between shows, we traveled on the road at least one hundred and ninety days a year!

"When Jack wasn't doing concerts with symphony orchestras, he was playing Las Vegas or Lake Tahoe. When he wasn't in Nevada, he was making a series of live appearances in big theaters, small ones, theaters in the round, college auditoriums, as well as playing state fairs and Expo's, like the ones he did in Montreal, Canada, in 1967, and San Antonio, Texas, in 1970.

"Naturally, I hadn't been with Jack during his early years in show business. But from all I'd heard and read, it seemed to me he was *reliving* his vaudeville days: playing small towns, contentedly using small dressing rooms, staying in quaint hotels, and reveling in the big crowds who came to see and adore him.

"For instance, when he played fifteen shows in six days at the Corn Palace in Mitchell, South Dakota, we checked into a marvelous little place called the Lawler Motor Inn. It was warm and comfortable and featured family-style cooking. Jack fell in love with the place and its almost boardinghouse atmosphere at mealtimes. The first night, he ate baked ham—'the best I've ever eaten.' For the rest of our stay, he kept raving about it. The management was so taken with Jack's sincere enthusiasm that, for the next few months, he and Mary received a baked ham, regularly as clockwork, every time the first rolled around!

"Whenever Jack played a big city for any length of time, Mary came to join him. In between times, she stayed home, receiving a regular running report of Jack's latest appearance through his unending phone calls, barrage of funny postcards, and the little gifts he'd send her from every town . . ."

In October of 1966, Benny played Caesar's Palace in Las Vegas for one full month—unheard of for an artist of Jack's caliber up until that time. John Davidson and Israeli singer Aliza Kashi were on the bill with him.

Whenever Jack played Vegas, whether at Caesar's, the Sahara, or the Tropicana, the hotel relaxed its rules for him on opening night. Ordinarily, each hotel gave an entertainer a specified amount of time in which to put on his show. Stars *never* ran over . . . These were gambling resorts. The management was anxious to get the audience out of their nightclubs and back into their casinos.

Jack was the exception. All the hotels' entertainment directors knew he *purposely* ran long the first night of an engagement. Jack was one of the few top performers who felt audiences were entitled to hear *fresh* entertainment from him, since he played the Nevada resorts so regularly. He not only met the challenge, but was eager to try out new material. Each management was aware of this and appreciated it.

Even Bill Harrah's hotel in Lake Tahoe indulged Jack. Their usual practice is to have a red light at the foot of the stage. Whenever that light goes on, it is the star's signal to wind up and get off stage within five minutes. It never flashed for Jack on opening night.

Immediately after his first show, Jack's mind would go to work like a computer. He knew exactly what and where to cut. There were even times he would edit his material while he was on stage performing it!

"How he did this, I'll never know," Marks commented. "All he had to depend on for timing was his own wristwatch, which never ran because he always forgot to wind it . . . and which he couldn't have read anyway because the numbers on it were too small for him to see!

"During this period, Frank Sinatra came to one of the shows and got hysterical looking at Jack struggling to time himself with a very expensive watch he could hardly see, let alone read. So Frank went out and bought Jack a fifty-dollar electric Timex with very large numerals. Jack was as delighted as a kid with a new toy . . .

"When the battery ran down, Jack bought another one—and sent Frank the bill—for two dollars! Along with it, he wrote a letter saying he hoped that Frank didn't feel his obligation was *over* with the *initial* gift. He expected him to *maintain* the watch. Sinatra sent back a note, enclosing the two dollars. He said that, while he had not anticipated having to pay 'yearly support' for its upkeep, he would continue to do so. He closed with a P.S. telling Jack what he *could do* with his original watch, the one he always forgot to wind and couldn't read anyway!"

It was quite apparent to those close to Jack that his "hyperkinetic," always-on-the-go personality had no intention of being slowed down just because he was in his eighth decade of life. Jack was *never* able to relax fully. Once satisfied with his Vegas opening, for example, he did not pass the remaining days of his engagement lying in the sun, or playing golf. Oh, he *did* play a round or two, each week. However, the main portion of every afternoon was spent with Hickey—working on a completely different act for his upcoming personal appearances. Benny liked to use some topical material, and also included a few local jokes about whatever town in which he was scheduled to appear.

It was also Jack's practice to use various guest stars on each bill. During an Indianapolis appearance, he hired Wayne Newton and a young musical prodigy, Doris Dodge. The violin routine used successfully by Jack and Giselle MacKenzie when they appeared at the Flamingo in 1966 was resurrected, with eleven-year-old Doris and seventy-two-year-old Jack playing the "Getting to Know You" duet. When the press asked Jack if he wasn't worried that the child was taking too much away from him, he said, "If she *didn't,* she wouldn't be with me."

"I'll never forget our flight to Indianapolis," Hickey recalled. "We hit some real turbulence. Doris and her mother were sitting across the aisle from Jack and myself. Just before we boarded, Mrs. Dodge admitted she had a fear of flying. Although both Jack and I tried to be very reassuring, the moment it got rough, she became terribly frightened . . .

"She knew I carried a bag of drugstore remedies for Jack, and said, 'Mr. Marks, please help me. I know you always have something to take . . .'

"Usually, she would have been right. This time, I had nothing with me . . . and it was too late to ask the stewardess for Dramamine. However, recognizing her condition, I calmly looked into my bag. With all the confidence of Dr. Marcus Welby, I offered her a Certs breath mint, which I removed from its package and handed her in a Kleenex.

" 'Let this tablet dissolve on your tongue. In a few minutes, you'll become very tired. Close your eyes . . . Before you know it, you'll feel drowsy.'

"Sure enough, a few minutes later, she was fast asleep. When she awakened, we were flying through an electrical storm. The turbulence was getting worse instead of better. She said, 'Oh, Mr. Marks, could you please give me *another* pill?'

" 'No, the first was strong enough. If I give you another one, we'll have to *carry* you off the plane . . .' There was a pleading look in her eyes. 'Well, okay, I'll give you half of one . . .' I said. She smiled with relief.

"I broke another Certs in two and gave it to her. A few minutes later, she was asleep again. Jack, seeing the results, asked me for a pill, too. I gave him the other half of the Certs—and *he* fell asleep!

"Finally, the plane ride ended. Once we were settled in our hotel, Jack came to my room.

"'Hickey, you're a genius. How in the hell do you always manage to carry just the right pills?'

"Like an idiot, I told him the truth . . .

"He was amazed. 'My God,' he said, *that really is mind over matter.* You son-of-a-bitch, you were so convincing, you even fooled me!'

"I didn't want to tell Jack that fooling *him* wasn't difficult!

"In all the hundreds of thousands of miles Jack flew—from prop planes to jets—the only close calls he had were over the war zones in the forties. He always remained a very calm traveler. But there *was* a flight from Memphis, Tennessee, to Duluth, Minnesota, one winter . . . It was rainy and foggy. When our plane came in for a landing, the ceiling was almost zero. The pilot made three passes at the airport . . . Things *were* a bit tense. Then the captain came on the intercom . . . 'We're about to make our *final* approach . . .' Just as he said that, I looked across the aisle and saw a priest sitting by the window. I leaned over and said . . . *'Where* and *when* did you come aboard, father?'

"All the years Jack and I traveled together, we were completely compatible except in certain *very basic areas,* where we were the exact opposites . . .

"Once, when Jack was playing the Palmer House in Chicago, we went to a matinee of *The Odd Couple,* starring Dan Dailey. All during the play, Jack kept tapping me and saying, 'My God, Hickey, Neil Simon wrote this story *based on us!'*

"In truth, Jack and I *were* the odd couple. Off stage, he was a slob, while I've always been as meticulous as Craig's wife, that literary paragon of virtue who kept emptying ash trays and driving people nuts being so meticulous. If we shared a hotel suite, I'd walk from place to place to keep dumping Jack's cigar ashes. He never finished one . . . There were half-smoked, half-chewed butts in every blessed ash tray . . ."

It was a completely crazy paradox in Jack—or maybe it *wasn't* so much a contradiction as it was a recognition of the *two sides* of Jack Benny. As Mary says, "The minute Jack was off stage, he couldn't have cared less how he looked, where his ashes fell, or if his sports clothes were hung up or slung over the nearest chair in his room . . .

"When we were going out to a party, Jack was the height of understated elegance. Always so handsome, so neatly dressed. But if just the two of us were going to dine in the neighborhood, then catch an early movie, or if we were going to a private screening at a friend's house, Jack dressed positively weird!

"He'd come walking downstairs in brown slacks, a green shirt, purple socks, and a blue sweater. I'd just look at him. In the early days, some of our friends thought Jack was color-blind! He wasn't. *He just didn't care . . .*"

Because of Jack's casual, often preoccupied nature, he came close, every once in a while, to getting himself and/or Hickey into trouble. During the time they were broadcasting from Palm Springs, Jack absent-mindedly drove off in someone else's Cadillac—and the car was tracked down by the local police. Jack couldn't believe it when they told him he had another man's automobile. He thought it very funny that his car and the one he had driven by mistake were the same style, year, and color. What amused him even more was that the *same* key worked in both cars!

"Then there was the time Jack was appearing at Buster Bonhoff's Star Theatre in Phoenix, Arizona," Hickey remembers. "As soon as the engagement ended, he and I planned to drive back to Palm Springs, where Mary was waiting for us, instead of going straight home.

"I was at the wheel and, as on many previous vacations, I was berating Jack for littering my car. He had the Hollywood trade papers, stacks of magazines, cigar wrappers, and half-finished crosswords puzzles on the front seat and floor of the car. The ash tray was full . . . His ashes were all over the floorboard . . .

"As I raved on, I saw a motor home in front of me, going rather slowly. I sped up and passed it. Almost immediately, I heard a siren, saw the flashing red light of the highway patrol, and pulled over. I stepped out of the car, and the officer informed me there were laws about the speed with which a passenger car could pass a motor home. He was very nice, and said this would be a warning—not a ticket.

"As he was talking, out of the corner of my eye, I could see Jack roll down his window and begin dumping ashes, cigar butts, newspapers, and other debris into a ditch by the side of the road. My heart stopped . . . I put my hand on the officer's shoulder in a friendly gesture and turned him in the other direction. When he got back into his patrol car and took off, I walked over to our car and yelled, 'For God's sake, Jack, what the hell were you trying to do, get us arrested?'

" 'What are you so mad about?' Jack asked.

" 'Just look out the window. There's a signpost right above you . . .' Jack stuck his head out and read the words:

WARNING $500 FINE
ABSOLUTELY NO LITTERING

"Jack just grinned. 'Next time, I won't *try to help* . . . Your car can stay *dirty!*'

"He had certain habits when we were on the road that, unlike his material, *never* varied. No matter the time of year, he always 'slept warm.' I'll never forget one June when we played Lake Tahoe. Whenever Jack went to bed, he always pulled the drapes in his room, turned the temperature way up, and slept with a warm bed jacket . . .

"That night, he made a golf date with a local jeweler friend. They decided to meet around two the following day. Jack usually slept until at least one in the afternoon, since his last show wasn't over until close to 2 A.M.

"He went to bed, had a good night's sleep in his completely darkened room, woke up early, and ordered room service.

"Every morning, we went through the same routine. He always would ask what *I* was having for breakfast, then ordered the *same* meal—corn flakes with fresh bananas or strawberries on top. Then he'd put on the lights—he never opened the drapes—shower, shave, and, on this particular morning, dressed in his golf clothes, complete to shoes and glove. His clubs were already at the course. By this time, I was long gone.

"He went downstairs and walked through the casino lobby. People were turning, laughing, and staring at him as though he were out of his mind. Lake Tahoe has an elevation of close to seven thousand feet. During the night, there had been a freak summer storm. Six inches of snow was on the ground. Finally, someone walked up to him and said, 'Mr. Benny . . . where are you going?' When he told them, the person said, 'If I were you, I'd look *outside* first . . .'"

All his life, Jack Benny was a very handsome man without the type of ego that usually accompanies good looks. Vanity was never Jack's thing. The only time he was the slightest bit concerned about his appearance was during the last five or six years of his life, and then, only about *certain areas*. When he was putting on his stage makeup in the dressing room, if Hickey was there, Jack would stare at himself in the mirror, take his hand, chuck himself under the chin, and say, "Look at these. If I ever have plastic surgery, that's *all* I'd want done—just to have these chins taken away . . ."

"Actually," Hickey said, "Jack always looked so good, people thought he already had gone through cosmetic surgery, which he never did . . . During one of Jack's appearances at Melodyland, a lovely theater in Southern California, I was in the dressing room and he started in again on how his extra chin made him look older. We were still talking when a stagehand knocked on the door. He said there was a woman outside from Waukegan, who claimed to be an old friend. She said Jack used to date her best friend. I went outside to talk with her . . .

"Jack had a rule for everyone who worked with him. *Never be rude to anyone*. Never slough people off. It happened that once, earlier in his career, a staff member had been abrupt and rude to someone who turned out to be Jack's friend. He was very annoyed and, ever since, it was a standing rule—never be rude to anyone, especially his fans.

"When I stepped outside, the woman repeated the story, giving me names, dates, and places. If she was a contemporary of Jack's, she would have been in her mid-seventies. But I swear, the sweet lady looked at least ninety. She was very heavy, bent over, and walked with a cane. Her hair was completely white. After she had spoken with me, I excused myself and went back inside.

"When I mentioned the names she'd given me, Jack stood right up and smiled with happiness. He knew who she was immediately, even though he hadn't seen or heard from her in nearly *sixty years!* I brought her inside, and left them alone. They talked until a few seconds before Jack had to go on stage . . .

"The minute he came off, I asked him if he had enjoyed his conversation. He was very enthusiastic about it. At which point, I started laughing, looked him straight in the eye, and asked, 'What was that you were saying a while ago about having too many chins?!'

"In 1972, Mary, Jack and I flew to Dublin, where he was to appear at the Gaiety Theatre prior to opening at the London Palladium. Jack always had a nervous habit of rubbing his fingers, fooling with his hands. Whenever he didn't have his violin with him, he liked to play with a violin mute, a small rubber device used to soften the tone. He used to roll it around and around in the palm of one hand until I told him he was getting like Captain Queeg in *The Caine Mutiny*—the officer who had to keep rolling steel balls around between his fingers.

"Jack lost his last mute and asked me to shop around Dublin and see if I could find any. Right behind old Trinity College, I discovered the violin shop of a Mr. Hoffman, who sold and repaired fiddles. We had already been playing in town for a few days, and when I told him I needed some mutes for Jack, he was thrilled. He refused any money for them saying they were a gift to a great artist . . . He raved about Jack's show.

"Then, shyly, he asked if that was really a Stradivarius Jack was using in his act. When I said yes, he confessed that, in all of his years working with violins, he had never seen a Strad close up. He wondered if he might come and take a look at it. I said I would try to arrange it. I returned to our hotel and told Jack. He said sure and asked me to call the man back. Jack made arrangements to go to the theater an hour early that Saturday to meet with Mr. Hoffman . . .

"It was a very touching moment when the gentleman came backstage, shook hands with Jack, and then, very tenderly, took the Strad in his arms and minutely examined it. 'What a magnificent instrument,' he kept saying over and over. 'Just magnificent!'

"Jack said, 'Mr. Hoffman, would you like to play it?' The expression on the man's face was enough of an answer. He tucked the Strad under his chin, closed his eyes, and began playing. It was a very special moment—all of us had tears in our eyes.

"While we were still in town, Jack received a beautiful thank-you note from Mr. Hoffman—it was so touching that, for months, he walked around with that letter in his wallet. *That was Jack!*"

CHAPTER FORTY-THREE

MARCH 20, 1968, was one of the happiest and proudest days of Jack's life. In a formal ceremony, he donated his memorabilia: clippings, radio and television scripts, tapes, films, recordings of shows, and thousands of photographs to the University of California, Los Angeles. UCLA, just a few miles from the Benny home, would become the permanent repository for Jack's lifetime body of work. He had dreamed of a place where students and researchers could come and freely have access to the records of his career. Now the dream became reality . . .

He had *two* seats of learning which had honored him: Jack Benny Junior High School in Waukegan, and the University of California, Los Angeles. Not bad for a tenth-grade dropout!

No one in Hollywood appreciated the significance of Jack's relationship with UCLA more than Johnny Carson. Recently, he sat discussing Benny's impact on his own life . . . and career.

"When I was a student at the University of Nebraska, Jack had a tremendous influence on me—on my understanding of comedy construction and timing. I still have a whole tape I did in college, in 1948. Jack never got to hear it. I wish he had—but I told him about it. It was a thesis I did on radio comedy . . .

"I was twenty-one at the time. What I did was to tape all the big comedy shows: Jack's show . . . Fred Allen . . . Bob Hope . . . Fibber McGee and Molly . . . Herb Shriner . . . everything that was on. Then I took excerpts from those programs to illustrate how jokes were constructed. The running gags . . . the toppers . . . the whole development of humor.

"Today, students interested in the arts will be allowed access to all of Jack's material. They will have the opportunity of looking at and studying the work of a master. A genius in our field.

"Many people say some of my mannerisms are like Jack's. Well, I think *all* comedians have 'ears.' They pick up, mimic, and eventually fall into certain patterns. I realize now that, in the early days of my career, I *was* too much like Jack. I tried to emulate him, which was wrong. But *I idolized* Jack. He had more influence on me than say Bob Hope, who is a joke-teller, a one-liner. Fred Allen had some influence on me, too. I enjoyed his wit, his construction of lines, his word pictures. But without question, Jack and his show were the most tremendous influences on my development . . . on what I tried to do . . . on what I've become.

"Like so many of my generation, I grew up listening to Jack on radio. I was a completely devoted Benny fan for as far back as I can remember.

"I was seventeen years old the first time I saw Jack," Johnny continued. "I hitchhiked to California, and went to see one of his radio show tapings at CBS. I was fresh out of high school, and about to go into the service. But first, I wanted to see Hollywood —and Jack.

"I can never forget what a thrill it was actually being in his audience. Frank Fontaine was his guest, doing the character of J. L. C. Sivoney, the sweepstakes winner. He subsequently appeared many times on Jackie Gleason's program as the drunk.

"Eight years later, in 1951, I had my first picture taken with Jack over at CBS. I had gone to a taping of his at the studio on Sunset and Gower. At that point, I had left the Midwest, come out here, and was doing a radio show, 'Carson's Corner,' on the local CBS station, KNX. I was on every morning for *five minutes,* from 8:55 to 9 A.M. Jack was very generous, posing with me for that publicity photo. I'm sure he had no idea who I was.

"Later, I did a program called the 'Sunday Show.' One week, when Fred Allen came out from New York to be on with me, Jack visited the studio. That was the first time I actually *met* him . . .

"Many stories have been written about Jack's influence on me. *They are all true*. I can show you things I did in the early days—twenty years ago—in which I was *so close* to his style, it embarrasses me now. But every comedian, when he's going through a formative period, takes a lot from everybody, for a while. All the comics I've talked to admit it . . .

"When I discussed this with Jack, he told me that, as a young man in vaudeville, he was influenced by Frank Fay. And I know Jackie Gleason picked up a little from Oliver Hardy . . .

"Most of all, from the standpoint of timing and structure, Jack was the key influence on me. Basically, I, like him, am a reaction comedian. I play off of the things that are happening around me. That is what works for me on 'The Tonight Show.' When things happen around me, I can play off them by reaction, timing, pauses, and looks . . .

"Over the years," Carson went on, "I learned another very important thing from Jack. If *other* people on your show are good, it makes *you* better. The stronger the other performers are, the greater it is for the *whole* program.

"I not only learned that—I've gained from it. On my show, the funnier and stronger Ed McMahon, Doc Severinson, and Tommy Newson are, the better it is for me . . . for the entire show.

"No matter how funny Rochester, Phil Harris, Don Wilson, Dennis Day, or Mary were, it was always the Jack Benny show people talked about and critics wrote about.

"When Jack had guest stars, he stood back, gave them the best material, and never was bothered when they got most of the laughs. He realized *instinctively* that it only strengthened him. But, in truth, there are very few comics who could have stood it. Most of them want and *need* all the funny lines for themselves . . .

"Most comedians are, by nature, very mercurial, especially in their anger—but not Jack. I never saw him display any temperament. He was the most disciplined performer I ever met.

"Overall, Jack seemed to be a very secure man. I know of only *one* area in which he had insecurities. We talked about it on several occasions. Jack felt he was not sufficiently well read. He regretted his lack of a formal education. One time, at my house, I started discussing something, and I recall Jack saying, 'I really don't know about those things . . .'

"I felt strange, being so much younger than he was. But he was being very honest. I heard that one of the few personal appearances he ever turned down was an invitation to address the student body at Harvard. He said he felt he just couldn't face all those university students!

"Still, he not only overcame a great deal of this, he made it *work* for him. His language was grammatically correct, but, because of his own lack of a formal education, he never talked down to his audiences, or used words that would have needed explanation . . .

"I think the reason Jack was able to sustain his career for so long is quite simple. *People liked him.* If an audience likes a performer, he can get away with anything. If they don't like you, it doesn't make any difference how clever or witty you are . . . it just won't work!

"Performers like Jack, who sustain over the years, are the ones people identify with—as a person as well as an entertainer. I have seen a lot of clever performers come and go simply because the audience just didn't like them . . . didn't care about them. Jack's audiences always *cared.*

"As far as Jack Benny, off stage, there were so many marvelous things about him. He was a man with no pretensions at all. It was the *little* things that pleased him, not the money . . . or the big house . . . or the fame. Although they *are* nice to have. But for Jack, the simple things were more important.

"He was completely unaffected. Whenever we'd walk down the street together in New York or Los Angeles, and he was stopped, Jack always talked with people if they said hello to him . . . I believe there is something to be said for Jack's Midwest background. I hate to sound corny and say *both* he and I came from 'solid roots.' But that small-town beginning—at least with Jack—helped him to keep his simplicity. I know how close he always felt to Waukegan. When they named the junior high school after him, it was the highest honor in his life.

"Jack never acted like he had a superior quality, that's why everyone could identify with him. It may sound dull to keep praising him, to make him sound so saint-like. People always look for *something* in a life like Jack's. Something to add pizzazz. But with Jack, what it comes down to is *the man was what he was* . . .

"One night, a few of us were sitting around, just talking. Sinatra was there . . . George Burns . . . a few others . . . We were discussing some mundane thing—like how to prepare a decent cup of coffee. Suddenly, Jack started to laugh. 'People think we lead such exotic, glamorous lives. They imagine the parties we go to are all wild orgies—and here we are talking about a cup of coffee. Wouldn't they be disappointed if they could hear our conversation!'

"Jack didn't have the jealousy you often find in the entertainment world—which is very much a *big ego* business—especially in the comedy field. Many comedians don't even like to go and see other comics because they would have to hear them get big laughs! Jack was the other way around. He was the *best* audience in the world. If he saw somebody he liked, he'd call me and say, 'Gee, I saw this great kid. Why don't you put him on your show? Invariably, I did . . .

"Jack was so secure about his talent perhaps because, down deep, he knew *nobody* could do what he could . . . Really, no one could steal from Jack. You had *to be* Jack to do what he did. It was his *attitude* toward comedy, the way he *delivered* his lines that made him so unique . . .

"I called Jack in Texas once when he was appearing down there. I had just come back from playing in the same place, and I had a line for him which I couldn't have used . . . They had just closed the oldest house of prostitution in the state of Texas . . . It was called Edna's Chicken Ranch. The incident started a big furor going. The people didn't want the place closed because it had a lot of glamour and nostalgia about it. It had been open since the 1880s.

"I told Jack I had a good opening for him. If he just walked out and said, 'I'm down here because I understand they're closing Edna's Chicken Ranch . . . The reason I came is because I was here for the *opening* and I'd like to be here for the closing . . .'"

"He used it—and the audience roared.

"I couldn't have used the joke. It wouldn't have made any sense at all for me. For Jack, it was perfect. There were just certain things he could do and say that wouldn't have worked for anybody else. He could go back in time. His character could use the so-called vanity lines, or the youthful lines. He had everything going for him, because his 'public role' was so wonderfully constructed . . .

"Women really adored Jack. In addition to being so good-looking, there was a gentleness about him that women sensed and found very appealing. Most men would have thought it *un-macho* to be so sweet. Jack couldn't have cared less. He adored women—and they him.

"There was a quality of tenderness about Jack, too . . . A *vulnerability* that women saw in him. My own wife, Joanna, adored him. There were times she'd be at the Benny house talking with Mary and Jack would walk in . . . and she would just beam. She only knew him for a few years, just since our marriage. But from the first time she met him, she told me she felt as if she had known him all her life. Jack had an ability to make people feel comfortable because he showed his interest in them . . .

"Another thing I loved about Jack, especially in his later years . . . He was frequently preoccupied . . . Also, he didn't hear very well, and often had *delayed reactions*. You would say something . . . He'd be busy thinking . . . But thirty seconds later, he would slap his knee and start laughing . . .

"Once, Jack and I were driving over to appear with Frank Sinatra at a benefit for the Mount Sinai Hospital. Mary, Joanna, and I were in the back seat. Jack and his violin case were up front. Suddenly, he said, 'Gee, Johnny, I hope my driver put the violin in my case . . .'

"I said, 'Well, Jack, how would he get a tuba in there?' We drove on in silence for a full minute before Jack slapped his knee and repeated, *'How would he get a tuba in there?'* and burst out laughing.

"Jack was a very special person in my life—in so many lives . . . And he always was so *concerned* about what he did and said . . .

"When he appeared on the dais at a dinner the Television Academy gave in my honor, in October of 1970, his monologue

250

was tailored to fit the situation so beautifully, I broke up. As usual, he had *anticipated* the others, and had taken the *opposite* direction. Frankly, testimonial dinners can become so repetitious —but not when *he* was on!

"That night was no exception. Jack was superb. Here's his material, exactly as he delivered it:

Ladies and gentlemen . . . tonight we are paying tribute to a man whose talent is exceeded only by his salary . . . In other words, this young Ted Mack discovery, with *no* particular background or schooling in show business, is now earning—or *making* rather . . . you know . . . *collecting* approximately twenty-five thousand dollars a week, which amounts to approximately a million three hundred thousand dollars a year . . . approximately meaning a dollar more or a dollar less.

Now, Johnny Carson's brother Dick is the director of his show . . . *His* salary is a thousand dollars a week . . . and Johnny, who acts as his agent, collects 11 per cent . . .

Johnny is *also* the contractor for the musicians—which is *another* nine thousand dollars . . . So this mercenary Marquis de Sade is making at least a million five hundred thousand dollars a year!

Now, on 'The Tonight Show,' Carson uses five or six guest stars —and no matter *how* important the guest star is—he receives approximately three hundred dollars . . . approximately meaning— he's a schmuck!

Just imagine—ladies and gentlemen—for the last nine or ten years on Johnny's show, the Vice-President of the United States has been getting the *same* amount of money as Phil Foster or Henny Youngman . . . and you can throw in Tiny Tim . . . and Carson *doesn't* have to pay it . . . So, outside of his lawyer's fees, this penurious Protestant *still* makes one million five hundred thousand dollars a year.

Now, ladies and gentlemen—I *like* Johnny Carson very much . . . In fact, *I love him*. But once in a while he can get just a little bit egotistical . . . Here's an example:

About six years ago, I stopped doing my weekly television shows, but continued to do two or three specials a year—and guest appearances . . . But *evidently* Johnny thought that I was having a tough time getting a job . . . So, about five years ago, I happened to be in New York City, and I was walking down

Fifth Avenue when I heard someone yell, 'Hello, Jack'—and it was Carson . . . I said, 'Hello, Johnny' . . . Then he told me how *glad* he was to see me—and I said I was *glad* to see him, too . . .

We talked for a little while—and finally he said to me: 'How are things going—*kid?*' . . . Right then and there I should have punched him in the nose, but *I* can't even lick *Don Knotts* . . . Anyway, he said, 'Jack, as long as you are here in New York, how would you like to come on my show? It certainly *can't hurt*' . . . And I *did* go on it . . . Needless to say—I've had many offers since then.

So tonight—just before dinner—Carson and I were talking, and he finally said to me, 'Jack, the *next* time you are in New York, I want you to come up and have dinner with me in my beautiful new apartment overlooking the East River.'

Now, *little does this miserable s.o.b. know that I own that apartment building*—and *part* of the river . . . And when his lease is up—it's going to cost him a bloody fortune to renew it!

And now, ladies and gentlemen, to get on with the show . . ."

CHAPTER FORTY-FOUR

JACK AND MARY celebrated New Year's Eve in 1969 with one of their usual smashing parties. Two days later, Jack flew to Miami Beach to tape a "Jackie Gleason Show," then returned to Hollywood to rehearse and tape a television special of his own.

At the end of January, he left for Hawaii, where he did four shows at the Illikai Hotel, one show at Pearl Harbor for the Navy guys . . . and gave three performances at Hickam Field, which was so devastated on December 7, 1941. Then, for the following few weeks, he crisscrossed the country, guesting on "The Joey Bishop Show" in California, flying to Kansas City for an athletic awards banquet, going on to New York for a "Tonight Show," and to attend several industry dinners.

In February, Jack was to be the star performer at the annual governor's conference being held in Washington, D.C. He and Hickey boarded a plane heading East along with the Bennys' close friend Nancy Reagan, wife of Ronald Reagan, then governor of California. Nancy and Ronnie had been dear Benny friends from Reagan's show business days. In fact, Ronnie considered Jack his "good luck charm." Years before Reagan had entered politics, while he was still hosting "The General Electric Theater" on television, Jack already had begun calling him "the governor."

As Hickey describes the scene, "It was very impressive and, for Jack, a bit embarrassing. As our plane taxied into Dulles Airport, outside of Washington, D.C., it came to a stop at mid-field. Two secret service men came on board and ushered Mrs. Reagan, Jack, and me off the plane. Waiting below was a long black limousine with the vice-presidential flags flying. 'Ted' Agnew had sent his car to meet us.

"After the show Jack put on for the governors, Agnew asked us if we would like to go to Cape Kennedy to see the launch of Apollo 9. Of course, Jack and I were excited. But bad weather moved into the Cape, and the launch was postponed for several days . . .

"Jack and I flew to New York for the weekend. On Sunday morning, we received a call from Washington, asking us to fly right back as the launch had been rescheduled for early the following day. Due to a snowstorm, we couldn't get a plane out, so we took the train. We were met at the station by Vice-President Agnew's aide, who told us President Nixon was due to arrive within the hour from his history-making trip to Russia. He asked if Jack and I would like to go out to Andrews Air Force Base and meet the plane. Naturally, we said yes.

"Jack and I were driven right out onto the field along with a small group of V.I.P.'s. The door to *Air Force One* swung open, and the President walked down the ramp, shook the obligatory hands, looked out, saw Jack, and couldn't believe it. He walked right over to us, clasped Jack around the shoulders and said, 'What the hell are *you* doing here?'

"Perhaps I should digress to say that Jack was *never* publicly political. He was friendly with *all* the Presidents—beginning with Franklin Delano Roosevelt. In fact, while we were in Washington during that trip, when a reporter asked Jack who he was voting for, he just grinned and remarked, 'I am always loyal to my party . . . *I'm a Whig.* If it was good enough for Millard Fillmore, it's good enough for me!'

"After greeting the President, we boarded another plane and flew to Cape Kennedy. We were among the honored guests for the launch of astronauts McDivitt, Scott, and Schweickart, which took place on the third of March.

"I don't have to tell you how impressed we were with the whole event. To Jack, who was the least mechanically inclined man I ever knew, the lift-off of the rocket was the 'greatest miracle' he had ever witnessed. I must say, you didn't have to be un-mechanical to feel that way!"

Only a short time after Jack's return from the happy exhilaration of the space shot, he learned of the very serious illness of his close and dear friend Billy Goetz. Goetz, a producer-banker, among whose films was the Oscar-winning *Sayonara,* was dying of cancer. As Mary said, "Billy Goetz had the funniest wit of any non-comic Jack ever knew. He was always pulling these outrageous gags on Jack, and my husband could never stop laughing at him.

"Once, we were at a dinner party given by Billy's sister-in-law, Irene Mayer Selznick, then David O. Selznick's wife. After a sumptuous meal, we were all standing in the living room talking, with Billy next to Jack, when our hostess walked by. Just as she passed us, Billy said, in a voice loud enough for her to hear, 'Gee, Jack, I don't know why *you didn't like the dinner* . . . Everyone else thought it was delicious!'

"Jack started to laugh, but turned three shades of red when he noticed Irene looking right at him. Then he began to sputter, telling her how *great* the meal was. But he was unable to keep a straight face. Billy was always doing things like that—and Jack always fell for the gags."

Recently, Billy's widow, Edie Mayer Goetz, daughter of famous film producer and head of Metro-Goldwyn-Mayer Studios Louis B. Mayer, sat talking about that last year of her husband's life—and the part Jack played in it:

"One of the things I remember most about Jack was his inability to travel alone, without Mary, or Hickey, or *someone* being with him," she began. "So, in 1969, when Billy was being treated as an outpatient at the Mayo Clinic in Rochester, and Jack showed up there *by himself,* I couldn't believe it. Originally, he had flown in just for one day. He wound up staying three extra days just to be with us.

"He was so wonderful with Billy. The moment he realized how happy my husband was to see him, he just couldn't leave. When he decided to stay over, he remembered he hadn't brought any clothes with him. Down below the Kaler Hotel, where we were staying, was an underground mall leading to the Mayo Clinic, as well as to numerous shops. I told Jack, and he said he would go and pick up a few things.

"An hour later, he returned lugging an enormous shopping bag bulging over with shirts, ties, pajamas, and underwear. In his other hand, he carried a box—all gift-wrapped with a corny little bow. When he came in, my husband was lying down. But the moment he opened his eyes, Jack, just like a little kid, said, 'Billy, I bought you a present . . .'

"And Billy said, *'Well, it's about time!'*

"Jack laughed so hard, the big bag broke, spilling all of his purchases on the floor around him. It was a marvelous moment between two old and dear friends. As ill as Billy was, he never lost his sense of humor.

"Inside the gift box was a lovely pullover sweater my husband wore every day when he went for his treatments . . . Jack's stay in Rochester could have been rather dreary, under the circumstances. Instead, it was fun. It gave my husband such pleasure. He didn't have time to dwell on himself . . .

"Before Jack arrived, Billy had spent most of his time in bed. With Jack there, he got up and walked. He and Jack went out for ice cream together. They were like young pals, these two men, Jack, then in his seventies, and my husband, dying of cancer.

"I grew up around people in show business. I've been with celebrities all my life. But Jack, without question, was unique. This may sound odd, but I saw in Jack some of the same qualities pianist Artur Rubinstein has. It's a *special genius.* A simple, *childlike* magical outlook toward life on one level, combined with complete, unmatched *professional excellence* on another . . . Today, they toss around the word 'genius' so loosely—it really *fit* Jack!

"As a man, his sweetness was overwhelming. Years ago, Billy and I rented a small house in Palm Springs, and Jack and Mary came to visit us. During the day, I found myself alone with Jack. Suddenly, he looked at me and said, 'Edie, I'm so grateful to Mary . . .'

"When I asked him exactly what he meant, he said, 'If it wasn't for her, I'd be a third-rate violinist in some little dump. She had the brains, the courage, and the ambition to push me forward. *She's* responsible for my success . . .'

"I thought that was the greatest thing I had ever heard any man say about his wife . . ."

CHAPTER FORTY-FIVE

WHENEVER THEY COULD, close friends of Jack's came to see him "on the road." Financier-philanthropist Armand "Ardie" Deutsch was no exception—even though, in one instance, that meant watching Jack perform in England.

"One of the last times I saw Jack on stage," Deutsch said, "was at the Palladium in London, in 1972. My wife and I were taking our thirteen-year-old granddaughter on a tour of Europe, and Mary had invited us to Jack's opening . . .

"It turned out to be one of the most memorable nights of my life. Jack was so terribly funny, and the English audience went wild over him. Watching the show through my granddaughter's eyes was a revelation. This child loved him so much, and she alternately laughed and wept at the joy of just being there. Earlier that day, I had been very disturbed about Jack . . . I even had doubts as to whether he could, or would be able to go on. Always before, he had seemed so ageless, so youthful. But the afternoon of his first performance, he was terribly fatigued—and I was concerned for him.

"That night, however, as we sat with Mary, waiting for the show to begin, an electric excitement and expectation ran through the crowd, and I was swept along with it. When the orchestra struck up 'Love in Bloom,' he came on—*looking fantastic*. It was like a miracle!

"It was Jack—as usual—striding so confidently on stage. Smiling out at us. Looking not a day over forty-five. The entire audience stood up and cheered. It brought tears to my eyes. I looked over and Mary was crying. All of us sensed that this wasn't a moment for laughter—but, to the contrary, a time to express our love and respect for Jack.

"After the show, we went up to his suite for a party. He was worn out, but still so gracious. He took my granddaughter's arm, led her over to a couch, and said, 'I'm very tired. Let's just sit down here . . .' She was with him while so many people came over to compliment him on the brilliance of his performance . . .

"Years before, as a young Dartmouth graduate, living in New York City, I had been to many show business parties. Often, I'd be at the same affair with the Bennys. But I was just one of the crowd. I didn't get to know Jack and Mary until 1945, when I got out of the Navy. I came to Hollywood and, through pull, got myself a job. Dore Schary, head of RKO at the time, was my mentor. I eventually became his assistant . . .

"Hollywood then, as now, was a stratified society. You traveled in circles comprised of people in your same salary and celebrity bracket. That restriction never seemed to apply to me because I already knew a lot of stars from my New York days . . .

"From the moment I arrived in Hollywood, I was taken into the Benny circle. We became close, dear friends. I regarded it as a most meaningful relationship in my life, not one of those transient friendships Hollywood is so famous for . . .

"Eventually, I left the movie business to go back into investments with a family-owned firm. That didn't in any way interrupt our relationship. Like all friendships, ours was divided into two parts: the times Jack, Mary, my wife, Harriet, and I were together, usually at parties or dinners; and the times when Jack and I went to the ball game together . . . or played golf.

"Jack was always fascinated by my 'indirect' connection with the infamous Loeb-Leopold case. Dick Loeb's father was executive vice-president of Sears, Roebuck. He and his family lived next door to my grandfather, Julius Rosenwald, president and chairman of the board of Sears. The senior Loeb and my grandfather went to work together every day.

"I used to be around there regularly, not only to see my grandfather, but also to play with Dick's younger brother, who was my age. I certainly knew Loeb well, as one kid knows another kid's older brother . . .

"There is *no* question that I was the *intended kidnap victim*. And, if they *had* asked *me* to get into their car, I would have gone with them. Fortunately, on the day of the crime, I had a dentist appointment, and the family chauffeur picked me up and drove me there. Obviously, that's how Bobby Franks became the standby victim . . . I was in the fourth grade, around eleven years of age. During all the months of investigation and trial, I never read about the case. Papers were kept from me. I was taken out of school. It never occurred to me something odd, something dreadful had happened . . . And that it had almost happened to me!

"Years later, when I was in my fifties, I played golf one day with Jack at Hillcrest Country Club Meyer Levin's best-selling book, *Compulsion,* which concerned the Loeb-Leopold case, had just come out and was all the rage. Jack and I finished playing a round, and were having coffee in the clubhouse, when he said to me, "Ardie, this new book about the Loeb-Leopold case has brought the whole thing back into everyone's mind . . . I just can never believe that you were the one they *really* intended kidnapping . . .'

"You have to understand, of all the comedians I ever knew, Jack was the *only one* who asked a question and really *listened* to the answer. So when he mentioned me as being the intended victim, I looked at him with a straight face and said, *'You know, Jack, the way I putted today, I wish they would have gotten me!'*

"Jack and I shared a box at Dodger Stadium from the time the team first came out to California. What a baseball fan Jack was!

He loved the game with a passion. If they were good games, he liked them better. If they weren't so good, it didn't matter because it was a lovely way to spend an evening. After a while, we frequently wound up sitting in the box of Dodger owner Walter O'Malley . . .

"It's funny, how you remember little things. One of Jack's great complaints was he couldn't eat sweets, especially ice cream, which he loved, because of his diabetes. But time after time, when we were at Dodger Stadium, in O'Malley's box—which always contained lavish food—Jack *would* eat ice cream. First, he'd always say, 'Don't tell Mary . . .'

"And I'd reply, 'I won't. But eventually *somebody*—like your *doctor*—will find out!' Then, one day, he said to Mr. O'Malley, 'Do you know what I'm going to get *you* for a present? And you can keep it right in your ice box . . . Some dietetic ice cream so that *I* can have it . . .'

"And Walter said, very seriously, 'Gee, Jack, that will be a wonderful *present* for me!'

"There's one very meaningful anecdote about Jack that, to me, is illustrative of the kind of man he was. I was in Aspen, Colorado, attending their marvelous annual music festival. A cousin of mine, Edgar Stern, Jr., was president of it He complained to me about the big deficit the musicians were up against. He asked if I could bring one of my celebrity friends next time to play at the festival—someone who wouldn't charge too much.

"I told him I had a friend who would come—and wouldn't charge a dime. When I mentioned Jack Benny, he thought I was kidding. I assured my cousin that, pending Jack's schedule, I knew he would be happy to come . . . and furthermore, that his appearance would *guarantee* the festival could make up its entire deficit.

"When I got back to Hollywood, I talked to Jack. He seemed to know his schedule way into the next year, and said he would be very happy to come to Aspen and do a concert. We even set a definite date. When I told my cousin, he was thrilled.

"Jack and I made plans to stay up there for a couple of days after the festival and play golf. But fate is very cruel. One year later, almost to the day, Billy Goetz died. He was a very dear friend of both Jack's and mine. When Billy passed away, Jack was playing an engagement in North Tonawanda, just outside of Buffalo, New York. Afterward, he planned to come to Aspen for the festival. We had arranged for him to fly to Denver, where my cousin's plane would pick him up and take him to Aspen, so he would have a chance to rehearse with the orchestra before the concert.

"When Billy died, Jack called me immediately. 'Ardie, what'll I do? I'm one of Billy's pallbearers. The funeral is the *same* day I'm supposed to be rehearsing. I feel awful. If it were a paid engagement, I'd pay them off and get out of it. I *want* to do the benefit, but I *can't* miss Billy's funeral . . .'

"Naturally, I understood completely. I told him not to worry, and assured him I would take care of things. I did some frantic phoning and was able to make arrangements. I called Jack back, and he was very satisfied with the new plans.

"Jack was no young man . . . Yet he flew from Buffalo to Denver, took my cousin's plane to Aspen, rehearsed with the orchestra, then flew to Hollywood. He spent the night at home, and got up early the next day, when we had the sad task of going to Billy's funeral . . .

"Immediately afterward, there was a car waiting to drive us back to the airport. We got on my cousin's plane and headed for Aspen. When we arrived, there were several hundred people waiting to meet Jack. We got off looking exactly like we were: two pallbearers in mourning. But as sad and tired as Jack was, he remained completely gracious and outgoing.

"I can't tell you how much it meant to me that Jack put himself through all that wear and tear, knowing the emotional grief he felt over Billy. But he realized all the tickets were sold—and he wouldn't let me down. *That* was Jack! And, because of him, the festival's deficit was wiped out.

"After the concert, the high-priced-ticket holders had been invited back to my cousin's house to meet him. Fatigued as he was, Jack went through with it all. He didn't rest until he had shaken the last hand of those who had come to meet him. I wonder how many other people in show business would have done what Jack did—under the circumstances!

"I've always felt that, in a way, *Jack wasn't egotistical enough*. Which is not to say that he didn't have a true appreciation of his own greatness. He understood it—thoroughly. He knew he was Jack Benny, but somewhere in his brain, he realized that, however other people reacted to their fame or good fortune, he would do very well in life to remain *untouched* by his success . . . He realized that if he ever became overly impressed with his position in the world of show business, and in the world of American life, he would lose the *very thing* which made him what he was.

"He disciplined himself so that he was able to accept all those honors which poured in to him with grace and dignity. He was never cynical, or satiated by them. Jack instinctively knew that if he began to take himself too seriously, after a while, he would no longer be Jack. That is the single most important thing about his character: he never took himself too seriously.

"The day Jack died, my granddaughter was so affected, she couldn't go to school. Being with Jack in London, seeing him perform, had been the highlight of her trip abroad. The *universality* of his humor was that a little girl could love him and, at the same time, her parents could love him, and a ninety-three-year-old person could love him—Jack's humor was for everybody!"

CHAPTER FORTY-SIX

ON A FRIDAY NIGHT in December 1974, five days before Christmas, Mary phoned her brother and asked him and his wife to come over—right away . . .

"During the fifteen minutes it took us to maneuver through the traffic on Sunset Boulevard and head out toward Mary and Jack's place Virginia and I conjectured about the obvious urgency I had detected in Mary's voice," Hickey said. "We knew Jack was sick —but I had just seen him the day before—and he had been resting comfortably . . ."

Five months earlier, Marks and his wife had been on the road with Jack when the first signs of Benny's illness had become apparent. They had flown to Washington with him, where Jack appeared at the Seattle Opera House. From there, they had gone on to Portland, Oregon, for his show at the Convention Center.

It was during their stay in Portland that, for the first time, Jack had complained of stomach pains, and a lack of appetite. Before going to bed, he felt so uncomfortable Marks had given him a Valium. The pill relaxed Jack. He felt much better and had a good night's sleep. The next morning, at breakfast, Hickey encouraged him to eat.

"Jack, forget about your diabetic condition. You have a show tonight . . . Tomorrow we have to leave for the Exposition in Spokane. Why don't you indulge yourself and have some pancakes? You need the energy . . ."

Jack ordered pancakes and smothered them with butter and syrup. Then he went up to his hotel suite and rested until show time. If he was uncomfortable on stage, no one in the audience had been aware of the fact. He gave his usual entertaining performance, and was enthusiastically received.

Later that same evening, however, he had complained of pain again. Marks gave him another Valium, which enabled Jack to get a second good night of rest.

Early the next morning, July 26, they took the short flight to Spokane in order to make a press conference which had been set up for Jack in one of the rooms of their hotel. Radio, television, and the print media were represented.

It was a long, free-wheeling, disjointed affair—as most spontaneous press conferences are. The questions, covering a whole variety of topics, began, ironically enough for Jack, with a controversial subject.

Several weeks before, the country's major newspapers had been full of reports of a gigantic oil swindle. What made the story so especially newsworthy was the fact that the list of people who had been "taken" was a literal Who's Who of show business figures, national politicians, highly respected financiers, and even a conservative foundation or two. Among those on the list of "victims" was Jack Benny.

Even though Jack had recently celebrated his eightieth birthday, his cheapskate public image *still* followed him. The media people were well aware of the "Benny legend" as contrasted with the *real* man, but few could pass up the opportunity to get a couple of laughs—at Jack's expense. As you will see, Jack was more than equal to the task!

No one had any idea this would wind up being Jack's *final press conference*. Despite any personal discomfort, he looked well, and was very sharp, witty, straightforward, and totally candid. He was also the best analyst of his own unique brand of humor—that comic genius which had made him a top star for close to half a century.

The words or phrases in italics are those in which Benny's famous rising vocal inflection was "in action."

PRESS: Mr. Benny, is it true you had to trade in the Maxwell to purchase your Home-Stake shares?

JACK: Did I trade in my Maxwell to buy shares? Oh, you mean in that *oil swindle?* Well, *that's* a kind of a silly question, isn't it? In the *first place,* I *never* really owned a Maxwell, and in the *second* place, *evidently* I didn't even *own* any oil stock! As a matter of fact, I didn't even know I was in that deal until I went over to my club one day to play golf and somebody ran over to me with the *Wall Street Journal* . . . I hadn't read the Los Angeles *Times* yet, so I read in the *Journal* where I was in there with everybody else. But when I read some of the *smart* names that were *hooked* in there—not in show business but people who should have known better—then I found out that it wasn't *too* embarrassing. I also found out that I didn't lose *that much* money. You always find *that* out later.

PRESS: Have you ever been in Spokane before?

JACK: I think so. But if I played here before, it was a *very* long time ago. During the time when we had the Orpheum Circuit going from Winnipeg to Calgary and Seattle. I think sometimes they would book us in for a half a week, or a week, in Spokane . . . It was so long ago. But I don't remember, outside of then, having been here. Except maybe driving through. I think I've driven through here several times . . .

PRESS: Exactly how thrilled are you to be here?

JACK: Well . . . *thrilled???* I'm *not* thrilled to be *anyplace.* But I'm *glad* to be here . . .

PRESS: Jack, you and Bob Hope are definitely superstars, and you certainly didn't come for the money. Why are you and Hope the first two big stars to come to Expo '74? Were you asked by the government, by any chance?

JACK: Well . . . you know, I played the Expo in Montreal. I played the Expo in San Antonio . . . and this is the third one. It's a place to work . . . the same as anyplace else . . . Bob Hope and I are *very much* alike. We'd rather work than not work, I guess. Bob Hope, *I* think, is *worse* than I am. He loves to work every minute. And he claims that *I am* the biggest ham in show business. He thinks *I* work too much. Now *nobody* works as much as Bob Hope! *He's crazy.* He *never* stops. He can't stand vacations. He's got to work all the time . . . and I'm *almost* like that. I only enjoy vacations when I also have something to do, when I have something on my mind . . . Something has gotta worry me or I won't enjoy my vacation.

PRESS: Are you on vacation now?

JACK: Well—in a way. Most of my engagements are vacations because I have all day to do what I want to do, really. Some places I'll play golf in the daytime. Now I just played a few days in Colorado Springs, which was a marvelous vacation. One show a night and you have all day. You live at the Broadmoore Hotel a block away from the theater. You play golf. You go swimming. You do anything you want. So *that's* a *real* vacation.

PRESS: George Burns appeared last night on the show in which they picked the Playboy Bunny of the Year. You must have a comment on that.

JACK: I didn't see it so I don't know . . .

PRESS: You *don't* have a comment on George Burns with all those Playboy bunnies?

JACK: I have *ninety comments* on George Burns . . . and if you come to the theater you'll hear a few of them because I wouldn't drop him. In fact, I *close* my show with *him*.

PRESS: Are you going to play the violin?

JACK: Yeah . . . I play a lot of it.

PRESS: Mr. Benny, when you play an engagement such as this, how do you determine what kind of material you might use? Do you kind of judge your audience? Do you have some standard stuff that you use? Do you play to the audience?

JACK: Well, I might change a thing or two for each town, but the audience is *exactly* the same in Spokane, in Seattle, in Vancouver, in London, in Sydney, Australia; in Singapore, in Israel. It's the same anyplace where they can understand and speak English. I played what they call a Sunday night concert about a year ago in London where I did *almost* the same kind of a show that I'll do here; and then, towards the end of my show, I would do some local things about London. But I would *always* start out with practically some of the things that I'll do here. They laugh at exactly the same things. They laughed just as loud at certain jokes as they'll do here. As long as they understand what you are talking about . .

PRESS: What kind of jokes do people like basically?

JACK: Anything that's funny . . . that's all. *Anything* that's funny. I talk a lot, not constantly, or always, about the town that I'm in. I might talk about the last time that I think I played here, and I'll get some laughs out of that. And I try to do a special routine . . . . You see, I *could* do the *same* routine every night that I play almost anyplace, except *I* would get tired of hearing *me* say the same things over and over again. The audiences *wouldn't* get tired . . . because they haven't heard 'em. But I change sometimes . . . arrange a program a little differently. I even make notes to myself to change my program . . . and I look at 'em in front of an audience and *tell* the audience that I've changed some material. And they go along with me and they laugh. But you could do the same show anyplace. Like I do concerts with symphony orchestras practically all over the world. I did a couple in Israel, in Tel Aviv. And the same things that I say and I do with the violin in Tel Aviv are the same things that they laugh at here . . . Because they speak English . . . most of 'em. And they understand the humor so you don't have any problem. Now, I *couldn't* play in countries where they don't speak English. *Then* I'd have a problem.

PRESS: With all the problems in the world . . . in the United States today, is it tougher to make people laugh now than it used to be?

JACK: No . . . I don't think it's tougher at all. And I stay away from most of the gags . . . I might do one or two once in a while about Watergate. About all the problems . . . that the President has . . . the problems in Washington. But I kinda steer away from that because in the first place I don't think it's always *particularly* funny. I also say that I think I should know more before I talk about it.

PRESS: Do you think the world should laugh?

JACK: Oh, sure. You gotta laugh. In the first place, they are not thinking of Watergate, or the problems right now that are going on in Washington while someone else is doing a show. And so they laugh . . . You know, they laugh at the same things now that they laughed at fifty years ago. Except you might have to be a *little* more sophisticated. For instance, if I do a stingy joke—because that's been my character—*now* I have to be a little wilder with the jokes, a little more sophisticated . . . A little bit funnier than it would've had to have been twenty years ago. And I steer clear *entirely* of jokes about being thirty-nine years old. That's corny now . . . *Others* do it *about* me, but I *never* do a joke about being thirty-nine years old. Nor do I talk about my Maxwell . . . or anything else that would be corny . . . I wouldn't talk about it any more . . . Today, a lot of people still introduce me at a banquet, or something, and they'll say—and they *think* they are going to get a scream when they say it—"And now, ladies and gentlemen, our guest of honor, that thirty-nine-year-old boy Jack Benny." They *think* they'll get screams, but *nobody* laughs at that any more. If they would come to me *first* and say to me, "Do *you* think that'll be funny?" I'd say, "Not only won't it be funny, but nobody's going to laugh at it any more." I *never* do those jokes about myself on television, unless some way or another there happened to be a great, great joke associated with that. But I can't think of what it would be, saying I was thirty-nine. That was funny *years ago* when I *was* just a little bit over *thirty-nine,* or even ten years over. But now that's just not funny any more.

PRESS: What's caused the change? Have audiences become so sophisticated that you stopped doing the jokes that you now call "corny"?

JACK: Yeah . . . Sure . . . Because they've heard it so much . . . And they heard it *years ago.* I can just hear an audience saying to themselves, wherever they are watching, whether it's on television, or live in a club, "Well, why doesn't he *stop* with that thirty-nine *already?*" Well, I *wanta beat 'em to it.* You *always* have to beat the audience to it. *Don't* let them get the best of it.

PRESS: How long ago did you stop doing those jokes?

JACK: Oh, I think it must be fifteen years or something like that . . .

PRESS: Do you find audiences different now from when you started out in show business?

JACK: I don't think so. Now, if you do a lot of topical humor there would be a lot of laughs about what's going on in Washington, but I don't think . . . it depends . . . If you are *constantly* doing topical material, like Will Rogers did, or let's say, Mort Sahl does, then they sort of expect that and it seems to be the right thing to do. But I *don't* think it's the right thing for *me* to do. I might throw in one joke about Washington, or something. Now, when I played London a little less than a year ago, it was just at the height of Watergate . . . The London audiences expected, I'm sure, that my first fifteen minutes would be all talk about Watergate. Well, *that's* where you *must* fool them. You *don't* do it, you see? At the *very end* of my show, I did *one* joke about Watergate, without mentioning Watergate, without mentioning Washington, without mentioning the President, and yet it *was* a joke *about* Watergate—and they all screamed. They knew all about it because they watched it on television over there. They saw all those proceedings that were going on from eleven at night until two in the morning. So *that's* what they expected from me. They thought: Right away, he's going to do fifteen minutes on Watergate—and *I didn't do it at all.* I did my first ten or fifteen minutes of stuff like I would do here. And they laughed . . .

PRESS: Do you see any more of the old radio group that you were with?

JACK: That used to be with me? Yeah, they were with me on television, too. I see Phil Harris once in a while in Las Vegas . . . and Dennis Day . . . Rochester, I don't see very much. He's been a little bit ill . . . I see my wife, *who won't work anyway.*

PRESS: How did that famous feud between you and Fred Allen get started?

JACK: It just started by accident, *like everything I've ever done.* I've always explained that everything I've ever done on radio or television *that was good* started by an accident . . . Because if Fred Allen and I had said to each other, "Let's have a feud," I'm sure it would not have lasted over three or four weeks. It would have been lousy. But the fact that it just came up out of nothing— which, incidentally, I explain in my show here—made it funny, because then you are saying the right things, you are ad-libbing . . . and when you feel they've had enough of it, you stop. There would be some shows that I wouldn't even mention Fred Allen, or he wouldn't mention me on his show. Then later on we would pick it up again . . . Everything good started by an accident. Like, you mentioned the Maxwell . . . Well, no matter what car I would have picked out to trade my old car in for, *that* would have been the car that would have been funny. It could have been any of the old cars . . . It could have been a Rio. *That* would have been the car then that people would have laughed at . . . Now, take my theme song "Love in Bloom," which I *certainly* did *not* pick as my theme because it has *nothing* to do with a comedian at all! It happened to be a number that I kept playing on the violin for a few weeks, *not dreaming* it was *ever* going to be my theme song. Then, all of a sudden, I'd walk into nightclubs or restaurants and the orchestras there would start playing "Love in Bloom." So *they* made it my theme song—practically against my will —and there was *no* way that I could stop it. So I left it that way. It's a beautiful song, but it *doesn't* fit a comedian! But I just couldn't do a *thing* about it . . .

PRESS: Did you actually get your radio start on a show with Ed Sullivan?

JACK: Yes . . . Because I had quit a big show. I was on the road with *Earl Carroll's Vanities* and I realized that radio was the thing to get into, so I got a release from Earl. I told him the reason. I said, "I want to try to get into radio." I was in New York for a couple of weeks, waiting for the opportunity . . . this was in 1931, or '32 . . . and finally Ed Sullivan saw me, or called me, or something, and asked me if I would go on a show with him. He was doing a sports show, sports news on radio. I said, "All right. What'll we do?" "Oh," he said, "we'll just talk about sports . . . I'll ask you some questions about your business and you ask me some questions . . . we'll just talk." So I went on . . . The next morning I had a call to be on my own very first radio show. So, eventually, I probably would have gotten into radio anyway, 'cause you *have* to get into whatever is important at

the time. Like when we had to make the transition from
radio to TV . . .

PRESS: Your age, needless to say, has always been a controversial thing. And, although you don't use that joke any
more, you really don't look a hell of a lot older than
thirty-nine. What is the secret to how you look?

JACK: Well, first let me thank you for *that* . . . *then* I'll answer
it. I *must* look a *lot* older than thirty-nine, but I still
don't think I look anything like my right age, so I should
be grateful for *that,* I guess . . . You know what I *think*
it is? I think it's because I'm constantly working. I think
that has a lot to do with it. Now, I imagine—I haven't
retired yet—I imagine if I was in the haberdashery business, selling neckties, or something, I'd be willing to retire
after a certain amount of time. But in show business it's
difficult to retire because we don't know anything else
. . . Most of us don't . . . Maybe *you* do . . . But I don't
know anything else but show business. So, if I *tried* to do
something else—'cause to retire entirely would be very,
very difficult, I think, because I don't *feel* my age, though
there *are* moments—and then I wouldn't know, actually,
what to do.

PRESS: Maybe the secret is to keep working.

JACK: Yeah . . . To keep working until you *can't,* I guess.
Right now, we just played a couple of engagements, and
the audiences have been better than ever. Business has
been fine. The audiences are laughing . . . I write better
than I used to. I find *everything* much easier, so therefore I don't think I should get out of it yet.

PRESS: Where do you go from here?

JACK: I go back home for about five days and then I go East
. . . I'll tell you the thing I do that I *enjoy* more than
anything else. Now, I could retire if I were doing *just*
concerts with symphony orchestras. I like *that* better
than anything. And maybe sometime I'll be able to do
that—that better come *pretty quick,* too, I think!

PRESS: You've probably heard about Sinatra's problems recently in Australia. Do you have any plans on making some acidy remarks about Spokane's press?

JACK: No . . . I have found the press pretty good . . . all over. Once in a while they would like to ask me something that would annoy me . . . I *also* have a little bit of a temper, but Frank *really* has. He gets very angry. Like for instance, he probably went to Australia to open and, instead of asking him immediately how he thinks he will enjoy Australia, although he has played there before, or did he enjoy working there before, or what kind of a show was he going to do, they probably started right in with maybe one of the problems that he has had. Excuse me for talking so long but *that* makes him angry . . . Once in a while they'll start right out by asking *me* something like, "How do you feel about losing $300,000 in that oil deal?" They won't say, "How do you feel about being in Spokane?" or "Do you think you're going to enjoy it here?" But *I* don't get angry. I might say to them, "Why don't you ask me that later, and then we'll go through a whole thing about that . . ." But Frank gets angry . . . and they *know* it. So, sometimes it *could be* Frank's fault . . . and sometimes it *could be* the fault of the press. But I'll tell you one thing about Frank Sinatra—because he is *one of the three closest friends that I have in the whole world*—for every fault that he has, he has *such great qualities* that make up for it. He is the *most* generous man in the whole world. Nobody does as much for people—even people he doesn't know. All he has to do is read something in a newspaper that somebody, let's say in Spokane . . . we'll make up a town . . . He'd read that some woman in Spokane has to go to a hospital and her husband can't afford to take her there; or maybe her child is ill. He right away calls his banker and says, "In this morning's *Times,* look on page three, column one. You'll read about so and so and so and so and so. Send them $10,000 or $20,000 immediately and *don't say* where it came from . . ." And *that's* been Frank Sinatra all his life. So I think *that* makes up for a lot of things. A

271

lot of people won't do that, you know. Or they'll do it for publicity, which Frank doesn't. Frank doesn't want anybody to know it . . . The first we knew about it—all of those good deeds—was a few years ago when he was on the Oscar show. Gregory Peck mentioned it. Frank would *never* mention it. But I've seen him do the nicest, *kindest* things for people. And yet, he *can* get very angry himself. Well, everybody can't be perfect, you know. But, if you can control yourself, you're better off in the long run . . . I don't remember ever having a problem with the press . . . Because I don't know why the press would pick on me—unless maybe it was like something that just happened lately—*which is news* . . . Because *it was news to me when I read it!* I didn't even *know* I was in that oil deal where I lost the $300,000. Then I came back to my office and I found out that I actually didn't lose that kind of money. You know, a lot of it was given back. Like all those swindle deals. They give you some of it back . . . They get money from somebody else and give it to you . . . But I *could* have lost an awful lot . . . I haven't the slightest idea at this moment how much. But *that's* news . . . and you've got to expect those kind of questions. But sometimes they might pick on Frank a little bit more than they should. And then he's ready, you know, he's ready to jump on you, you see? But I think I'm right about one thing . . . And I think you will all agree with me . . . When a fellow can take a lot of money—fortunately *he's got the money* to do it with. But there are a lot of people that are very rich and won't help as much as he does. And he doesn't want anybody to know about it except his banker. Then his banker gets mad, because he says, "Whenever Frank sends something, *I* have to send something . . ."

PRESS: Could I ask you about your movies, Jack? How many did you make?

JACK· Well, that's a good question . . . and I've got a good answer . . .

PRESS: I loved *The Horn Blows at Midnight*.

272

JACK: Well, yeah, a lot of people liked it. You know why? Because *I* panned it so much that everybody said, "Gee, it can't be *that* bad." And they looked at it and said, *"It isn't."* I had somebody just the other day in Portland say to me, "Gee, I saw *The Horn Blows at Midnight* and I liked it." And I said, "Well, *you* liked it because *I* didn't." I was on Merv Griffin's show about a year ago and I said, "Merv, let's talk about things that I haven't talked about much on these shows. Why don't you do some research and find out how many pictures I've made, or I can find out, and we'll discuss my movies." Now, I actually thought I'd only made about seven or eight pictures in my life . . . Well, I made twenty-two. And most of 'em were *good* . . . and most of 'em made *money,* because in those days if you made a picture for a million dollars, that was a lot. Today, it's fifteen or sixteen million, you see. So, they all made money. Today, one picture is considered a classic, *To Be or Not to Be,* the one I made with Lubitsch. And there was *Charley's Aunt* and *George Washington Slept Here* . . . I made a lot of good movies. But I've always kidded so much about one, you know, deprecating myself about that one picture, so a lot of people think I never made any others . . . I should have shut up really! . . .

PRESS: Thank you very much.

JACK: Thank *you* . . .

Although Jack continued to be troubled with intermittent pain, he did six shows in the next three days. After each performance, a table was set up for him so he could autograph souvenir programs. In between times, he, Hickey, and Virginia also managed to tour the fairgrounds.

Jack enjoyed his stay in Spokane . . . but after the last show, he seemed very anxious to get back home to Mary.

CHAPTER FORTY-SEVEN

"JACK ARRIVED HOME, walked through the door, kissed me, and said, 'Doll, I don't feel well . . .'" Mary began.

"He went right to bed and, the following morning, I took him to see the doctor. Over the next few days, Jack took a whole series of tests. They all turned out negative. The doctors couldn't find any reason for the cause of his pain . . .

"During the next couple of months, he occasionally felt uncomfortable and complained, yet he continued to stick to his schedule. That August, he played a week's engagement at the Candlewood Theater in New Fairfield, Connecticut . . .

"In mid-October, Jack flew to Dallas, Texas, to make a personal appearance on behalf of our good friend Stanley Marcus, of the Neiman-Marcus department stores. During rehearsal, he became ill—and never completed the show. The doctor in attendance called me in Los Angeles, and I immediately made arrangements for Jack to be flown back home in a hospital plane . . .

"That afternoon, Joan, my brother and sister-in-law, doctors Rex Kennamer and Gary Sugarman, and I all met at Cedars of Lebanon Hospital, where we waited for Jack to arrive. He was due in at four-thirty . . .

"By five o'clock, when he still wasn't there, I called Burbank Airport. They said his plane had landed, and that he was en route to the hospital by ambulance. I couldn't understand why it was taking so long . . .

"Finally, around five-fifteen, Jack arrived, and we asked about his delay. He told us he had felt hungry, so the ambulance driver *waited* while he went into the airport cafe and had a cup of coffee and a doughnut—*that was Jack!*

"He remained hospitalized for five days. After going through

L. to R.: Jack, Mary, George Burns, Gracie Allen, and Eddie Cantor at a B'nai B'rith Award Dinner for Jack. (Photo courtesy Peter Banks)

Jack and his sister Florence. (Benny Family Personal Collection)

Zubin Mehta conducting the Israel Philharmonic Orchestra with guest soloist Jack Benny, taken at Mann Auditorium in Tel Aviv. (Photo courtesy Zubin Mehta private collection)

Jack and Pablo Casals. (Benny Family Personal Collection)

Veronique and Gregory Peck in front of the Bouchet caricature of Jack. (Photo courtesy of the National Broadcasting Company, Inc.)

Jack and Maurice Chevalier. (Benny Family Personal Collection)

Jack with his grandchildren, Michael and Maria Rudolph. (Benny Family Personal Collection)

Jack and his daughter Joan in the last photograph ever taken of them. (Benny Family Personal Collection)

exhaustive tests, he was released. Once again, nothing showed up. His tests were still negative . . ."

Ironically, this period in Jack's life was one of his busiest. His schedule for the balance of 1974, and way into 1975, was already crowded with commitments.

On October 29, he was due to play the Fontainebleau Hotel in Miami Beach. From November 8 through 21, he was booked into the Tropicana Hotel in Las Vegas. On November 26, there was a Benny concert scheduled in Santa Barbara, California . . . And early in December, he was to be one of the honored guests at the Hollywood Women's Press Club luncheon. They were to present him with the coveted Louella O. Parsons Award. He and Louella had been great friends. Even though he was not feeling well, he attended the party. George Burns went with him. Midway through lunch, however, Jack felt worse and had to leave. George stayed and accepted the award for him.

After that event, Jack remained in bed quite a bit of the time. He was scheduled to rehearse his television special on December 14, 15, and 16, and then to tape the show on the eleventh of January. The guest stars were to be Mr. and Mrs. Gregory Peck, conductor Zubin Mehta, and Engelbert Humperdinck. His "Third Farewell Special" had an air date of January 23, 1975, over NBC.

One day after the TV show was seen coast to coast, Jack was scheduled to begin another week's engagement at the Tropicana in Vegas. Then he was to return home and take four days of rest before checking onto the M-G-M lot to begin rehearsing Neil Simon's *The Sunshine Boys,* co-starring Walter Matthau. Actual shooting on the film was to begin on February 23.

Under the circumstances, however, everything was canceled—except his television special and the film.

During the next few weeks, while working on the script for the special, Marks would pick Jack up at his house, and they would drive to the office where they were writing. Invariably, Jack would complain about not feeling well.

"Then, one morning," Hickey recalls, "while Jack was working along with the writers, Al Gordon, Hal Goldman, Hugh Wedlock, Jr., and myself, I saw him unbuckle the belt of his trousers. Immediately, I said, 'Well, that's it, boys . . . Let's stop writing.'

Ironically, we had just completed a rough draft of the show—that was the last day we all worked together . . ."

Once again, Mary had called the doctors. This time, they suggested Jack *stay* in bed, and a nurse was hired to be in attendance during the day.

It was a few weeks after this period when Mary had phoned Hickey and asked him to come right over.

"The night I finally called my brother and sister-in-law . . . I already *knew*," Mary said. "In fact, I had known for a couple of weeks.

"Jack's physicians had called in Dr. Max Lippman, a stomach specialist, for consultation, and he had discovered the reason for Jack's severe discomfort—cancer of the pancreas. They call that a 'silent cancer' because it's almost impossible to detect—until it's too late . . .

"When Hickey and Virginia first arrived, I didn't tell them. Instead, the three of us went right upstairs. When we entered his room, Jack looked great. His color was good. He said, 'Hello,' and kissed Virginia. After a few minutes, she and I left the room, and my brother stayed with Jack . . ."

Hickey continues:

" 'I don't think we'll be able to do our TV show, Hickey,' Jack said.

" 'Yes, Jack, I know.' Then I told him a made-up story. 'We've *already* postponed the show for the time being. We've arranged to do it *after* you finish *The Sunshine Boys*. Zubin's in Israel this week, so I couldn't reach him. But I phoned Engelbert Humperdinck and Greg Peck. They were willing to postpone until you get better. Besides, if we wait and do the special *after* you finish the picture, the publicity will be even greater . . .'

"For a few seconds, Jack just looked at me. Then he said, 'I don't think I'll ever be able to go on again . . .'

"I tried to humor him. 'Jack, let me say one thing I've said to you a hundred times before . . . I'll have to use the hook . . .' Whenever Jack played Las Vegas, or made other personal appearances where he was required to do more than one show a night, he'd usually say, 'Hickey, I don't think I can do the second show.' But he *always* went on—and, invariably, the second show was *longer* than the first one. When he'd make his final exit, I'd be standing in the wings, smiling, and I'd repeat that old vaudeville expression: 'I thought I'd have to use a *hook* to get you off.'

"He looked up at me. There was a smile on his face. In a few minutes, the medication took over. That was the last time Jack was lucid . . .

"He just fell asleep. He was not in pain. I left his room and joined my wife and sister.

"Then, when we were all together, Mary broke down and told us the news . . ."

CHAPTER FORTY-EIGHT

Two of Jack and Mary's closest friends were Gregory Peck and his wife Veronique. They joined the Benny "inner circle" in 1969, after Greg guest-starred on one of Jack's television specials. But actually, because of Jack's willing participation in any cause organized to help Hollywood, he and Greg originally became acquainted twenty-five years earlier.

Peck spoke with great warmth and affection about a man he had grown to love and respect deeply.

"When we heard Jack was terminally ill, we couldn't believe it. Age never meant anything to him. When Mary told us, we were stunned.

"I met Jack in the early forties in connection with the Actors Studio. A group of us who thought Los Angeles did not have enough legitimate theater, John Garfield, Hank Fonda, Dorothy McGuire, and Mel Ferrer, asked Jack to join us in raising money to build a legitimate theater on Wilshire Boulevard and Doheny Drive in Beverly Hills.

"Our plan was to put on a special radio production of *The Man Who Came to Dinner,* with Jack starring in the Sheridan Whiteside-Monty Woolley part. The show was a success and earned

277

nearly $200,000, which we intended to use as good money for what we called the Actors Company Playhouse . . . Each of us was to commit ourselves to doing one live production at the theater every year. In organizing the company, and in rehearsals, I met Jack.

"Frankly, he was not too happy about playing the Whiteside role—a very acerbic, sarcastic character, not really a 'Benny-type' part. But he was such a good sport, Jack did it just to help our cause . . . Ultimately, we couldn't buy the property we wanted. We couldn't get enough people to make a firm commitment to the project . . . so it fell through.

"During that period, I ran into Jack every once in a while socially, or on the dais at an industry function. But our close friendship dated from my appearance on Jack's television program in December 1969. It was the very first comedy show I had ever done on TV.

"I was scared to death. To overcome my fear—of doing comedy and singing and dancing—I wanted to rehearse a lot. I was perfectly willing to do my lines with a stagehand, or anyone else who would cue me. But Jack insisted on staying with me for hours at a time.

"He rehearsed our sketches . . . and went over and over our dance routine. He and George Burns, the other guest star, already knew it. But I needed more assurance—and Jack gave it to me.

"He really got a kick out of it. He said he never saw anybody rehearse as much as I did. He confessed that he enjoyed it, too, but didn't often run into people who wanted to really rehearse. He said, 'The best ad libs are the ones you rehearse . . . If you believe in spontaneity, and inspiration *doesn't* strike, you're nowhere. If you are prepared, and inspiration *does* strike, you're that much further ahead.'

"Jack was a great comic actor with a unique audience sense and empathy. He knew how to communicate . . . how to reach out and get an audience's attention. He was a *highly skillful actor*. So much of his humor depended on character, and the transmission of thought . . . sharing an idea with an audience. Sometimes, he didn't even need words . . .

"Alec Guinness, Laurence Olivier, and Noel Coward were big

278

fans of Jack's. A great many *dramatic* actors learned from him
. . . *Most great performers take their time.* They don't go too fast
for an audience. They stay just a little bit ahead, and give people
time for the point to get across. Compelling speakers like Winston
Churchill and Franklin D. Roosevelt took time to make their
points. All great speakers are instinctively slow—Jack knew that
secret!

"There was an elegance about Jack, and an innocence, too. He
never gave an audience the impression he was smarter than they
were, or superior to them. *Yet, they looked up to him.* There was
a generosity about him. A warmheartedness that came through.
Jack was unique. He had a very aristocratic style. Yet, at the same
time, he was down to earth. *That was his secret.* People simultaneously loved, admired, and empathized with him.

"Socially, he was often quiet. We would have dinner—say at
Chasen's—and he never knew what to eat, or how to tip . . .
Also, he never went out of his way to be funny. But he was *always
ready* for a friendly, good time . . .

"We were in Las Vegas with him one time, and after his midnight show, he got to playing blackjack with Mary. Finally I said,
'Let's do something really silly. Let's go to a topless show. There's
one on at 3 A.M.' Mary wanted to stay and play blackjack, so
Veronique and Jack and I went to a sort of second-rate place and
watched some rather tired girls bounce up and down. After a few
minutes, Jack said, 'What am *I* doing here?' We all laughed—and
stayed for another two hours! Even stupid things like the girlie
show gave him a kick.

"He was not a sophisticated man in the sense that he was jaded,
or cynical. Yet, in the purest sense of the word—because *he was
an aristocrat of the spirit*—he *was* sophisticated. Jack was a rare
blend of simplicity and complexity," Greg continued. "I don't
think you can ever fully explain a man like that. He had a touch
of genius, and you just can't put an easy definition to it . . .

"Certain things made him laugh . . . One night, at dinner, he
said he thought he and Mary should have a dog—a big, strong
dog. Veronique and I just happened to have a ninety-pound German shepherd. A few days later, a man whom I work out with, a
physical trainer, a big husky guy, was at my house, when I got an

idea for this gag. I bought a new leash, put a big bow on his collar, and sent my friend, the muscle man, down to Jack's office with our dog.

"He walked in and told the secretary he had a *present* for Mr. Benny from Mr. and Mrs. Peck. When he was shown into the inner office, he just handed Jack the leash. Jack was speechless! We had sent along a letter which included a whole list of instructions: what the dog had to eat; the fact that he was *not* fully housebroken; etc. The trainer left the dog and walked out. Jack was flabbergasted. The man was all the way to the parking lot before Jack ran out, calling after him . . . 'Hey, *I don't want this dog* . . .' But he carried our note around for a long time. He got such a kick out of it!

"For Jack's eightieth birthday, Veronique and I were stuck in London. We racked our brains trying to think of what kind of a message we could send him. We knew he'd be receiving wires from presidents and senators . . . that there were to be three days of parties. Rosalind Russell gave one. There was another in a restaurant in Palm Springs. Then Frank Sinatra gave him a party. It was to be the *big event* . . .

"That's when Veronique got an idea. We sent him a cable that just said: DEAR JACK . . . BIG DEAL—and that's the wire he kept and carried around with him. Funny little things like that made him laugh.

"In 1972, while Jack was in London, my wife and I took him to see the Joe Frazier championship fight. Ava Gardner came along, too. Afterward, we picked up Mary and all of us went out to dinner. Jack really seemed to enjoy himself so much at the fight. He was like a kid out for a Saturday matinee!

"In the fall of 1974, when the Muhammed Ali fight was going to be on closed-circuit TV, Veronique and I took a table at the Century Plaza Hotel in Los Angeles and invited Jack, and our close friends Natalie and Robert Wagner, to come with us. That was around the period *after* Jack had been in Dallas, had gone to the hospital, and subsequently had returned home feeling much better.

"When we picked him up, he was in very good spirits. But just as the fight started, he said, 'Greg, I don't feel so hot . . .' The fight didn't last long. Instead of going on to dinner, we took Jack home. Subsequently, he and I had a couple of telephone conversations regarding his 'Third Farewell Special.' He kept telling me about the part he had written in the script for Veronique and me to play. He loved to talk out sketches—almost as if, by going over them, they became more visual in his mind.

"It was to be a sensational part of the show, a take-off on violent movies. Because he sounded so enthusiastic, we never realized how ill Jack was. Then Hilliard called and told us the TV show was being postponed until after Jack did *Sunshine Boys* . . ."

Veronique Peck, a lovely, shy lady, born in France, has been married to superstar Gregory Peck for more than twenty years. Although a journalist prior to her marriage, she very seldom *gives* interviews. Yet, she wanted to add her own memories of the love and respect she felt for Jack.

"I first met him at a large dinner party given by Gloria and Jimmy Stewart in the late 1950s," she began. "It was a few years after Greg and I were married and I had come to America. *For me,* it was a memorable meeting. Gloria had seated me next to Jack. It was such a large party, I never even met Mary that evening.

"Jack had no idea who I was, and we never spoke. *Not a word.* I noticed he didn't speak to the women on the other side of him, either. But I was so enchanted *just to be next to him.* I thought, if he feels like being quiet and reserved, he's perfectly entitled to do so.

"I discovered, when I first came to Hollywood, that many women who meet important male stars are *very upset* if a big fuss is not made over them. They'll say, 'Well, so and so certainly isn't at all what he's supposed to be like . . .' I've never felt that way. Living with a star myself, I know there are times when Greg prefers to be quiet, too.

"I didn't meet Jack again until almost ten years later. During the interim, we must have attended the same parties, but I actually *met* Jack and Mary in 1968. Again, it was at a social event. This time, we were *properly* introduced and hit it off immediately. It was an instantaneous love affair between all four of us. We became close, true, and very loyal friends.

"It was the following year when my husband did his first television special with Jack. I was happy for Greg—because *he* was so happy working with Jack. There were always these wonderful emanations from him. These vibrations that made you know you were absolutely safe *professionally*. That show became, for both Greg and myself, a wonderful memory. By then, we were devoted friends. We would have done anything for each other. We were close as family. Today, Mary is still very much part of our clan . . .

"Early in the fall of 1974, Greg and I were in New York. I was out shopping one day and when I returned, I found several messages saying Jack had phoned from California. When I called him back, he was so dear, so excited. For years he had been teasing me—*I thought*—that one day he would find a TV script which would not only be perfect for Greg, but for *me* as well. As we spoke, that's exactly what he told me. He and his writers had come up with a sketch for his 'Third Farewell Special' which had been written for Greg and me . . .

"I can't tell you how excited I was! I had never been a performer. To be offered a large part on a Jack Benny show was, for me, terribly special. Jack even assured me that I was to be paid a *separate* salary. I couldn't believe it! For several nights, I dreamed about all the wonderful things I was going to buy with *my* money! Every woman will understand what it means to suddenly receive quite a large sum. It can set your head spinning! However, in the end, I made a very practical decision. I knew how much Jack loved music, how close he was to Zubin Mehta and the Los Angeles Philharmonic. I am a member of the Blue Ribbon Committee, whose function is to directly support the symphony. I decided to donate all my salary to that charity.

"By the time we returned to California, Jack was not feeling well. We were all supposed to meet at NBC and pose for some publicity photos. Jack was too sick to keep the appointment. That's when NBC came up with the idea for Greg and me to pose in front of a large blowup of the Bouché caricature of Jack . . .

"It's so hard to think of Jack not being here . . . When I speak of him, I have to reach for the most wonderful things someone could say about another human being. He was a unique artist. People like Picasso . . . Casels . . . Jack . . . they created their *own* art. Each was such a master, and made not only a lasting impression on their peers, but left behind a mark for future generations—forever.

"Jack Benny, *the* man, was an extraordinary person. So loving, so generous. Once, he told me *quite seriously* how much he regretted being such a moody man He said he was sorry most of all because Mary, whom he deeply loved, was the one who had to live with him—and his moods.

"Jack adored her in a fantastic way. It was a magnificent union. He took such delight in buying things for her . . . Whenever we were at dinner, for even the simplest things, he would invariably turn to her and say, 'Doll, what do you think I should have?' Mary *always* had the answers that were right for him . . .

"What a privilege it was just to know a man like that! Most artists are not even-tempered, or always able to be 'up.' I don't think people who are capable of creating greatness, who are able to reach such high artistic heights, could achieve what they do *without* the other side of their nature for balance.

"Jack's generosity was unsurpassed. He never thought in terms of money or amounts. He just wanted to give. I'll never forget Mary telling me about the 'Julius affair.' Julius is the gentleman who has done Mary's hair for years. Jack loved him because, in addition to his creative talent, he has a marvelous sense of humor . . .

"One time, Mary decided to go to Ireland and England with Jack while he was making a series of appearances. Jack always wanted Mary with him, but *never* when he felt she would be uncomfortable, or bored. He was scheduled to do ten performances in ten days in Dublin, which would have left him no time to be with her. It was during February, and Irish winters are aways so cold. Then he was to go right on to London to do several television shows requiring endless rehearsals. But at this stage in his life, Mary *wanted* to be with him. She insisted on going along, although she realized it wouldn't be much fun . . .

"Jack was so appreciative, he wanted to do something extra special to show his feelings. Unbeknownst to Mary, he invited Julius to come to England as his guest. They devised the whole scheme. Julius was to fly to London on a certain day and be waiting for them when they arrived from Ireland. Everything went off on schedule. Jack and Mary spent ten days in Dublin, then flew into London and arrived at the Dorchester Hotel.

"As they walked into the lobby, there was Julius. Mary was shocked into one of her rare silences. I mean, Mary *always* has a comeback for everything, but she *was* taken totally off guard seeing Julius there. As for Jack, he, *too,* looked surprised. He walked over and said, 'My God, what are *you* doing here?' Julius thought Jack was pretending, until he noticed a *completely straight expression* on Jack's face. Finally, Julius said, 'Don't you remember, Jack, *you invited me* to come to London to surprise Mary!'

"Jack indeed had forgotten! Can you imagine? First of all, what other husband would have been that considerate? And second, what man but Jack could have forgotten a good deed so fast?

"As for the giving part of Jack—I'll never forget in 1972, when he went to appear in Israel with Zubin Mehta. On his return, he came over with Mary and brought me a beautiful bracelet. I had tears in my eyes. Only Jack would have been able to take a trip, do his concerts, and *still* have time to remember a friend in such a loving way.

"Jack also had gold money clips made for his close friends. The clip had the Bouché caricature of Jack etched into the gold. From the moment he gave one to Greg, my husband treasured it. A few years ago, in the South of France, Greg and I were robbed. All of Greg's jewelry was taken—and never recovered. The only two things which remained were a watch I had given him, which Greg was wearing, and Jack's money clip, which he is never without. As Greg said, 'If we had to sustain such a loss, I'm happy that, at least, the watch and money clip are still with me.' That's how much value he placed on something with which Jack had gifted him . . .

"You cannot ever *totally* analyze Jack Benny. It would be like trying to evaluate the sun. How could you ever fully describe sunshine? It transcends definition. This is hard to say, but I can't think of Jack without Mary. It is a blessing he went first . . . I cannot imagine him surviving without her . . .

"Greg and I have kept our television script—the one we never had a chance to do. We will always cherish it with such loving care . . ."

The Pecks' part on Benny's "Third Farewell Special" went this way:

Up on section of sitting room at the Pecks' home. Door opens, Gregory Peck enters carrying a bouquet of flowers.

(APPLAUSE)

As he walks into the middle of the room . . .

GREG: Oh, Veronique, Veronique . . .

              (Veronique enters)

              (APPLAUSE)

GREG: (hands her flowers) Happy birthday.

VERONIQUE: (kisses him) Oh, thank you, Greg, they're
              beautiful.

              (She puts flowers down on table)

GREG: Well, after all, your birthday only comes once
              a year.

VERONIQUE: Thank heaven.

              (Greg goes to chair, picks up newspapers, starts to read)

VERONIQUE: Oh, Greg, I was on Beverly Drive today and
              I saw Jack Benny.

GREG: (still reading paper) Oh really?

VERONIQUE: You know, I was thinking . . . you and Jack
              are such good friends and yet in all the years
              we have known him, we have never once had
              him to the house for dinner.

GREG: We haven't?

VERONIQUE: No, and I don't understand why.

GREG: I'm sure there must be a reason.

              (Resumes reading his paper)

VERONIQUE: I think Jack is so nice, don't you?

GREG: (absently) Jack who?

VERONIQUE: Jack Benny.

GREG:	Oh yes, yes . . . I like Jack very much.
VERONIQUE:	I think I'll invite him for dinner Saturday night.
GREG:	That's only two nights away, Veronique. You can't give a man like Jack Benny such short notice . . . after all, he's a big star . . . He's probably booked weeks in advance.
VERONIQUE:	Then I'll find out when he *can* come.

(looking through her address book)

. . . I don't seem to have his number in the book.

GREG:	Try the Yellow Pages . . . under entertainer.
VERONIQUE:	Oh, here it is.

(She dials the phone on her desk)

JACK:	Hello.
VERONIQUE:	Jack, this is Veronique Peck.
JACK:	Veronique, how are you?
VERONIQUE:	Wonderful. Jack, Gregory and I were just talking about you and we were wondering . . . well, when could you come over to dinner?
JACK:	Six-thirty . . . seven . . . seven-thirty . . . If I don't shower I could be there in a half hour.
VERONIQUE:	(holding hand over phone) He wants to come tonight.
GREG:	(half-whisper) Tell him it can't be tonight . . . we're going out.
VERONIQUE:	Jack, tonight is my birthday and Gregory is taking me to La Parisienne.
JACK:	Oh, that fancy French place . . . Do you have reservations?
VERONIQUE:	For eight o'clock.
JACK:	I'll be there.

(He hangs up)

(We now see the Pecks in full screen)

VERONIQUE:	(weakly) He's joining us.
GREG:	Oh no . . . and I wanted to be alone with you tonight.

VERONIQUE:	Maybe we should just go somewhere else.
GREG:	He'd find us . . . he'd find us.

Dissolve to:

The elegant French restaurant. Five or six tables are occupied. Jack and the Pecks are seated at their table in the foreground . . . having their drinks.

JACK:	It was *so* nice of you to insist that I come . . .
	(Veronique and Greg exchange glances)
	(Jack looks around room)
	Gee, what a beautiful restaurant.
GREG:	It's one of the finest in Beverly Hills.
JACK:	I've never been here before . . . When did it open?
VERONIQUE:	Twenty-eight years ago.
JACK:	Well, it's certainly nice . . . there's something about French atmosphere. As a matter of fact, when I was in Paris, I ate in French restaurants all the time.
VERONIQUE:	Yes, they *have* quite a few there.
JACK:	(raising his glass) Well . . . to your birthday, Veronique . . . May we do this again next year?
GREG:	Next year we'll be out of town.
JACK:	Where are you going?
GREG:	We don't know yet.
	(Downs his drink)
	(They pick up their menus)
VERONIQUE:	Well, I don't know what I want to order . . . What're you going to have, Jack?
JACK:	(looking at menu) I don't know . . . let's see . . . grenadine of beef, seven fifty . . . Long Island duckling . . . nine seventy-five . . . Filet mignon . . . WHOOPS!! . . . OH BROTHER!!
CAPTAIN:	(French accent) Are you ready to order, monsieur?

JACK:	I'll have the grenadine of beef.
VERONIQUE:	And I'll have the Long Island duckling.
CAPTAIN:	Very good, madame . . .
	(to Gregory)
	You, sir?
GREG:	I'll have the whoops, medium rare . . .
	(Captain takes menus and leaves)
JACK:	(leaning over to Greg) Say, Greg, did you tell them it's Veronique's birthday? If you did, they'll bring you a free cake.
GREG:	(embarrassed) Oh, Jack, I wouldn't think of it.
JACK:	Don't be silly . . . you're entitled to it. If you don't eat it, you can take it home and put it in the freezer.
VERONIQUE:	Oh, Jack, we don't want it.
JACK:	Then I'll take it . . . Oh, gendarme . . . gendarme!! I wonder if that waiter heard me.
GREG:	If he did he went out to get a policeman.
VERONIQUE:	Jack, "gendarme" in French means officer of the law.
JACK:	No, no, it's waiter.
VERONIQUE:	Jack, I'm French.
JACK:	Then you of all people should know . . . But look, it's your birthday, I won't argue with you.
GREG:	I suddenly feel I could use a drink.
JACK:	What happened to the one you had?
VERONIQUE:	I'm drinking it.
JACK:	Now Greg, as one leading man to another . . .
GREG:	What?
JACK:	You know I'm starting a motion picture, too.
GREG:	Oh yes, *The Sunshine Boys*.
VERONIQUE:	Isn't that the one you're doing with Walter Matthau?
JACK:	That's right, and if this movie clicks, Walter and I may do more together. Who knows, we

288

	could be another Robert Redford and Paul Newman . . . What's that, Greg?
GREG:	I didn't say anything.
JACK:	I thought you said "Oh no."
VERONIQUE:	That was the man at the next table.
JACK:	Oh by the way, Greg, I hear great things about that picture you produced, *The Dove*.
GREG:	Well, we thought it was quite intriguing, a true story about a boy going around the world alone in a twenty-three-foot sailboat.
VERONIQUE:	And it's such a nice departure from those violent movies they're making these days.
JACK:	Yeah, it's getting so if they only have two murders, three bombings, and five beatings, it's a comedy.
GREG:	You know, the thing that bothers me, Jack, is that audiences are impressed and they react to what they see on the screen.
VERONIQUE:	If they see a musical, they are very happy.
GREG:	Right, and if they see a drama, they are emotionally moved . . . and when they see a lot of violence and brutality, it's got to affect them.
JACK:	Well, I guess you're right, Greg, I think they are going too far.

(The waiter comes up with their soup course
and starts placing the bowls before them)

GREG:	Jack, this week I saw four movies that were absolutely disgusting . . . the violence was put in there without rhyme or reason.
JACK:	(as they start eating their soup) I know what you mean.
GREG:	Waiter . . . this soup is cold.
WAITER:	(politely) I don't see how that can be.
GREG:	(leaping to his feet in violent anger) If I say it's cold, it's cold!!

(He gives the waiter a right and left to the stomach . . . then a
right to the jaw that knocks the waiter into a back flip, which ends

with him falling unconscious over a table. Jack looks at this . . .
then out at the audience . . . then steps over and stares down at
the unconscious waiter . . . then comes back to Gregory.)

GREG: (dazed) I don't know what got into me.

(The manager now steps up to Gregory
and taps him on the shoulder)

MANAGER: (politely) Monsieur Peck . . . that was one
of my finest waiters. I cannot imagine what he
did that could have provoked you so.

VERONIQUE: Oh you can't huh? Well, he gave us cold
soup!!

(She karate-chops the manager . . . slaps him back and forth . . .
knees him in the stomach . . . and when he sinks to the ground,
she kicks him in the head.)

(Again Jack looks at this . . . Hand to cheek)

JACK: (to camera) All this? For a little cold soup?

(Large lady at another table stands up)

LADY: You knocked him into my pâté de foie gras.

GREG: (to lady) You can't talk to my wife like that.

LADY'S HUSBAND: Who says so?

(He brings a chair down over Greg's head. Greg retaliates. And
everyone now gets into the act, with fists and furniture flying.)

(Jack looks at all this in amazement)

JACK: (to camera) Gregory was right . . . it's all
these violent pictures.

(The fight now ends with everyone lying all over each other. Only
Jack is left standing. He can't believe what he has seen.)

(A waiter comes up to Jack with the check)

WAITER: Your check, monsieur.

JACK: Check? . . . They invited *me* . . . but all
right, I'll take it.

(He looks over the check)

Wait a minute . . . you're a dollar off.

WAITER: (reasonably) But I myself checked it twice.
That total is correct.

JACK: (explodes) Don't tell me! If I say it's a dollar
off . . . it's a dollar off!!

(He beats the waiter to a pulp. When the waiter is done for, Jack straightens his suit and adjusts his tie.)

JACK: (to camera) I don't know what all the fuss was about. I thought the soup was delicious.

(As he starts out of the restaurant)

MUSIC: PLAYOFF

(APPLAUSE)

(Jack walks to center stage)

JACK: Ladies and gentlemen . . . once again my special guests, Mr. and Mrs. Gregory Peck.

(They come out brushing themselves off)

JACK: Of course, Greg, you're always great . . . but Veronique, you've never been in pictures . . . you've never been on the stage . . . and this is your debut on television   and I must congratulate you . . . you were just marvelous.

VERONIQUE: Oh, I didn't think I was that good.

GREG: (turns to Veronique, grabs her by the shoulders) If Jack says you were great, you were great!!

(Lets go of her)

JACK: Wait a minute, Greg, you didn't have to do that to your wife.

(Veronique grabs Jack by the lapels)

VERONIQUE: If he wants to, he can, buster . . . and you keep out of it.

(She releases Jack and they walk off)

JACK: Hmmmmm . . . I can't wait to get home and kick Mary.

There were still more memories Greg Peck wanted to share:

"I can tell you for sure one thing, that Jack changed part of my whole life. He saw that I could play—or he could *set it up for me to play*—comedy. No one else did. As a result of that show, I found out the joy of making people laugh.

"In my picture career, I had only made five comedies out of fifty films. I always felt, with the right kind of comedy, I *could* do it. I did have one or two comedy successes—*Roman Holiday* and

Designing Woman—but generally, nobody thought of me for comedy—except Jack.

"Because of doing his show, I received comments, warmth, and friendliness from people that, during a twenty-five-year career, I had never heard from before. To be in front of an audience like Jack's, to make people laugh, to sing and dance—no matter how bad you were—had the effect of humanizing me. It made a big difference in my life. *It was as if Jack had given me a great gift* . . . Any time you came in contact with Jack Benny nothing but good could come of it . . . Every time I was with him, something good brushed off on me. That went for everyone else . . .

"I loved Jack. That was true of so many people who passed through his life. Once you had an intimate association with him, you were the beneficiary of his talent, his warmth, his human-ness . . .

"Twenty-five years after he had done his first radio show, he was still working as hard as he had been from the beginning. For Jack, comedy was an art. He did it *seemingly* without effort. Yet behind the scenes, it took years and years of constant work until he had refined his art to the point where he could do *more* with *less* than anyone in the business . . ."

CHAPTER FORTY-NINE

THE NEXT SIX DAYS following Mary's disclosure of Jack's condition were a nightmare. Those closest to Jack functioned on one level, doing whatever had to be done. Still, as they went through the motions, none of them could actually believe—or accept—what was happening.

In reality, Jack was, after all, *eighty years old*. But that is *not* how his loved ones thought of him . . .

Jack looked twenty years younger than the calendar reflected. He was always such a vital person . . . so remotely connected with death . . . To Mary, to all those who knew him, Jack was the man who had found the fountain of youth. He seemed to be indestructible.

"After first hearing Mary's sad news," Marks said, "I made two phone calls. The first was to Florence in Chicago. We made plans for her to fly to California right after Christmas to be with Jack. My second call was to our other sister, Babe. She and her husband, Clem Stanley, immediately rushed over to be with Mary. They stayed there off and on for the rest of the week . . . Who could have known that eight months later, on August 8, 1975, Babe would be gone, too . . ."

Meanwhile, Mary had called her daughter and the grandchildren. Joan and her two eldest came and stayed at the house almost constantly.

The doctors had told Mary they could not be sure how much time Jack had. It could be a matter of weeks . . . months . . . perhaps as much as a year.

But on December 24, after examining Jack again, both Drs. Kennamer and Sugarman suggested Hickey phone Florence and tell her to come right away. Jack's condition was worsening more rapidly than they had anticipated.

Florence was notified, and she immediately booked a flight for Los Angeles scheduled to arrive on Christmas Day.

On December 25, Marks and his wife met Florence at the airport and drove her directly to the house so she could be with Jack. Meanwhile, on behalf of the Benny family, a press release was issued. It contained information of Jack's serious illness, without going into specific details as to the exact nature or cause of his condition. Almost immediately, the news media took up a vigil outside the Benny home. Overnight, word of Jack's critical illness had been printed and broadcast around the world.

Once the gravity of Jack's situation was known, there was a steady stream of the Bennys' closest friends at the house—day and night. They all wanted to be near, in case Mary needed them.

Outside, the security guards were doubled. Fans, who knew where Jack lived, came by the dozens, just to stand and offer their own silent tributes. Finally, out of respect to the family, the news media left en masse, with just a few reporters remaining behind, along with a small television crew, knowing the whole world would be interested in Jack's progress.

Only a few people were allowed to go upstairs and see him. The doctors wanted Jack kept as quiet as possible. On the last morning, George Burns walked up the stairs . . . crying . . . and talking out loud to himself.

"Why did it have to happen to *you,* Jack, not *me* . . . I've already been through so much . . ." (George was referring to his recovery from a then recent miraculous heart operation.)

At 11:30 P.M., on December 26, Jack slipped away . . .

"The reason Jack got all that space in the newspapers when he died is very interesting," George Burns commented. "Many show-business greats have died. Valentino died. Jolson died. A lot of great comics in the world have died . . . and none of them got the tribute Jack did . . .

"It was the little things, the nice things in Jack's life that so endeared him—to *everyone* . . . All his adult life, Jack used to write at least fifty postcards a week to people. He would stop off downstairs of his doctor's office and buy cake. Then he'd go up, and the nurses would make coffee. Jack would sit with them, share the goodies, and have long conversations . . .

"It was all those countless nice gestures Jack did for people, big stars, secretaries—*just people.* I would like to say I do those things, too. But I don't. I can't. Yet, to Jack, they came naturally. None of it was ever done for effect . . . If there was a single uniqueness to Jack's character, I'd say that he was simply such a very nice man . . ."

CHAPTER FIFTY

"I NEVER SAID GOODBYE TO DADDY. When he lapsed into a coma, I was out of town. I had no idea he was so ill, or that the end was so near. I knew he wasn't feeling well those last few months, but I didn't think he was *that* ill," Joan Benny Blumofe recalled sadly.

"With hindsight, I realize it was stupid of me not to have recognized the signs and put all the pieces together. Partially, I was fooled because of circumstances. Namely the *kind* of man my father was. One of his favorite jokes—he used to tell it all the time —was the story about the hypochondriac who kept telling everybody he was going to die. No one believed him because he *always* said it. One day, he finally died. On his tombstone, there was only a single word: 'See!' Daddy loved that joke—because it was absolutely *him* . . .

"Ours was a traveling family. From the time I was seventeen, I did a lot of traveling, too. As soon as jet travel came in, my parents were always taking off for someplace. Sometimes, my father went on the road alone to fulfill various engagements. Occasionally, Mother took a trip to New York on her own. We all flitted around. As close as we were, I didn't always know where Daddy was. Frequently, he'd be gone only a day or two, so we didn't say goodbye. We instinctively knew we'd be talking together in a few days. We never met each other at the airport, either. *That* could have become a lifetime occupation!

"Once, after I was grown, I flew to New York and checked into the Sherry-Netherland. When I walked down to the lobby after unpacking, I ran into Daddy! I was momentarily startled. I hadn't a clue he was in town.

"He told me Kenneth Tynan had given him tickets to *Oh! Calcutta!* I asked if I could go along. He said, 'No, I won't take you to see that off-color show . . .'

"I protested, but Daddy was firm. He must have called Mother in California, because a while later he phoned. 'Joanie, the tickets are for tomorrow evening. I'm sorry I was being so stupid . . . I'd love to take you!'

"Daddy was *always* so funny about such things. When I was little, he and my mother went to *Hellzapoppin* with Olsen and Johnson. I heard him say it was the most risqué show he'd ever seen. He also felt that way about the play *The Little Hut*. The plain truth is, Daddy was an old-fashioned romantic, easily shocked and embarrassed—at least in front of females . . .

"The following night, we had dinner, then went to see *Oh! Calcutta!* Daddy didn't know exactly how to react—whether to play it cool, or be embarrassed. During the first act, I tried not to look directly at him. At intermission, we both admitted we were bored. By then, his embarrassment was gone!

"My generation doesn't find anything shocking. But my parents had a hangup that way. They watched their language in front of me. I didn't hear the word 'shit' until I was practically out of high school! During the last ten years or so—ever since I became a *real adult* in their eyes, Daddy loved to tell dirty jokes he had heard at his golf club. He'd come in and say, 'This story had a bad word in it . . . but I guess I can tell you.' He always had that delightful naughty little boy quality around ladies . . .

"There are so many things to remember about Daddy," Joan continued. "Little things that made him special to me. For instance, his love of walking. I used to live on Walden Drive in Beverly Hills, which wasn't too far from his office. He adored strolling over . . . staying to talk . . . sometimes, he'd have dinner with me and my children. He liked my cooking, and it was a real kick for me, 'to entertain' my father in my *own home*. To chat with him, confide in him . . .

"Yet, there was a paradox about Daddy. He was an *absolute coward*—about certain things. In *personal* matters, there were times where he had okayed something, or had told me something good would happen. Then, for some reason, at the last minute, they fell through. I did *not* receive the news from him. I heard from an attorney . . . someone he had call me. That really bugged me. It made me furious. It was one of the things I wanted to talk to him about, but never got around to. *He was just scared to be the bearer of bad tidings* . . .

"Over the years, I had lots of *imaginary* conversations with myself, planning what I'd say to Daddy about his failure in that area. But, of course, I never did. *I guess I'm a bit of a coward, myself.*

"When I was growing up, he turned all decisions over to my mother. As a kid, that really hurt. I wanted *him* to go out on a limb—even if he said no. But he loved me so much, he never wanted to disappoint me. It was easier for him to have my mother say no, even though she loved me equally as much.

"Still, Daddy was *supportive* in so many other areas. He was always proud of me. Proud I was a good student and brought home

296

top grades. He thought I looked pretty, and never failed to compliment me on what I was wearing. I loved being with him. Anywhere. Everywhere. He taught me to appreciate so many things—even baseball.

"The last game we saw together was in September of 1974, three months before he died. It turned out to be a very odd, funny evening. He suggested we take a limousine. I said I'd drive. He said okay, but it would be *easier* to take a limo. I said, 'Daddy, don't be silly. I don't mind driving.' You have to understand, I'm a person with an absolutely keen sense of direction. I never get lost. So, naturally, *everything* went wrong . . .

"It was horrendous. I got into a heavy traffic jam, and decided to make a U-turn and go the other way. I knew it would be faster, but I wound up in a *larger* traffic jam. Then there was an accident in front of us. We didn't arrive at the game until the second inning! Daddy was furious. But he was trying to control himself, so he was quiet—*very quiet*. He was in a rather bad mood that evening, and got very aggravated with me. As the moments passed, I became more and more apologetic . . .

"Once we were at Dodger Stadium, it turned out to be one of the most boring games of the season. We decided to leave in the seventh inning. Meanwhile, I had gotten Daddy a hot dog and something to drink, trying to make him feel better.

"We headed home early. I was glad to be avoiding all the stadium traffic. But I made a turn out of the parking lot and wound up on the *wrong* freeway. I can laugh now. It was awful *then*. We wound up circling and circling. Finally, we got off the freeway in the San Fernando Valley, miles from home . . .

"I had to backtrack to Beverly Hills. I started over Coldwater Canyon—and ran out of gas—fortunately, right near a station. By this time, Daddy was dying to get home. He kept looking at his watch and asking me how much longer. Poor Daddy. Why did I have to lose my sense of direction on *that* evening?

"Still another paradox is that, in his entire career, Daddy never missed more than a handful of performances due to illness. For fifty years, Jack Benny worked constantly—yet, he was the *hypochondriac of the world!* He always surrounded himself with pills. He had more bottles of medicine than a pharmacy! There were

297

bottles in his bathroom . . . pills on a nightstand by his bed. Altogether, there must have been hundreds of bottles of various little colored tablets. It became a joke to all his friends—Jack and his pills—most of which he *never* took.

"So, when he complained about not feeling well, to us, he was the little boy who cried wolf . . .

"On Thanksgiving Day, 1974, the children and I had dinner with my parents. Daddy wasn't feeling well and didn't even come down to dinner until someone went up and got him. Afterward, we sat in the den. He complained of pain and went upstairs. Still, I didn't think what he had was anything out of the ordinary.

"I had plans to take my children skiing over the Christmas holidays. My two youngest, Bobby and Joanna, had never skied before. I couldn't get reservations for Christmas and New Year's, but I was just as happy. We decided to go up to June Lake the week before Christmas, so we would be home to spend the holidays with my parents.

"Before we left town, I went over to the house and found Daddy lying in bed. I became angry with him because I thought he was just babying himself . . . Now, looking back, I think *inadvertently* I did the right thing. I treated him *normally*. He seemed afraid something was seriously wrong. Had I thought there *was* anything out of the ordinary wrong, I would have handled things differently. *Then* my father would have been suspicious . . .

"It was early afternoon when I saw Daddy in bed and a bit groggy. The minute I walked into his room, he started complaining . . .

" 'Daddy, you're being such a baby,' I said. 'It's silly. There's nothing worse for you than lying around here dwelling on your "condition." There's not a damn thing wrong with you. Why don't you get up, get dressed, and go over to Hillcrest. Tell jokes—or at least *listen* to some. I know you'll feel better . . .'

"I couldn't convince him . . . That was the last time I saw him —*to talk to*.

"I planned to let the kids ski until Christmas Eve morning, then to drive straight home in time to be at Mother and Daddy's for Christmas Eve. But the weather turned bad, so we left a day early. When we got back, I didn't call my parents. I intended just going over there Christmas Eve. The following morning, Mother called. She hadn't expected me to be there, and was phoning to find out if anyone knew exactly when we'd be home. When I answered, she said, 'Who is this, the maid?'

"I laughed. 'No, Mother, it's your daughter!'

"She asked me to come over right away. By the tone of her voice, I knew she was very upset. When I arrived, she told me about Daddy. He already had lapsed into a coma. I went up to see him . . . stayed awhile, then came home. There was nothing I could do, and I wanted to prepare the children. I told the older two, and we decided to put off saying anything to the younger ones. We didn't want to spoil their holiday.

"Christmas Day, I went back to the house and kept going in and out of Daddy's room. The next day, I went back early in the morning and sat by his bed—until he died . . ."

Maria Rudolph, Joan's teen-age daughter, shared some thoughts about her grandfather:

"My first memories of Granddad were playing with him on Friday nights when we used to go over to the Roxbury Drive house, or when we spent the night there. He was always silly. Michael and I used to laugh at him because he was always laughing at *us*. Things we said and did naturally struck him funny . . .

"His outstanding quality was kindness. I know it's a cliché, but it's also *the truth*. He was the kindest, simplest man. He enjoyed his work for the sake of *it*, not for the popularity, or the glamour. He just loved to make people laugh.

"I used to enjoy seeing his shows—mostly in Las Vegas. I would sit backstage and watch, or I'd be in his dressing room with him just before he went on.

"He was very special to me. I always thought of him as being out of the ordinary—even before I was old enough to realize he was! But I never talked about him at school. I thought the other kids might like me just *because* I was his granddaughter. If it ever came out that Jack Benny *was* my grandfather, then I'd talk about him and the special experience I had being related to him . . .

"It *was* a very special experience. I liked the way people treated me when I was with him. Everyone loved him and was so happy

299

to see him, it made *me* feel special being with him. Just walking down the street with him . . . Just being associated with him.

"He was such a generous man," Maria went on. "He gave me so many things—like the ring he brought me from Hawaii. It had a raised heart on it, and was very beautiful . . . But it was too wide. It didn't fit well on the crack of my finger, if you know what I mean. It pinched when I put it on. But I wore it, and loved it, because *he* gave it to me . . .

"Everything he did was concentrated on his work. He never thought of money, or material possessions. He would never even have worn matching socks if Miss Mary (We always call her that. She doesn't *look* like a grandmother!) hadn't selected them for him. He was not the 'average' celebrity. You know, the way stars always act so complex and try so hard to be stars. With Grand-dad, things just seemed to come without him *pushing* for them.

"I watch the reruns of his shows today and marvel at his ability. You'd never know he had it in him just seeing him. Especially the last few years—his age was showing—*off stage*. But the minute he walked on, he seemed as young as ever. That proves he was more wrapped up in his work than in day-to-day living . . .

"My only wish is that he could have lived longer. I'm a biology major in college now. But I never really had a chance to know him from a grown-up point of view . . ."

Maria's older brother Michael remembers how much he enjoyed being with Jack. "My grandfather was really such a nice man, and very funny. When I was little, he used to take me to Hillcrest Country Club. We'd have lunch and he'd play a game with me. He would hold his napkin over his face and pretend he was behind a stage curtain. Slowly, he'd roll the napkin up and down—enough to set me off into fits of glee! Today, even from my vantage point as a college student, I still think of him the same way: kind, generous, and funny.

"He took me exciting places. In the summer of 1969, we went to Cape Kennedy to watch the launching of Apollo 11—the first moon shot. That was one of the happiest times of my life . . . A very *special* birthday for me, July 16, which coincided with the launch. I met Neil Armstrong, Buzz Aldrin, and Michael Collins. I had lunch with all the other astronauts, and my big idol, Dr.

Wernher von Braun. Even at that age, I was a nut about science. Sitting across the table from those people was like a dream come true.

"Colonel Frank Borman showed us the computers, the rocket ready for launch, and took us for a tour all around the control building. Granddad was fascinated, although he didn't know too much, technically. He kept asking me questions. I would try to explain things, even though, back then, I didn't know too much myself.

"We spent a few days at the Cape, then went to Indianapolis, where he was appearing at the Starlight Theatre with Shani Wallis. While we were there, the capsule prepared to land on the moon. I remember Granddad was upset because people in the room were talking. He wanted to watch TV, to see that historic moment in silence . . .

"I also went to the Montreal Expo '67. He was appearing there with Jack Jones. I had a great time. They gave me a pass, and I ran all over to visit the pavilions, see the exhibits, and get in everyone's hair—as usual. I was even part of his show a couple of times. At intermission, Granddad announced that it was time to go out for refreshments. He said, 'Be sure and drink a lot, *I* have the concession.' Then I came in carrying a sign. On one side, it said, 'INTERMISSION.' On the other, 'Cokes: 35¢ . . . Marked down to a Quarter!'

"When I was small, he used to sit me down and play the fiddle for me. I loved listening to him . . . being with him. Even when I didn't know he was somebody special, I *thought* he was.

"We had a lot of fun going to baseball games. We'd either sit in the dugout, or in Mr. O'Malley's box—and I got all the Dodger autographs.

"I spent a lot of time in Las Vegas, too. I'd sit backstage with him before he went on, then watch from the wings, or from a ringside table. He also took me to Palm Springs . . . And, when I was at Millbrook prep school in New York, I went to meet him when he played the Westbury Theatre with Roberta Peters . . .

"Once, in Las Vegas, while he was appearing at the Sahara, something funny happened." Michael grinned. "At the time, *he* didn't think it was too funny. I was sitting in his dressing room when he decided to go out for a while. I wanted to stay and watch 'Mission: Impossible.' He said when I got ready to leave, to be sure and lock the door, because he had his violin there. A few minutes after he left, I felt like getting a Coke. But I wanted to come right back, and I *didn't* want to lock myself out. I decided to hide his Stradivarius in the shower. I reasoned that no one would look *there* for it. A few minutes after I'd gone, Granddad came back.

"The moment he walked in, he noticed his violin was missing. By the time I returned with my Coke, the room was full of security police. I took one look and sized up the situation. I was used to getting into trouble all the time *without meaning to*. I went over to him and whispered where I'd hidden his violin. He went into the shower and retrieved it. The police left . . . and we were alone. He wasn't really mad at me. He just couldn't figure out why I'd done such a thing!

"I wish we would have had more time together now that I'm grown up. I'm a physics-pre-med major in my senior year at college. I want to become a surgeon, and also teach. I like to think my grandfather would have been proud of what I'm trying to accomplish. His encouragement always meant so much to me . . ."

Once more, Joan began to reminisce. "Daddy loved Michael and Maria so much. He was proud of how they were growing into young adults. As for my two youngest, Bobby and Joanna, he adored them . . . and spoiled them.

"To go back to my not saying goodbye to Daddy. Perhaps I've rationalized *now*. At first, I took it very hard. I thought, 'My God, the last time I talked to Daddy, I was angry.' But today, I *do* think I did what was *best* for him . . . I acted normally.

"During his last few years, Daddy was just beginning to show his age. He was almost eighty-one when he died. There are some people who are ninety but act twenty-five . . . Some who are old at fifty. *My father became old at eighty*. There were little signs of him slowing down. Had he lived another five or ten years, he probably would have had to retire—and *that* would have killed him. He couldn't have gone on much longer . . . Thank God, he didn't suffer too much. His illness was brief—and he died knowing he was still in demand.

"I never had a chance to say a final goodbye . . . I loved him so much. I'll always be grateful that, to the end, his timing was perfect . . .

"Daddy died on top—still a star!"

CHAPTER FIFTY-ONE

"EVERY DAY SINCE JACK has been gone, the florist has delivered one long-stemmed red rose to my home . . ." Mary began. "For the first few weeks, I was in a state of deep mourning. It never occurred to me to ask who the roses were coming from.

"I can't begin to express the grief I felt. Jack's loss . . . Our separation after forty-eight years of complete togetherness . . . My feelings of utter loneliness, even though I was surrounded by relatives and dear, dear friends who tried to cheer me up.

"Jack died the day after Christmas. The New Year of 1975 came and went without my noticing it. I heard of people 'being numb with grief,' but I had never *fully* understood what those words meant—not until I went through it myself.

"It must have been seven or eight weeks before I finally asked the maid who the daily flower was from. To my surprise, she had no idea. I called David Jones, our florist, and asked him . . ."

Jones remembers the call very well. "I told Mary that, quite a while before Jack passed away, he stopped into my shop to send a bouquet of flowers to a friend. As he was leaving, he suddenly turned back and said, 'David, if anything should happen to me, I want you to send my doll a red rose every day . . .'

"When I related Jack's conversation, there was complete silence. I could tell she was crying as she thanked me and said goodbye. Subsequently, Mary learned that Jack actually had included a provision for her flowers in his will. One red rose was to be delivered to her every day . . . *for the rest of her life.*

"I never knew a kinder or more generous man," Jones continued. "And I certainly never met any two people who adored each other more than Jack and Mary . . ."

"God, I loved that man," Mary said, touching the wedding band she has never removed since her marriage in 1927. "I was the luckiest woman in the world to be his wife. Jack was such an easy man to live with. Can you imagine the sweetness, his wanting me to have a red rose every day to remind me of him? As if I *could* forget!

"All during our marriage, he constantly sent me flowers and gifts. Invariably, when Jack enclosed a card, he never signed his name. He would always draw a smiling face . . . For me, *that* was his signature. He would write:

Doll,

I love you . . .

Then he'd end with that happy face. Every once in a while, I *also* received flowers with a card signed:

Love . . .

Underneath, he would draw a sad face. The corners of the mouth would be turned down. A trace of teardrops would be falling from his eyes. I got that card whenever we had an argument!

"Jack was such a romantic. Such an idealistic, loving man. During nearly fifty years of marriage, if we *did* quarrel, nine times out of ten, I started it . . . The *only time* Jack and I were ever separated—in anger—was during the early months of our marriage. Jack was appearing in San Francisco. As usual, I sat backstage every night waiting for him to finish At one point in my life, my family and I had lived in San Francisco, so some dear old friends invited me to dinner to show off my new husband . . .

"I watched Jack while he changed out of his stage clothes and put on a rather loud sports jacket and plain slacks. Then he pulled a tie from his coat pocket and began putting it around his neck. It was the ugliest, most garish thing you can imagine. The years have *enhanced* my memory of that tie. I can *still* see it: a fusion of red, orange, green, and purple. I couldn't stand looking at it!

"Very sweetly, I asked Jack to please put on another tie. Just as sweetly, he said, 'Doll, I *like* this tie—and that's the one I am going to wear . . .'

"I guess you could say I pulled a typical bride's tantrum. I refused to budge until he changed ties. I sat and fumed, getting madder and madder. Finally, Jack left me sitting there and just walked out. I followed after him, protesting that I just *couldn't* take him to meet my friends looking *like that* . . .

"He said, 'Well, *that's* fine. We won't go at all! Let's just go home . . .'

"I shouted, 'That's exactly where I *am* going—*home*—back to Los Angeles!' I packed a few things and left him. Obviously, you can measure the *extent* of my maturity at the time! Imagine, going home to Mother over something as trivial as a lousy-looking tie!

"That was the one and only time in our married life we were apart—for forty-eight hours. Jack flew down from San Francisco to get me. After telling my parents I never wanted to see him again, the minute he walked through our front door, I fell into his arms . . .

"I still can't believe he's gone. Last November, just before the Christmas holidays, I walked into the Beverly Hills branch of VanCleef and Arpels. I told the manager, Mr. Ryan, that I wanted to buy myself a present—from Jack. He just looked at me, but I *knew* he understood. Jack always took such delight in picking out jewelry for me. He hated wearing any himself, but he loved to see me with it.

"I selected a pair of earrings, then sat down and wrote myself a card:

Doll . . .
All my love,
Doll

"That's how I got last year's Christmas present from Jack!

"Several months ago, Frank Sinatra took me and a few other friends out to dinner. He's such a marvelous man. He loved Jack —and Jack loved him. During our meal, they served an especially good bowl of soup. When I'd finished, I turned to Frank and said, 'I can't wait to go home and tell Jack how great the soup was . . .'

"Everybody heard me. *Nobody stopped me.* They let me go right on . . . I can't help it . . . I talk about Jack all the time *as though he were still here.* If I read a good book, I automatically want to walk into his room and tell him about it. After forty-eight years of being together, I miss him terribly. I know he's gone—

and yet he *is* here. He made such an imprint on my life, on *every* life he ever touched. Everybody he knew is better off for it . . ."

In an interview with Irv Kupcinet, the syndicated Chicago *Sun-Times* columnist and television talk show host, he echoed what Mary had just said. "Never a day goes by that someone in the business doesn't bring up Jack's name. I can't think of a guest celebrity I've had on my show lately who hasn't worked Jack into our conversation. With all the networks celebrating anniversaries and birthdays, you can hardly turn the dial without seeing Jack's face on the screen. I think Jack *started* the whole trend when he did his own 'Twentieth Anniversary Show' years ago.

"Still," Kup went on, "who can ever tire of those clips of Jack with Mary and the rest of the cast? Jack with the Marquis Chimps. Jack and that troupe of roller-skating penguins, and the follow-up show, where only *one* penguin roller-skated in. Jack looked at it, and said, 'I've told you ten times, I'll send you the check next week.' Then he turned to the audience and commented, 'That was their agent!'

"What an influence he had on this whole business. I saw a commercial the other day with a penguin in it, and I immediately thought of Jack and the first time he had those tiny creatures on his stage.

"You know," Irv continued, "there is something else very interesting. A few years ago, while Jack and Tony Martin were playing the Mill Run Theater, about forty-five minutes outside of Chicago, I went backstage to visit. Jack looked so damn tired, and I asked him when he was going to start taking it easy.

"I'll never forget the expression on his face as he replied, '*Irv, the day I stop working is the day I die!*'"

Mary shook her head as she recalled what Jack had told Kupcinet. "Jack *did* work up until the last few weeks of his life. When he slipped away, he was completely convinced he would be starting to film *The Sunshine Boys* within a few days. I'm so grateful he went that way. No lingering illness. No months of pain. Just a few weeks of discomfort in a life that spanned eighty-one years. My husband was a blessed man—and he led a blessed life.

"Not a day goes by that I don't catch a glimpse or a mention of

Jack on television or radio. Or a friend will call to tell me some new anecdote about him. Two years after Jack passed away, Zubin Mehta phoned. He had just returned from Israel.

"'Mary,' Zubin said, 'you'll never guess what I saw a few days ago—*To Be or Not to Be*. It's the biggest hit in Tel Aviv!'

"Zubin went on to tell me he had never seen the film before himself. 'Mary, when Jack first came on the screen, I began to choke up just hearing his voice. But soon, I was lost in the humor of the movie. It was *unbelievable*. Israelis are flocking to see it. One would think a picture about Nazis wouldn't go over in Israel, but it was done with such good taste. I haven't laughed so much in years. It's an absolute classic . . .'

"Shortly after Jack died," Mary went on, "I went down to the Los Angeles Music Center to present Jack's two violins. The day Zubin called, he again told me how much that had meant . . .

"Then he said, 'You know, Mary, we have several *special* fiddles in use. Our concertmaster plays a violin which belonged to Fritz Kreisler. Our second concertmaster uses Jack's Stradivarius, and another member of our violin section plays his Pressenda. Jack really *is* with us. He always will be . . .'

"More recently, Dina Merrill called and asked if I would permit her to use Jack's name to raise money for diabetes research. Dina had a son who was a diabetic, too. I have been very careful about allowing the use of Jack's name. But when Dina told me of her plans, I readily agreed . . .

"The First Annual Jack Benny Memorial Pro-Celebrity Tennis Tournament to benefit diabetes research was held in Houston, Texas, in April 1977. It was a joint effort of the Juvenile Diabetes Foundation and the American Diabetes Association. Six months later, George Burns was honored with the First Annual Jack Benny Memorial Award from the March of Dimes. Both affairs raised a lot of money in Jack's name. *That's* what I mean, he *is* still with us . . .

"This past Thanksgiving, Joan and her children were here for dinner. During the meal, her littlest one, Joanna, suddenly blurted out, 'I miss Granddaddy . . .' It was a very emotional moment.

Our third Thanksgiving without Jack. But kids are kids—and she's adorable. Meanwhile, Joanna kept eating. Stuffing herself, actually. When she finished the last morsel of pie, she said, 'Miss Mary, I'm so full, I'll never eat again until I'm twenty-one . . .' Then she proceeded to walk into the den and open the first candy dish!

"Four years ago, when Joanna was seven and her brother Bobby was eight, he came home from school all excited. My daughter was in her living room when Bobby said, 'You'll never guess what happened today at school. The teacher asked who our favorite comedian was, and the *whole class* said Granddaddy.' At which point Joanna piped up, 'Big deal—he only has *twelve kids* in his whole class!'

"I read somewhere that Jack was a worrier. That *wasn't* true. He never worried. He *was* anxious . . . but only about his work. Before a performance, he sometimes would express anxiety about a show. But the minute he walked out on stage, he was as cool as the proverbial cucumber. I'll never forget when we played the London Palladium for the first time. Everyone else was a nervous wreck. Not Jack. He walked on stage like he had been playing that house all his life . . .

"It's strange, what I've just said was true for his entire life—*until* he reached his eightieth birthday. That's when everything happened . . . when I saw Jack really worried for the first time. Even though he was looking forward to his television special, and eagerly getting ready to make *The Sunshine Boys,* and to play Las Vegas, just the *thought* of being eighty worried him.

"Things that never bothered him before suddenly began to annoy him. During those last months, he wasn't eating well. I knew he had cancer before anyone else did. But I didn't tell my family until the last week of Jack's life. I'm so grateful—if he had to go—that he *never knew* what he had. We told him it was stomach flu, and he accepted that.

"As you've read, Jack was a diabetic. Not the type who had to take insulin. His was controllable with a diet and oral medication. He had to keep away from everything that had sugar in it. During the last weeks of his life, however, *everything* I gave him had sugar . . . All those things he loved, but had denied himself. Sodas. Parfaits. Candy. *I* was sick having to eat all that sweet junk in front of him. I did it because I wanted to *share* the pleasure of eating things he loved.

"After a few days, he questioned me. 'You know, doll, I'm not supposed to have all this stuff . . .' I told him the doctor said it was good for him, to help build himself up while he had the flu. I even suggested he call the doctor to double-check.

" 'No, doll,' he said. 'You have never lied to me. I believe you . . .'

"It was only the last few weeks of his life that Jack suffered any real pain at all . . . Finally, he just went to sleep . . . He just *fell* asleep. It pleases me that, when he passed away, he was on top, as much in demand as ever . . ."

She paused for a moment, then continued speaking.

"I can't help myself. Every day, around this time, I *listen* for Jack's footsteps. I expect him to come walking into this room any minute . . ."

CHAPTER FIFTY-TWO

JACK ALWAYS TOLD everybody Frank Sinatra was one of the most incredible men he'd ever known. Seeing him take charge of the situation after Jack passed away, watching him comfort Benny's family and friends, only served to confirm Jack's faith in him.

On Saturday, December 28, the day before the funeral, Sinatra called and talked to Marks.

"Frank reassured me. 'Please, don't worry . . . Just see that Mary is as comfortable as possible. I'll take care of everything else.'

" 'But Frank, it's pouring outside . . . The forecast is for rain tomorrow, too . . .'

"Don't worry, Hickey,' he said, 'it won't rain . . . I've arranged everything. I've talked with Mayor Bradley. There will be helicopters and police diverting traffic. Just take care of Mary . . . I promise you, it won't rain!' "

The crowd at Hillside Cemetery was overwhelming. The procession of traffic seemed endless, but flowed smoothly. The world's most famous celebrities had come to mourn Jack's passing. And fans who had never known Jack personally came, too, this one last time to honor a man they loved.

Inside the chapel, Bob Hope delivered the eulogy, putting into words the feelings all of those present had in their hearts . . . and wanted to say . . . and have said on the pages of this book.

"It is said that a memorial service is for those who are left behind. For those who mourn the loss of a loved one. If this is the case, then this service is for the world, because last Thursday night the world lost somebody it loved a lot.

"When Benny Kubelsky was born, who in their wildest dreams would imagine that, eighty years later, at the event of his passing, every television program, every radio show would stop . . . and that every magazine and newspaper would headline it on their front pages. The millions of people who had never met him . . . who had only seen him, or heard him, would feel the pain of a very personal loss.

"The void that is left with us at Jack's passing is quickly filled with the happy memories that we have of him. That's the way Jack would like it to be. He wants us to remember the happiness we shared with him rather than the sadness of losing him. Any path that Jack Benny crossed was left with more laughter, not less.

"How do you say goodbye to a man who was not just a good friend, but a national treasure? It's hard to say that no man is indispensable. But it's true just the same that some *are irreplaceable*. No one has come along to replace Jolson, or Bogart, or Gable, or Will Rogers, or Chevalier. I think it's a safe bet that no one will ever replace Jack Benny. Jack had that rare magic—that indefinable something called genius. Picasso had it. Gershwin had it. And Jack was blessed with it. He didn't just stand on a stage . . . He owned it.

"Jack Benny, a gentle man, crossed all barriers, all boundaries, all countries, all races, all creeds. I'll never forget, in 1958, when I made my first trip to Moscow, and it was announced in the papers that America's leading comedian was visiting. That night I went to Ambassador Thompson's home and Mrs. Thompson met me at the door and said, 'How wonderful that you could come. Did you bring your violin?'

"His first love *was* the violin . . . which proves once again, as Jack used to say, you always hurt the one you love. And yet, with that violin, Jack raised more money and benefited more worthwhile causes and charities than a dozen violin virtuosos. His technique wasn't much, but God sure loved his tone.

"It is a cliché to say that, in time of darkness, Jack Benny brought light with his gift of laughter, making us forget our troubles. For Jack was more than an *escape* from life. He *was* life. A life that enriched his profession, his friends, his millions of fans, his family, his country.

"Perhaps what made Jack Benny such a great laugh maker was that he himself loved to *laugh*. He was the greatest audience a comedian could ever want . . . and all of us would play jokes on him just to break him up and hear him laugh. I know it might sound corny, but there will be times from now on when the lightning will crackle with a special kind of sound, or thunder will peal with a special roar, and I'll think to myself that Cantor, or Fields, or Fred Allen must have just told Jack a joke.

"Jack had *another* quality that's become as rare as nickel candy bars . . . *taste*. When Jack was on the tube, you didn't have to chase the kids out of the room. And he was a perfectionist, a meticulous craftsman. His radio show was classic, a masterpiece of ensemble playing.

"I think, how many generations grew up to the sound of Jack Benny? To the names of Mary Livingstone, Don Wilson, Dennis Day, Rochester, Phil Harris, Anaheim, Azusa, Cucamonga? For over forty years, first on radio, then on television, Jack was a pioneer, ever extending the frontiers of humor. He was one of the first, if not the first, to have great film stars on his show, playing themselves and getting big laughs. The Ronald Colmans, the

Jimmy Stewarts, the Greg Pecks . . . They were on for Jack because they trusted him and his superb sense of what was exactly right.

"Jack knew that the best laughs were the ones you worked the hardest for. He and Mary felt the same way about friends. They both cultivated lasting friendships because they were friends in return. This is the kind of love that surrounds Mary now, and will surround her as long as people remember Jack Benny and Mary Livingstone . . . That is the best definition of eternity that I know of.

"When a man can leave as much of himself as Jack left us, then he can never be truly gone. He has to be immortal.

"In his book *You Can't Go Home Again,* Thomas Wolfe might have written these words about any of us . . .

> 'If a man has a talent and cannot use it
> He has failed
> If he has a talent and uses only half of it
> He has partly failed
> If he has a talent and learns somehow to use
>   the whole of it
> He has gloriously succeeded
> And won a satisfaction and a triumph
> Few men ever know . . .'

"Jack had a great talent . . . and he learned somehow to use the *whole* of it. In his beautiful, full lifetime, Jack succeeded . . . gloriously. Jack found a great joy in the joy he brought to others.

"I cannot say it better than these words . . .

> 'His life was gentle, and the elements
> So mixed in him that Nature might stand up
> And say to all the world "This was a man!" '

"God keep him. Enjoy him. We did—for eighty years."

When the services were over, the mourners walked out into the warmth of a brilliant sun. Frank said it wouldn't rain—*and it didn't!*

As Jack was being laid to rest, hundreds of fans, who heard the services over a loudspeaker outside the chapel, wept. Families stood, silently, many with children holding tiny bunches of flowers. Wherever you looked, the cemetery grounds were dotted with colorful blossoms.

Jack's theme song—the one he felt had never really suited a comedian—became, at the end, the perfect expression in all of our hearts . . . It was truly "Love in Bloom."

INDEX

321